History and Nation

Aperçus: *Histories Texts Cultures*

a Bucknell series

Series Editor: Greg Clingham

Aperçu (apersü). 1882. [Fr.] *A summary exposition, a conspectus.*

Relations among historiography, culture, and textual representation are presently complex and rich in possibilities. *Aperçus* is a series of books exploring the connections between these crucial terms. Revisionist in intention, *Aperçus* seeks to open up new possibilities for humanistic knowledge and study, and thus to deepen and extend our understanding of what history, culture, and texts have been and are, as these terms are made to bear on each other by new thinking and writing.

Titles in the Series

Critical Pasts: Writing Criticism, Writing History
ed. Philip Smallwood

History and Nation
ed. Julia Rudolph

Europe Observed: The Reversed Gaze in Early Modern Encounters
ed. Kumkum Chatterjee and Clement Hawes

History and Nation

Edited by
Julia Rudolph

Lewisburg: Bucknell University Press

Associated University Presses
2010 Eastpark Boulevard
Cranbury, NJ 08512

The paper used in this publication meets the requirements of the American National Standard for Permanence of Paper for Printed Library Materials Z39.48-1984.

Library of Congress Cataloging-in-Publication Data

History and nation / edited by Julia Rudolph.
p. cm. — (Aperçus)
Includes bibliographical references and index.
ISBN-13: 978-0-8387-5640-9 (alk. paper)
ISBN-10: 0-8387-5640-9 (alk. paper)
1. Historicism. 2. History—Methodology. 3. Nationalism and historiography.
I. Rudolph, Julia, 1962– II. Title III. Series: Aperçus (Lewisburg, Pa.)
D16.9.H558 2006
901—dc22

2005026013

PRINTED IN THE UNITED STATES OF AMERICA

Contents

Acknowledgments

MY THANKS ARE DUE NOT ONLY TO THE CONTRIBUTORS TO THIS volume but also to Dominick LaCapra and David Armitage who, along with Colin Kidd, delivered lectures on this topic of "History and Nation" as part of the Social Science Colloquium at Bucknell University in 2002–2003. This volume is an outgrowth of that lecture series and I am grateful to Jim Rice, Assistant Vice President for Academic Affairs and Development at Bucknell, for providing the funding and institutional support necessary for organizing such a series. My thanks are also due to my colleagues in the History Department at that time, especially Leslie Patrick and Richard Waller, who provided intellectual and moral support and were vital participants in the series. Finally, Greg Clingham first approached me about organizing a lecture series and editing this subsequent volume for Bucknell University Press, and he has offered much encouragement and excellent advice. I'm very glad to have had the opportunity to get to know him not only as an editor but also as a friend and colleague in the course of preparing this volume.

Two of the essays included here appeared first in earlier collections: Jorge Cañizares-Esguerra, "Whose Centers and Peripheries? Eighteenth-Century Intellectual History in Atlantic Perspective," in *The Atlantic World: Essays on Slavery, Migration and Imagination*, eds. Wim Klooster and Alfred Padula (Prentice Hall, 2005) and J. G. A. Pocock, "The Treaty Between Histories," in *Histories, Power and Loss: Uses of the Past—a New Zealand Commentary*, eds. Andrew Sharp and Paul McHugh (Bridget Williams Books, Wellington, 2001). They are reprinted here, with some minor changes, by the kind permission of the original publishers.

History and Nation

Julia Rudolph

Introduction

A COLLECTION OF ESSAYS CONCERNED WITH THE RELATIONSHIP between "history" and "nation" might be conceptualized in a variety of ways. For example, one might survey the kinds of histories of nations historians produce. And following a spectrum of such histories, suggested by John Breuilly, would afford principles of selection and interpretation: from histories in which the nation is simply assumed as a kind of "framing device" or, more actively, in which the nation "as a real historical force" appears as an agent of change; to histories in which the formation of a nation is analyzed, or in which the imagination, rather than formation, of a nation is exposed.[1] Yet it might be fruitful to focus instead on the question of history's impact—to ask what has been the influence of history-telling on the "process" of nation? This would be, in one sense, to pursue Ernest Renan's insight that "historical error is essential to the creation of a nation" and to trace the vexed connections between nationalism and the historian. History has clearly functioned as a form of propaganda for the nation, just as surely as it has served as a vehicle for self-reflection and for hostile challenges to the nation.[2]

The purpose of this volume, however, is not primarily to confront these aspects of the relationship between history and nation, but rather to reflect on the consideration of this topic and this relationship by historians. The concern here is with the ways in which historians understand, envision, and theorize their actions and their impact. The subjects of these essays are historians—Florentine and Maori, British and Spanish, New Zealander and French, Spanish-American and Dutch, early modern and modern—who are seen to be engaging with these issues. Two of the essays, those by Colin Kidd and John Pocock, provide examples of the authors themselves transparently considering ways in which to conceptualize the relationship between history and nation, and the definition of both history and nation, in their own work.

Colin Kidd's essay, for example, offers a powerful critique of the concepts—in particular that of "identity"—through which historians have interpreted nation. Kidd builds upon recent trends in the historiography of nation, and the growing sensitivity of historians to the constructed or imagined nature of nations. His essay begins by surveying some of the most important historical analyses that have portrayed the construction of nation as a product of a variety of ideological, economic, and cultural changes in nineteenth- and twentieth-century Europe. These analyses and this appreciation for the construction of nation and nationalism stem, I think, from the uncomfortable recognition of the vital role played by historians in that construction and in the rise of modern nationalisms. Examples of the destructive effects of a powerful merger between history and nationalism in the nineteenth century have led many historians to be deeply skeptical about positing a productive or optimistic relationship between history and nation. The same concern to repudiate past nationalist histories is betrayed from a slightly different perspective in the language of "infection" and "toxicity" used by historians like Rees Davies and Patrick Geary; here the goal is to expose the fabrication of ethnicity that was achieved as part of an earlier historical construction of what Geary terms a "myth of nations."[3]

This new sensitivity to the dangers of anachronism in formerly transhistorical notions of nation and ethnicity is perhaps also evidence of awareness among contemporary historians of problems associated with decolonization and devolution. How we recount the past is, some have argued, inflected with current concerns about the claims and status of so-called ethnic and indigenous groups. How we recount the past may also be increasingly shaped by an awareness of globalization and by a new ambivalence about the fluidity of national boundaries. This ambivalence is characteristically expressed in the contributions made by historians to recent debates about European Union; it is also evident in the turn towards imperial, postcolonial, and subaltern studies, and in the drive to trace the legacies of "encounters" in successive waves of colonization in the early modern and modern worlds. Linda Colley's *Captives* is just one recent example of the ways in which historians have begun to explore the global context of national histories and to rethink the ways in which we have divined the past along national, continental, and oceanic lines.[4] Finally, another way to explain these trends is to point to historians' confrontation with multiculturalism and further, with the recognition of multiple histories, a confrontation with the possible denial of facts characteristic of postmodernism. What Donna Gabaccia charts as a "transition from homogenous national to multicultural histories . . . in Europe, Latin America and the English-speaking world" not only describes the emergence of typical concerns about anachronism, categorization, and certainty, but also, in general, a confrontation with problems of historical method.[5]

The question of the relationship between history and nation, then, speaks to many of the most important questions debated by historians today. As long-accepted national categories of historical research and teaching have been challenged, fundamental questions about methodology, evidence, and narrative have become even more pressing.[6] The focus of this volume on historical theory and method is in part motivated by a desire to counter the familiar but unfounded complaint (probably articulated most often by historians themselves) that historians do not adequately investigate the principles on which their work proceeds. It is also motivated by a desire to view some of the current trends towards methodological self-consciousness more explicitly in relation to trends in the historiography of nation. Peter Burke has argued that this self-consciousness has been especially notable among intellectual historians and economic historians[7] but there is evidence, of course, that many historians are becoming vitally interested in connecting questions about the philosophy of history with questions about nation and nationalism. Recent investigations into collective memory and national memorial cultures by social and cultural historians, for example, have included questions about methodology, psychology, and epistemology. The work of historians and theorists like Pierre Nora and Dominick LaCapra has generated a rich field of historical inquiry focused especially on problems in the remembrance of modern war and on questions about the effect of traumatic experience on individual and collective memory.[8]

Most well-known, perhaps, are debates about the proper public recollection of the Second World War within a French or German national narrative, but these kinds of questions have also had implications for the recollection of conflict in postcolonial Africa and India. The special question of the history of the Holocaust has generated enormous debate not only about the relationship between history and nation, but also about the status of historical evidence, and about the status of the historian herself. Here questions about the reliability of memory often merge with concerns about national (or nationalist) bias, and this has led to very public debates about objectivity and revisionism. For example, again from a French context, questions about the role of a historian in national life may be seen in the 1998 trial of Maurice Papon. In this case prominent historians of France, most notably Robert Paxton and Henri Rousso, articulated and acted upon conflicting arguments about the reliability of historical evidence and the appropriateness of historians' testimony in the courtroom and in the public sphere more generally.[9] Very different indications of a current concern to define a proper public role for historians may be found in debates among American historians over the construction of a set of "National Standards for History"; this concern is also apparent in British historians' attempts to come to terms with history's role not only as education but also as entertainment within the burgeoning "heritage industry" and within the mass-media of television and internet.[10]

The essays in this collection take up some of these questions and introduce many others. One of the most important questions addressed by contributors reflects a now familiar concern with language, with questions about the role language plays in historical and cultural understanding. What language is available to a people to think about and write history? Here language may be understood in two ways: as native forms of expression—whether Maori, Nahuatl, or Etruscan—and intertwined with a world-view; or as forms of discourse—whether humanist, juridical, or biblical—and indicative of traditions of meaning. Some eighteenth-century historians' approaches to sources in non-alphabetical scripts provide an illuminating example. As Jorge Cañizares-Esguerra explains in his essay, this concern with language was central to debates about the status of historical evidence among historians in the early modern Atlantic world. These historians expressed skepticism about the veracity of Mesoamerican sources, but they also demonstrated an awareness of fundamental problems of translation. Particularly interesting is the example of a Spanish-American historian like Antonio Leon y Gama: his understanding of the particularity of expression and knowledge embedded in Nahuatl logograms and ideograms led to a deep skepticism about non-native (i.e., European) ability to comprehend these historical records.

Cañizares-Esguerra's interest in complicating the traditional Western understanding of the influence between historiographies and cultures is shared by other contributors to this volume. Both he and Daniel Carey encourage questions about categories used in the understanding of history and nation—categories of indigenous and dominant, core and periphery, European and non-European—as they focus on developments in notions about science, truth, and the reliability of sources within the construction of historical narratives. Carey explores important connections between geographical, historical, scientific, and philosophical approaches to "the dilemma of authentication" through a careful analysis of John Locke's reading of travel narratives. Concern with the epistemological status of historical accounts, and a particular interest in the formation and influence of a British historiographical and philosophical tradition, are themes evident in John Pocock's as well as Daniel Carey's contributions to this volume. Pocock articulates broad questions about how to conceptualize the relationship between different histories, and different forms of historical narration, as he proposes his concept of "a treaty between histories." Here recognition of the contestability of history is matched by a commitment to understanding the role histories have played in the formation of communities, and in the determination and exercise of sovereignty in New Zealand and elsewhere. Similar interests are also apparent in Ann Moyer's claim that sixteenth-century Florentine history was central to a cultural program launched as an expression of Medicean sovereignty. Moyer, like other contributors, asks historians to reconsider traditional temporal boundaries. This questioning of national boundaries in historical understanding has also encouraged a reconsideration of traditional historical periods—such as "Renaissance" and "Enlightenment," or "modern" and "pre-modern"—as well as reflection on the methods historians use to establish periodization. The challenge Moyer's essay poses to our periodization of Renaissance and decline, as well as her evidence of developments in the understanding of feudal history among these Florentines, remind us that theories about time are a central part of the historical understanding of nation. In these and many other ways contributors to this volume seek to uncover the practices and problems of historians in relation to the question of nation.

Notes

1. John Breuilly, "Historians and the Nation," in *History and Historians in the Twentieth Century*, ed. Peter Burke (Oxford: Oxford University Press, 2002), 55.

2. Ernest Renan, *Qu'est ce qu'une Nation? What is a Nation?*, trans. Wanda Romer Taylor (Toronto: Tapir Press, 1996), 19; Breuilly, "Historians and the Nation," 84; E. J. Hobsbawm, *Nations and Nationalism since 1780: Programme, Myth, Reality*, 2d ed. (Cambridge: Cambridge University Press, 1993).

3. R. R. Davies, "The People of Britain and Ireland 110–1400. I. Identities," *Transactions of the Royal Historical Society* 6th ser. 4 (1994):1–20; Patrick J. Geary, *The Myth of Nations: The Medieval Origins of Europe* (Princeton: Princeton University Press, 2002).

4. Linda Colley, *Captives: Britain, Empire and the World, 1600–1850* (New York: Random House, 2002).

5. Donna R. Gabaccia, "The Multicultural History of Nations," in *A Companion to Western Historical Thought*, ed. Lloyd Kramer and Sarah Maza (Malden, Mass.: Blackwell, 2002), 433. Cf. also Peter Burke, "Historiography and Philosophy of History," in Burke ed., *History and Historians*, 238–39.

6. Some good surveys, in English, of these trends in historical writing can be found in the work of Peter Burke, Michael Bentley, Georg Iggers, Ludmilla Jordanova, and Peter Novick.

7. Burke, "Historiography and Philosophy of History," 235–38.

8. Pierre Nora (ed.), *Realms of Memory. The Construction of the French Past*, 3 vols., English-language ed. Lawrence D. Kritzman, trans. Arthur Goldhammer (New York: Columbia University Press, 1996–1998); Dominick LaCapra, *History and Memory after Auschwitz* (Ithaca: Cornell University Press, 1998), *Representing the Holocaust: History, Theory, Trauma* (Ithaca: Cornell University Press, 1994), *Writing History, Writing Trauma* (Baltimore, Md.: Johns Hopkins University Press, 2001); Jay Winter and Emmanuel Sivan eds., *War and Remembrance in the Twentieth Century* (Cambridge: Cambridge University Press, 1999).

9. The important connection between the recollection of conflict and crime in WWII and in the Algerian War in the Papon trial, and its relevance for thinking about the relationship between his-

tory and nation, is discussed, for example, by Richard Vinen, "Papon in Perspective—implications of Maurice Papon's trial for crimes against humanity," *History Today*, 48, 7 (1998): 6–8.

10. Gary B. Nash, Charlotte Crabtree, and Ross E. Dunn, *History on Trial: Culture Wars and the Teaching of the Past* (New York: A. A. Knopf, 1997); Peter Mandler, *History and National Life* (London: Profile Books, 2002); Felipe Fernandez-Armesto, "Epilogue: What is History *Now?*" in *What is History Now?*, ed. David Cannadine (Houndmills: Palgrave Macmillan, 2002).

Colin Kidd

Identity before Identities: Ethnicity, Nationalism, and the Historian

FAILURE, USUALLY HONORABLE, SOMETIMES DISTINGUISHED, lies at the heart of the historical enterprise. The past itself is gone and does not provide the historian with opportunities for direct empirical observation. Historical empiricism is limited to scrutiny of material survivals from bygone eras. What the historian tries to do is to resurrect as far as possible the life of the past from the various relics that have been bequeathed to the present. These relics are in themselves lifeless. A living past has to be inferred from documentary and other forms of evidence. The job of the historian is primarily one of imaginative reconstruction, the reconstitution of past life from its dry bones. While the surviving evidence permits the historian to go a long way in recovering the significant contours of various stories from the past, the whole life of any past era is too vast and moth-eaten in too many places to be recoverable. Every story told by the historian inevitably involves many acts of abridgement. If the wholeness of the past presents an unattainable object for academic historians, another prize appears at times to be within tantalizing reach: the holy grail of past centeredness. Historians aim to recover the past, or as much of it as can be recovered, on the past's terms rather than on our own. Indeed, the best way to avoid the delusive traps of teleology and anachronism is to study the past for its own sake.

Nevertheless, what differentiates historians from mere antiquarians is that the former aim not only to recover as much of the past as they can, but to ask, as far as possible, lively and pertinent questions about the nature of the past worlds they have in some measure recovered. These questions, and the categories they employ, should also, as far as possible, conform to the value systems of the past. Otherwise, such questions become pointless. In this regard, the incautious historian is in danger of generating nonsensical answers to ridiculous questions, indeed perhaps to non-questions, ones that have no purchase in the past. The deadly historical sin of presentism derives from the unwarranted assumption that the preoccupations of today were those of the past. Ideally, the categories of historical analysis and interrogation should be commensurable with the mentality of the past society under investigation.

This is not always the case in practice. For practising historians—ears stopped against skeptical warnings issued by philosophers of history[1] —blithely operate as if it were possible to penetrate the particularity of past cultures. However, some historians remain alert to the dangers that their techniques, their tools, their technical vocabulary, their research agenda, are themselves particular to, or at least to some extent inflected with, the values of their location in the present. What historians do and the ways in which they think are themselves parts of the historical process. Of course, we inevitably import our own values into the past; and very occasionally we are right to do so. Immersion in the evidence can have very odd results. As John Vincent reminds us, nothing is better attested in the records than the miracles performed by saints and the real existing practice of witchcraft.[2] Sometimes we do just have to concede that we know better than the past. Yet, putting such exceptions aside, as far as possible past-centered historians are—and should be—prepared to modify their research strategies, even to abandon their inherited disciplinary terminologies in the light of their immersion in the language and values of the past. In this way, through the sensitivity of historians to avoidable anachronism, the past—though existing only as a lifeless static body of materials—is capable, on occasions, of having the last word.

As it happens, a close attention to anachronism has, over the past twenty years or so, revolutionized the historical study of nationhood and ethnicity; though, as this essay shows, the concept of identity has not been treated with the same level of analytical rigor or sensitivity. Whereas identity remains an ahistorical given, a label applied to all periods and all peoples, nationalism has been exposed as a product of modernity, a historical phenomenon found, according to several influential historians, sociologists, and political scientists, only in the period from the late eighteenth century onwards, and at first, only among European populations, whether in Europe or its colonies.[3] Historians disagree, however, about the features of modernity that gave rise to nationalism. Did nationalism develop because of the articulation of new ideologies and political doctrines, including popular sovereignty, the ideal of autonomy and a reappreciation of folk cultures as the embodiment of the untainted primal values of the ethnic group? More specifically, did the ideas of Herder or the example of the French Revolution inspire nationalist movements?[4] Or did nationalism evolve because of commercialization and the attendant transformations—and politicization—of the cultural infrastructure of economic life, including education, language, and culture? In other words, did the needs of commerce and industry, as Ernest Gellner argued, erode the horizontal divisions within traditional hierarchies between a cosmopolitan upper layer of clerics and aristocrats and a lower rung of identity-less peasantries, replacing these with new rigidities between the cultures contained within distinct national frontiers?[5] Alternatively, did nationalism spring up in the way suggested by Benedict Anderson, as a by-product of the emergence of new modes of communication, most notably print capitalism, which permitted the raising of a new kind of communal consciousness?[6] On parallel lines, historians have also investigated whether nationalism proceeded in step with the extension of powerful state bureaucracies into localist peripheries.[7] Or was nationalism, as the most sophisticated Marxists like Miroslav Hroch and Eric Hobsbawm have argued, the product of various political, technological, and social changes in modern society that manifested itself in a series of phased developments, spreading first within the middle classes from folkloric and literary intellectuals to a wider grouping of agitators, and only later issuing in a mass movement supported by peasants and workers?[8] More crudely, was nationalism, as some clumsier Marxists have claimed, an expression of the reformist class-consciousness of the bourgeoisie?[9] In spite of such disagreements, the protagonists in this major historical battleground are allies of a kind in a modernist coalition. All agree that nationalism is an expression of the conditions of modernity and is not found in earlier periods of history.

The modernists are opposed—halfheartedly in certain respects and in certain quarters—by the perennialist-primordialist school, whose most sophisticated champion is Anthony Smith. Perennialists and primordialists argue that some form of ethnic group association or national consciousness is an ongoing feature of history from antiquity, and can be found in the medieval and early modern eras. Emphases differ within this broad school as to whether the links between historic communities and their modern namesakes are actually continuous or merely recurrent. Moreover, Smith carefully distinguishes between nationalism proper, which he concedes is a product of the modern world, and earlier forms of national identity. Smith rejects the notion that nations are "invented" in the modern era, but is happy to endorse a modernist position that nations have been "reconstructed" in modern times out of preexisting materials.[10] In a similar vein, the medievalist John Armstrong has discussed the existence of national communities in eras long before the formulation of nationalism itself in his book *Nations before Nationalism* (1982).[11]

Lexicography lends some endorsement to the modernist position. The words "nationalism" and "nationalist" do not appear, for example, in Dr. Johnson's celebrated *Dictionary* of 1755. Johnson did, however, include entries for "nation"; "nationally"; "nationalness"; and "national," whose secondary meaning, after the primary definition of "public" is rendered—perhaps significantly in the absence of "nationalism"—as "bigotted to one's own country."[12] The modern observer is struck both by the absence of "nationalism" itself and also by a pejorativeness in Johnson's usage. In *Keywords,* his fascinating tour round the foundational concepts in the humanities and social sciences, the late Raymond Williams noted that while "nation" was in currency from the seventeenth century, "realm," "kingdom" and "country" remained more common until the eighteenth century. "Nationalist," Williams argued, appeared in the early eighteenth century, "nationalism" in the early nineteenth. Both became common only from the middle of the nineteenth century.[13]

The modernist turn in the study of nationalism has further repercussions for historiography in general. It is accompanied by a growing recognition that nationalism is implicated in the rise of modern academic history. The modern historical enterprise is itself a product of the nationalist moment of the nineteenth century,[14] and, despite the passage of time and reconfiguration of political arrangements, has remained subject to the gravitational force exerted by nationalism. As a discipline moreover, history exhibits nationalist inflections. For history as a body of knowledge is centered on the nation and seems to conform to a nationalist template, partly, in some places because of an overt nationalist ideology, more often in the liberal democracies because of a less articulate and subconscious type of nationalist assumption—what Michael Billig refers to as "banal nationalism."[15] The nation is, after all, an unconscious yet quotidian part of what we are. In the case of historians, of course, laziness and the availability of a convenient ready-to-hand framework for the organization of our material draws us into a diluted, low-intensity, non-ideological variant of the nationalist interpretation of history. This complaint is not new, though it has become more strident in recent years. As early as 1962 David Potter complained in the pages of the *American Historical Review* that not only had the national group become the "major focus" of the historian, but that nationalist assumptions had "warped" the historian's analysis as much as they had "assisted it."[16] In *Historians' Fallacies* (1970), David Hackett Fischer detected an inescapable nationalism as the factor underlying the "fallacy of cross grouping," in particular the common "conceptualization of all group types in terms of the nation state." The organization of history, Fischer noted, is national. Records are sorted into national piles. Historians are trained to study the pasts of particular nations. The very structure of historical interpretation depends on the idea of the course of a nation's history, the particular story that history tells of a specified national community.[17] Nations are the building blocks of history. Underpinning such approaches are assumptions about national continuity, that the ancient histories of the territories of England, Scotland, Ireland, France, and so on, yield the origins of the modern nation, even when the ancient inhabitants of these territories were divided into various different entities, whether regnal, ethnic, or tribal. Historians occasionally tell stories about individuals, towns, county communities, and ethnic groups; but most historians spend most of their time telling stories about nations. The rhetoric and grand narrative structures of history tend to be unreflexively or subconsciously nationalist. Historians tell, and their publics expect them to tell, "the story of Scotland" or "the story of Ireland," or the story of some other equally contingent and time-bound land.

Such inconsistencies seem most obvious in the medieval field, and it is here that historians have been most sensitive to the unfortunate nationalist legacy. Rees Davies, who has pioneered an archipelagic approach to the history of these islands during the Middle Ages, notes a "growing recognition that the centrality that academic historians have so long given to the unitary nation state as the natural, inevitable, and indeed desirable unit of human power and political organisation is itself a reflection of the intellectual climate in which modern academic historiography was forged in the nineteenth century." Davies adds that "the notion of a people is not only utterly elusive and fatally wishy-washy, it is also infected with the biological and racial descent-myths so widely propagated in the nineteenth century."[18] Even more outspoken is the medievalist Patrick Geary in *The Myth of Nations: The Medieval Origins of Europe* (2002). Geary is forthright in his attribution of a nationalist provenance to the historical discipline: "Modern history was born in the nineteenth century, conceived and developed as an instrument of European nationalism." Indeed, according to Geary, "the very tools of analysis by which we pretend to practice scientific history were invented and perfected within a wider climate of nationalism and nationalist preoccupations." One does not have to accept the emotive descriptions advanced by Geary of a "poisoned" historical landscape replete with the "toxic waste" of nationalist misinterpretations to sympathize with his anxiety about the ways in which modern preoccupations with the nation have distorted understanding of the medieval origins of Europe and its supposed nations. Geary locates the origins of modern professional historiography in the practices of nineteenth-century German scholarship. By this Geary does not simply mean the German seminar method, but also the accumulation of a corpus of texts, such as the *Monumenta Germaniae Historicae* and the development of a philological method linked to the Indo-Germanic classification of languages. The German world in Geary's eyes gave birth both to the basic methods and trappings of academic history and what Geary calls "pseudo-historical nationalism."[19]

A very similar, though more rhetorically restrained, picture emerges in Patrick Amory's book *People and Identity in Ostrogothic Italy,* 489–554 (1997). Amory finds that many of his colleagues are still in thrall, somewhat unwittingly, to nineteenth-century ethnic, nationalist, and racialist categories, including a model of ethnogenesis or people-formation based on nineteenth-century assumptions of ethnic invasion or migration. According to Amory, today's emphasis on ethnicity in the world of late antiquity is simply nineteenth-century volkish racialism "minus the racial value-judgments." Amory complains that the "notion of barbarian culture, translated into the nineteenth-century philological construct 'Germanic culture', continues to provide an easy way to translate classical ethnography into modern terms." According to Amory, ethnicity is an easy—but fundamentally misleading—way of describing "barbarian group coherence." Amory describes the way in which armies are redescribed as tribes. Indeed Amory insists upon the primacy of profession—in addition to region—in the formation of fifth-century groupings, delineating a more precise transformation by which a "royal clan and its polyethnic armed following" might become "a nascent gens, a people cleaving to an ancient ethnographic group-name." Indeed, Amory pursues a more subtle line than Geary, arguing that it is not simply the back-projection by historians of nineteenth-century nationalist and ethnocentric perspectives onto the past that distorts it, but also the currency in the fifth century of a classical ethnographic nomenclature that had its own distinctive appeal to contemporaries, witness the sixth-century *Getica* of Jordanes, a Gothicist fantasy that long predates the Gothicist fantasies of nineteenth-century romantic-nationalist scholarship.[20]

The cultural turn in history has served to eradicate in several places some of the most obvious fallacies associated with the nationalist interpretation of history. Historians have become more reflexive, aware of the provenance of their own discipline. Michael Biddiss notes that the nineteenth century held to the view that "nations had an entirely objective existence—including even those which were simply slumbering unawares, like princesses awaiting the fairy-tale kiss that would rouse them into consciousness of their identity and destiny."[21] A belief in the objective existence of nations (or embryonic proto-nations) across history has given way to an awareness of the contingency of nations and of the bogus teleologies that accompany histories of national origins. Hobsbawm, for example, has alerted historians to the dangers of identity history, most influentially perhaps through his demystification of "invented traditions."[22] In addition, students of nationalism have increasingly drawn attention to the active role of historians in the process of nation-building.[23] Some of today's historians are conscious of a need to atone for the participation of their professional predecessors in the sins of nationalism.

As a result of these various promptings, the national categories inherited from the nineteenth century seem to be of declining relevance for many types of historians. Where nations were until recently concepts that provided a long, continuous framework for the study of the past, particular nations are now seen more as episodes or sets of episodes in the history of a specified territory. What relevance, some historians ask, do today's national identities and national borders have to a past with very different patterns of culture and community? Historians have also begun to explore the possibilities attendant upon liberation from nationalist categories. This has led to a new emphasis on the margins, on borderlands, and on transnational fields, such as Atlantic history or the new British history that explores the interactions of the histories of England, Scotland, Ireland, and Wales.[24] Obviously, there is another side to this story: witness the series of books on cultural phenomena "in national context" edited by the late Roy Porter and Mikulasc Teich. Here the nation was used deliberately to insinuate a critical wedge into tired transnational concepts, such as the Renaissance, the Enlightenment, and Romanticism.[25] Nevertheless, this is a relatively minor counter-current to the dominant trends in historiography.

In the wake of the modernist interpretation of nationalism and greater historical reflexivity about the role of nationalism in shaping the subject has come an anxiety with the terminological baggage that the discipline inherits from its nationalist founders. In his book *Ethno-*

nationalism, Walker Connor, one of the leading political scientists in the modernist camp, not only devotes a chapter to the question "When is a nation?," but also devotes another to the vexed problem of "Terminological chaos."[26] In response to the growing delimitation of nationalism to the modern world, the medievalist Susan Reynolds has coined the term "regnalism" to describe the sense of belonging to a medieval kingdom.[27] This coinage is also applicable to early modern allegiances that were, to be precise, more regnal than national. In parallel, Anthony Smith has used the term "ethnocentrism" to describe communal self-image in periods prior to the modern rise of nationalism proper.[28] Terminological exactitude is not necessarily a mere sign of pedantry; it can also shed fascinating insights into wider historical problems, not least in the anglophone world between the early modern and modern periods, a field where it is possible to construct semantic histories of the basic terminology used in the history of ethnicity and nationalism.

To some extent language imprisons the historian's imagination. One obvious danger is where familiar terms appear in other eras, and one assumes an exact or even rough equivalence of meaning. The ethnic provides just such a minefield. Not only do historians need to be sensitive to the historical contingencies of ethnogenesis; they also need to be aware of the conceptual contingency of the very idea of the ethnic. What, for example, constituted the "ethnic" in the early modern era? Here there has been a subtle but very significant shift in meaning since the eighteenth century. Ethnic was a pejorative label often attached to people of color; but it was not attached to people because of race or nationality per se. Rather the ethnic denoted quite another kind of difference, though one which overlaps with today's understanding of the ethnic.

Johnson's *Dictionary* defined "ethnick" as "heathen; pagan; not Jewish; not Christian," and also included an entry for "ethnicks," meaning "heathens; not Jews; not Christians."[29] Other dictionaries reiterate the same broad definition of ethnic as "heathenish." Thomas Blount's *Glossographia* of 1656 defined "ethnick" as "heathenish, ungodly irreligious: And may be used substantively for a heathen or gentile."[30] In Nathaniel Bailey's *Universal etymological dictionary* (6th edition, 1733) "ethnick" is given a similar definition: "heathenish, of or belonging to heathens."[31] This usage can be traced throughout the early modern British world. Sir Robert Gordon of Lochinvar's proposal of 1625 for the establishment of a Scots colony on Cape Breton had as its principal declared aim the propagation of Christian truth and the enlightenment of "those that are captivate in ethnicke darknesse."[32] The early eighteenth-century English rendering of Herbert of Cherbury's *Ancient Religion of the Gentiles* spoke of the "ethnical superstitions" of pagan peoples.[33] The mid-eighteenth-century Irish Catholic antiquary Sylvester O'Halloran described the pagan rites of the ancient pre-Christian Gaels as "our national ethnic worship."[34] Indeed, it appears that early modern confusion to the effect that the Greek word "ethnos" was the source of the English word heathen, prompting further English variants "hethnic"and "heathenic."[35]

There has been a subtle but significant shift in the meaning of "ethnic" over the past couple of centuries, from an original association with religious otherness towards a more secular description of racial, national, or cultural distinctiveness. However, one can detect areas where ancient, early modern, and modern meanings overlap. Whereas the original Greek category of *ethne* in antiquity bore some resemblance to the modern sense of ethnic community,[36] the term *ta ethne* was also used in later antiquity to denote the non-Israelitish nations—the *goyim*—in the New Testament and Church Fathers.[37] This latter religious emphasis was to prove influential in later contexts. By the early modern era, the term ethnic was redolent of collective otherness, but religious rather than racial; though, of course, pagans would tend not to be white Europeans. There is a hint here that the primary badge of group identification in the premodern world was religious and did not pertain primarily to the secular marks of cultural particularity. One can see a similar ambiguity in the English domestication of *gens,* the Latinate parallel of the Greek *ethnos.* Most obviously, of course, there is the word "gentile," meaning non-Jewish, and the seventeenth- and eighteenth-century English term (borrowed from the Portuguese *gentio*) for a Hindu, pagan or non-Muslim Indian, a "Gentoo."[38] Alien religious practices and beliefs rather than physical appearance or color seem to constitute the primary descriptors of early modern ethnicity.

The ethnic was a concern of our early modern forebears; but their ethnic concerns were quite different from our conception of ethnicity. It requires an act of historical imagination to reconstruct early modern ethnicity. At the heart of the matter was the concern to uphold one of the central and most threatened tenets of Christian orthodoxy, monogenesis, the notion that all mankind was descended from an original pair of parents, Adam and Eve. The expansion of Europe during the early modern era and the discovery of new continents, other races, and alternative models of civilization posed a serious intellectual challenge to Christendom. Christian theology rested on a hitherto underexamined anthropology. Monogenesis was integral to the coherence of the story of the Fall, the biological transmission of original sin, and Christ's redemption of mankind. How was one to account for the pronounced and obvious differences between white and black and Amerindian types of mankind? Did all mankind have a single racial origin, or was the scale of human racial diversity so enormous that it could only be explained by polygenesis, the notion that the races of man sprang from multiple origins? Race was ultimately and most profoundly a theological problem. Racial difference, moreover, comprised only one part of the heterodox subversiveness of ethnicity. Christian scholars not only had to reconcile racial diversity with monogenesis; they also had to accommodate other features of alien cultural difference to Christian norms. Differences of language were easy. The story of the dispersal of nations after the construction of the Tower of Babel provided theologians with a convenient off-the-peg solution to this problem. The existence of pagan religions in the great civilizations of the world beyond Christendom required bespoke solutions. As early modern Europeans saw it, how could one explain the rise of these axiomatically false religions? The problem of the ethnic revolved as much around what we might now think of as comparative religion as it did ethnology proper.[39] Scholars devised a number of solutions, largely variations on the idea of the corruption and degeneration of the patriarchal religion of the Old Testament. The general story was one of a gradual neglect and corruption of the original monotheistic religion of Noah into pagan cults that over the course of time came to have less and less superficial resemblance to the patriarchal religion. One of the central features of early modern theology was the detection of the latent resemblances that revealed pagan religions to be degenerate offshoots of the religion of Noah. Euhemeristic techniques—which demystified pagan gods as mere humans, though prominent enough historical figures in their day, whose ancient celebrity was perpetuated by their peoples through posthumous deification—permitted a more precise delineation of degeneration into polytheism. In these versions the founders of nations in the post-Babelian dispersal, namely the sons and grandsons of Noah, had been set up as gods after their deaths by the nations that lapsed from the monotheistic truths of their patriarchal inheritance, memories of which were further usurped by the polytheistic deification of further national leaders. The example given by Johnson's *Dictionary* of the word "ethnicks" was derived from a euhemeristic passage in Sir Walter Raleigh's *History of the World:* "This first Jupiter of the ethnicks was then the same Cain, the son of Adam."[40] The racial-cum-theological issue of monogenesis and the problem of paganism were equally part of the European response to "ethnic" difference.

A similar investigation into the semantic history of the term "identity" yields even richer pickings. Ironically, the modernist displacement of nationalist perspectives has coincided in part with the importation of another possible distortion into the study of nationhood and ethnicity, namely the notion of "identities." In recent years, identities, particularly ethnic and national identities, have become a staple feature of historical enquiry. Identity has indeed become a ubiquitous concept in the humanities and social sciences. Questions regarding identity have been applied across the board to every country and to every age. This ubiquity is troubling. Identity has become an idolatrous concept; it often serves to inhibit thought, and worse, to distort the past. Have historians, one wonders, become addicted to "identity"? Might its deployment have become unreflective, lazy, and conventional? In particular, have historians become overly dependent upon a conceptual tool which, far from being sterilized and neutral, carries with it the germ of anachronism (reflecting indeed not only the values of modernity in general, but of western bourgeois modernity in particular)? Might the vast corpus of academic work on the subject of past identities say more about the present than the past? Do our analyses of identity—in the words of fiction's most skeptical historian—merely throw a "pseudo-light" upon "non-problems"?[41]

Identity has become one of the fundamental building-blocks of historical analysis. However, as Keith Jenkins warns, although historical concepts "look impersonal and objective," they are not, in fact, "obvious and timeless." Jenkins, who urges historians to "historicise history itself," believes that even such basic concepts as time, evidence, and cause and effect are provisional and culture-bound.[42] Identity, I would argue, is no more robust than these core concepts. Richard Handler reminds us that identity is a term "peculiar to the modern Western world."[43] It is worth noting that "identity" does not even feature in Raymond Williams's *Keywords* (1976: revised edition, 1983). Even as late as the mid-1970s in Britain had "identity" not yet become a "key-word"? If "identity" is not applicable to societies in the past, then what term did they use to capture the projection of their ethnic or national being? Ultimately—and a question for anthropologists rather than historians, I fear—one wonders whether some sense of group "identity" (as opposed to something like loyalty or supposed kinship) is in fact a universal attribute of humanity? Nevertheless, my remit here is a more limited one. It is limited by language to the anglophone world. How far is the English term identity applicable even within the anglophone world to past eras?

What does identity actually mean? What is its ultimate provenance? Within historiography and the humanities, identity now seems to signify difference; yet the basic meaning of identity is likeness or sameness. The modern English noun is formed out of the Latin word "idem," meaning the same, and the *OED* lists "idemptitie" as an obsolete form of the word. In later Latin, moreover, there was a noun "identitas." However, the recent history of this simple term for sameness has been accompanied by some exotic and profuse semantic proliferation. Identity has come to mean not only sameness, but the sameness of a person or thing at all times and in all circumstances.[44] By extension, this has become the condition whereby that person or thing is itself and not someone or something else. This has led to a total reversal of the original meaning of identity as sameness, as now identity has come to mean "individuality," "personality," something distinctive rather than something that is the same as something else. Somehow a word denoting sameness has come to mean an unchangeable sameness, or authenticity, and hence distinctiveness and difference from other persons, groups, or things. Identity now denotes the essence of individuality either for a person or a group. This new definition has in good measure within academic discourse at least supplanted and indeed subverted its former signification. Did the term "identity" have our meaning of "individuality" in the past? If not, then how could people in the past have "identities" in our sense, if they did not possess the requisite vocabulary to express such identities? Historians need to confront a history of change in one of their own fundamental categories of analysis. When did identity first find itself applied to matters of ethnicity and nationhood, and was its meaning in that sphere similar to that which it enjoys today? Further, when and how and why did identity come to acquire its present meaning?

Identity has a very illuminating, ironic, and ambiguous semantic history that calls into question our unqualified reliance on this category of analysis. The word identity can be found in seventeenth- and eighteenth-century literature, but its meaning was much narrower than that of today. Johnson's *Dictionary* defined "identity" as "sameness; not diversity," a position echoed by the first edition of the *Encyclopedia Britannica* (1771), which stated that identity "denotes that by which a thing is itself, and not anything else; in which sense, identity differs from similitude as well as diversity."[45] Identity was to most intents and purposes the noun from which the adjective "identical" was drawn—and no more.

Discussions of identity were a staple feature of eighteenth-century British philosophy. David Hume, in particular, has a lot to say about identity, and devotes a chapter of *A Treatise of Human Nature* to the subject "Of personal identity." At first glance personal identity sounds promising and familiar; but is it quite what it is now taken to mean? Hume asked, "What then gives us so great a propension to ascribe an identity to these successive perceptions, and to suppose ourselves possest of an invariable and uninterrupted existence thro' the whole course of our lives?" Selfhood for Hume was nothing but "a bundle or collection of different perceptions," the whole held together by the action of memory, which he established as "the source of personal identity."[46]

However, what matters to us is not Hume's powerful critique of personal identity, but what Hume understood personal identity to be. Hume offered a clear definition of identity: "We have a distinct idea of an object, that remains invariable and uninterrupted thro' a suppos'd variation of time; and this idea we call that of identity or sameness."[47] By personal identity, Hume meant the sense of the continuous sameness of the self, an entity whose existence he set out to challenge. Personal continuity and invariableness denoted nothing about the quality of personhood. Personal identity for Hume did not amount to a matter of being true to one's sense of self or to one's background, ethnic heritage, or adopted lifestyle. "Personal identity" in Hume's philosophy did not encompass any sense of our personality or character, our lifestyle choices, the sense of what kind of person one might be. Personal identity for Hume did, of course, amount to a sort of personal myth; but only in a very restricted philosophical sense far removed from its modern associations. Identity for Hume was strictly a type of philosophical relationship, the others being resemblance, quantity, quality, contrariety, and causation, plus the relations of space and time.[48] In the eighteenth century, identity was a technical term of extreme desiccation, entirely lacking in the lush and luxuriant connotations that the expression currently suggests.

As a descriptor of ethnicity and nationhood, "identity" has a rich and surprising semantic genealogy. Identity possessed a fascinating semantic history—indeed a couple of quite distinct semantic histories—in the field of ethnicity and nationhood long before it assumed the meaning it currently holds within that area. The earliest usage of "identity" in the field of ethnicity is essentially the application of the restricted meaning of sameness to different groups and cultures. For instance, in 1669 Theophilus Gale claimed that the Canaanite origin of the Phoenicians was "manifest from the identitie of their languages."[49] No less an authority than Thomas Jefferson can be found using the term "identity" in this way. In a letter of May 27, 1813 to his loyal correspondent and former political opponent, John Adams, Jefferson discusses the contemporary debate over the ethnic origins of the native Americans. Amerindian linguistics were at the heart of the debate. Did native American languages provide evidence of descent from the

Hebrews (as argued by Adair), the Trojans (as advanced by Moreton), the Tartars (as championed by Brerewood), or the Mongol followers of Kouli Khan (as claimed by Reinold Foster)? Jefferson takes into account the theological import of the question, noting that some polygenists, such as Bernard Romans, suggest that "God created an original man and woman in this part of the globe," while others, such as Brerewood, argue that the Amerindians "must of necessity fetch their beginning from Noah's ark." Monogenist orthodoxy suggests that all the languages of the earth bear some affinity to one another. At this point Jefferson points out that this raises a vital and highly subjective issue of definition: "To wit, what constitutes identity, or difference in two things? (in the common acceptation of sameness). All languages may be called the same, as being all made up of the same primitive sounds, expressed by the letters of the different alphabets." But this doesn't really suffice for the critical ascription of unity of language insisted upon by the monogenists. Jefferson then proceeds to discuss the classification of languages into groups, such as the Celtic, the Gothic and so on, and suggests that in the process of constructing such family trees "we then ascribe other meanings to the terms 'same' and 'different'. In some one of these senses, Barton, and Adair, and Foster, and Brerewood, and Moreton, may be right, every one according to his own definition of what constitutes 'identity'. Romans indeed takes a higher stand, and supposes a separate creation. On the same unscriptural ground, he had but to mount one step higher, to suppose no creation at all . . . " Jefferson's letter to Adams provides a vivid example of the deep theological implications of ethnicity, as well as a clear indication of how differently the word "identity" was used in this sphere of discourse.[50]

Consider some other mundane examples. In 1799 Robert Macfarlan appended to his translation of George Buchanan's *De Iure Regni apud Scotos* a dissertation that dealt with "the pretended identity of the Getes and Scythians." In 1829 an anonymous treatise was published in London entitled *Identity of the Religions called Druidical and Hebrew; demonstrated from the Nature and Objects of their worship* while in 1866 the Reverend Donald McIntyre published *On the antiquity of the Gaelic language, showing the identity of the present vernacular of the Highlands with the Gaelic of ancient times.*

Within the sphere of ethnicity and nationhood, "identity" did once have the meaning of the common brotherhood and unity of the human race. In other words, whereas now identity has come to signify that which divides humanity into nations, ethnicities, and other minorities of one sort or another, it once stood for the underlying unity of human kind. It also had another meaning in the ethnic and national field of indicating where two ethnic or national labels disguised a sameness in the ethnic composition of two apparently—but only superficially—distinct groups. This usage can be found in the emerging field of ethnology or science of races. In 1848 W. B. Carpenter, reviewing the prominent Bristolian monogenist racial theorist James Cowles Prichard in the *Edinburgh Review,* wrote: "Independent of the aid which philological research affords to other departments of ethnology, it directly bears upon the great problem of the unity or identity of mankind." Carpenter went on to discuss the common provenance of what were then reckoned to be the five major language groups of the Old World: the Indo-European, Turanian, Chinese, Syro-Arabian, and African: "No scientific philologist, we believe, any longer retains a doubt that all these languages have been derived from one primitive stock, deviating from their original identity by variations at first merely dialectic, but gradually increased."[51] Other reviews of Prichard's work in the *North British Review* and *Blackwood's Magazine* used the term "identity" to mean a shared humanity sprung from a common stock, as in the expression both deployed, "identity of species."[52] In a similar fashion, the controversial anatomist and racial theorist Robert Knox spoke in *The Races of Men* (1850) of "the asserted identity of the Red Indian throughout the entire range of continental America."[53]

Even doctrinaire nationalists used identity in this restricted sense. William Burns, one of Scotland's first explicitly nationalist historians, denied that "nationality" was "always, or necessarily, synonymous with identity of race." On the other hand, wrote Burns, "a common history, identity of memories and associations, of institutions and interests, of ideas and aspirations, are even more efficient in producing that sympathy which is the essence of nationality." Here is a self-consciously nationalist writer, dealing with the subject of national identities (as we might put it), and using the term "identity." But Burns is not using the term identity to refer to racial or ethnic or national identity; rather Burns is using identity in the dry, technical sense of sameness of relationship,. basically the same usage as that of his countryman Hume over a hundred years previously.[54]

Indeed, identity only became fixed to ethnic and national subjects during the nineteenth century. There are three quite distinct semantic histories of the term "identity" in this particular field of the ethnic and national. The language of "identity" was first intensively deployed in the spheres of ethnicity and nationhood not to emphasize ethnic or national distinctiveness, but in the restricted sense of one ethnic group or nation being identical to another, and this is the case with two of the three distinct usages of "identity" in this area.

The first decisive conjunction of identity with ethnicity and nationhood came in the early stages of a movement whose later trajectory turned out to be sinister and deeply disturbing. The British Israelites, who argued that the true children of Israel were not the modern Jews, but the white Anglo-Saxon and Celtic peoples of Great Britain and the United States of America, hijacked the term "identity" during the nineteenth century for their own particular purposes. British Israelites, the forerunners of today's Christian Identity movement, were not a Protestant denomination as such, but a loose cross-denominational organization that upheld a particular reading of Israelite history. In particular, the British Israelites contended that they had a solution to the mystery of the dispersal of the northern kingdom of Israel. After the defeat at Megiddo in 722 BC, there were mass deportations of Jews from the northern kingdom, which comprised ten of the dynastic tribes descended from the patriarch Jacob, namely the tribes of Reuben, Simon, Issachar, Zevulun, Manasseh, Ephraim, Dan, Naphtali, Gad, and Asher. The southern kingdom of Judah, which comprised the remaining two tribes of Judah and Benjamin, survived. Nobody knew the whereabouts of the Ten Lost Tribes, though there was plenty of speculation. The primary begetter of British Israelism, John Wilson (d.1871), an autodidact from a radical weaving background, claimed that the peoples of northern Europe were the offspring of the lost tribes of Israel, the British Isles themselves being the province of the tribe of Ephraim. Moreover, these peoples also inherited from their ancient

Israelite ancestors the divine promises that God had given to the northern tribes, and therefore had a central starring role in the fulfilment of prophecy. Wilson pressed bogus etymology into the service of his argument, with the suggestion that the very name of Britain derived from the ancient Hebrew word for covenant, "brit." Wilson promoted his ideas on the lecture circuit in Ireland and Britain, and in 1840 published his *Lectures on Our Israelitish Origin*, which ran through five editions by 1876. The British-Israelite ideology that it spawned is a quasi-heresy with sinister implications. For although inspired to some extent by philo-semitism, at best it excludes modern Jews from the promises made to the northern tribes of Israel, or worse, offensively treats modern Jews as impostors, certainly by contrast with the supposedly authentic claims of the white Anglo-Saxon Protestant peoples to the status occupied in sacred providential history by their supposed Old Testament ancestors.[55]

Anglo-Israelite literature was drenched in the language of identity. The author of *The Remnant in Assyria ready to Perish* (1842) spoke of the "identity" of the Nestorians with the ten lost tribes. Protheroe Smith wrote *Identity of Israel with the English and Kindred Races* while the pseudonymous Philo-Israel published *A Resume of the Scriptural Arguments, Proving the Identity of the British Race, with the Lost Ten Tribes.* Edward Hine's publication, *The Forty-Seven Identifications* indicates precisely how the term identity was used in British Israelism. John Gilder Shaw, in *Israel Notwithstanding* (1879), spoke variously of "Identity Truth," "The Identity," and "the subject of our Identity," a usage clarified by his references to the "valuable testimony in favour of our [British] identity with Israel." Shaw also referred to "the Identity of the British race with the Lost Tribes" and the "Identity of the Anglo-Saxon race with the Lost Tribes." Similarly the theme of George Bullock's *The British not Gentiles* was "the identity of the British nation with the Lost Ten Tribes of Israel." In *The British Nation Identical with the Stone Kingdom of Nebuchadnezzar's Dream* (London, 1880?), J. M. Grant, the President of the Cheltenham Anglo-Israel Association and Vice-President of the Metropolitan Anglo-Israel Association, discussed "the question of our [English] Identity with the House of Israel." In another paper given before the Cheltenham Anglo-Israel Association, Major-General A. M.

Rainey mentioned "Identity writers." Frederick Danvers in *The Covenant or Jacob's Heritage* (1877) produced evidence in chapter ix, entitled "The Identification," which to his satisfaction provided "proofs of England's identity with Israel." If there were no reasons for doubting that "the Israelites and Scythians were the same people," then concluded Danvers, "the identity of the Anglo-Saxon race with God's chosen seed is so far established." The leitmotif of identity recurs in late nineteenth-century British-Israelite organizations, such as Edward Hine's unsuccessful British-Israel Identity Corporation or the Lost Israel Identification Society of Brooklyn established by the Reverend Joseph Wild. This usage was accepted by opponents of Anglo-Israelism. In an attack on the mistaken "identifications" of the British Israelites in his work *The Mystery of the Jew* (1872), the Reverend Rushton Talbot utilized the term "identity" in a similar fashion: his subtitle was *A Refutation of the theory as to the Identity of the English Nation with the Lost House of Israel.* The modern heirs of British Israelism are in fact known as the Christian Identity movement. In the ethnological system of Identity Truth, ethnic or national identity meant being of the same racial stock as another people. Identity meant being one and the same people; it was not used to indicate the values or character or peculiarities of any one group.[56]

A second surprising usage of identity in the field of ethnic relations emerged in South Africa in the early part of the twentieth century. Here "identity" was used to denote an anti-racist policy. Identity was the opposite of "differentiation," that is of racial segregation. Edgar Brookes, Professor of Public Administration and Political Science and Lecturer in Native Law and Administration at Transvaal University College, Pretoria, in *The History of Native Policy in South Africa* contended that there were "three great lines of policy" on what he termed "the Native problem," namely "identity," "subordination" and "differentiation." Describing "the liberal policy of identity" and its likely consequences, Brookes claimed that the "liberal policy of identity means sooner or later that Natives will govern Europeans or that all distinctions will be lost in a fusion, complete politically and considerable even physically." Indeed, he argued, "the result of the thoroughgoing application of the policy of identity would be, in a few generations' time, that South Africa's population would consist of a small class of white aristocrats, a large and increasing mixed population, a diminishing number of 'poor whites', rapidly intermarrying with Natives and Coloured people —and for the largest class of all—large masses of semi-Europeanised natives." Brookes found "identity" to be too liberal a prescription for South Africa, denying that "kindliness, courtesy and dignity" were "necessarily" or exclusively "bound up with the policy of identity."[57] Almost half a century later the term still enjoyed some currency among commentators on colonial issues. Marjory Perham in her Reith Lectures on "The Colonial Reckoning" described the "policy sometimes known as 'identity'; of regarding all men as much the same, of simply extending the government and law of the existing white colony over the local Hottentots and Bantu."[58] This specific South African definition of "identity," which is listed as a separate definition in the *Oxford English Dictionary*,[59] serves as a reminder of how treacherous the English language can be. Whereas identity might be presumed in such a context to refer to black identity or white identity, to Xhosa or Zulu or British or Afrikaans identity, the term referred instead to the obliteration of ethnic distinctions in the cause of a common humanity.

The third meaning of identity is our own. Yet the current usage of identity with which the modern academic community has become overfamiliar is of very recent vintage. Consider, for example, the most famous juxtaposition of "identity" and "community" in the first half of the twentieth century, which appears in the opening lines of Aldous Huxley's dystopian novel *Brave New World* (1932): "A squat grey building of only thirty-four storeys. Over the main entrance the words, CENTRAL LONDON HATCHERY AND CONDITIONING CENTRE, and, in a shield the World State's motto, COMMUNITY, IDENTITY, STABILITY." Here, identity and community are not yoked together as they would be later in the twentieth century. The significance of "Identity" in the World State's motto is soon revealed in Huxley's description of the Bokanovsky process at the Hatchery. "Bokanovskification" involved arresting the development of the fertilized eggs of future lower-caste Gammas, Deltas, and Epsilons. In response to this check to their growth, the eggs then bud, up to a limit of ninety-six embryonic buds per original egg, though seventy-two was the average. The Bokanovsky process contributes significantly to the central political aim of the World State, social stability, by creating enormous batches of identitical siblings who as children are then subjected to massive doses of psychological conditioning to stamp out any traces of individuality: "Standard men and women; in uniform batches. The whole of a small factory staffed with the products of a single bokanovskified egg. 'Ninety-six identical twins working ninety-six identical machines!' The voice was almost tremulous with enthusiasm. 'You really know where you are. For the first time in history.' He quoted the planetary motto. 'Community, Identity, Stability.'" Later in the novel, and much less centrally than this major usage, Huxley does use "identity" in a different way. Discussing the weekly Solidarity Service, a ritual bonding session for a group of twelve more highly individuated Alpha caste members, Huxley uses identity—quite casually and more peripherally—in a more familiar way: "Man, woman, man, in a ring of endless alternation round the table. Twelve of them ready to be made one, waiting to come together, to be fused, to lose their twelve separate identities in a larger being."[60]

Despite Huxley's secondary employment of identity in a recognizably modern way, this was still a somewhat unusual usage and, one suspects, as yet far from common. Indeed Philip Gleason has traced the origins of the modern academic usage of "identity" to the social science and psychology of the 1950s.[61] A key figure in the transmutation of identity in Anglo-American usage was a non-native speaker of English, Erik H. Erikson. Identity, in its current usage, seems to have been coined by a figure we might be tempted to describe—anachronistically, of course—as a man of confused, multiple, and overlapping identities, ethnic, national, and personal. Erikson's father has not been solidly identified; his mother, Karla Abrahamsen, was from a prominent Copenhagen Jewish family. Born in 1902, Erikson grew up in Germany where his mother went on to marry Theodor Homburger—not his biological father—in 1904. During the late 1920s, after a period of dislocation and aimlessness of the sort he was later to analyze professionally, Erikson was drawn into the Freud circle in Vienna. Erikson traveled from Copenhagen to America in 1933, and assumed naturalized citizenship in the United States under the chosen name Erik Homburger Erikson.[62]

Erikson formulated his identity concept in the mid- to late-1940s and his classic work *Childhood and Society* was published in 1950. Erikson used identity in the first instance to denote a specific stage in the life cycle. Identity formed a crucial part in the transition from youth to adulthood. In youth there was a struggle between identity and identity diffusion. Identity diffusion involved a breakdown in an individual's sense of continuity and sameness, a meaning to one's life story. Identity diffusion was the basis of a personal identity crisis. Erikson warned of the dangers of a synthetic identity apart from one's true self. Significantly, Erikson's psychohistory *Young Man Luther* (in which the word "identity" is bandied around more cavalierly, in such formulations as "negative identity," "identity crisis" and "Super-identity") started life with the provisional title *Varieties of Identity Diffusion.* Erikson's use of identity did much to impart a meaning of authenticity to the term identity.[63]

Erikson's story indicates that the modern sense of identity has another particular historical provenance. It emerged in the context of the disorientating immigrant experience, in a sense of being uprooted from one's native soil, of a loss of solid moorings. The immigrant was prone to some of the same bewilderment and disorientation felt by adolescents, feelings of alienation and uprootedness that were exacerbated by the pressures of modern urban society. Identity, in the sense of authentic individual autonomy, enabled one to resist the pressure to conform to the dictates of mass society. Erich Fromm, an immigrant from Germany, responded in a similar way to Erikson, warning of the dangers of lapsing into a "pseudo-self"-hood. The notion of authenticity resonates too in the work of the sociologist David Riesman, author of *The Lonely Crowd* (1950).[64]

Erikson enjoyed considerable acclaim, and his concept of "identity" seeped further and further into circulation, not only through the universities, but also through the media. It seems very likely that the provenance of our current usage of identity is American higher education during the third quarter of the twentieth century. In a review article published in 1955, Margaret Mead announced that "a new concept is clamoring for acceptance—the concept of identity." "Identity" entered into a much wider circulation during the 1960s and 1970s. Quoted in a *Newsweek* article of December 21, 1970, entitled, "Erik Erikson: The Quest for Identity," Robert Bellah, a prominent sociologist of religion proclaimed: "If there is one book you can be sure undergraduates have read, it is Erikson's first one. You can't always be sure that they've read Shakespeare, but you know they've read Erikson."[65]

Ironically, Erikson was criticized toward the end of his life for evasiveness on the question of his own personal identity. Marshall Berman accused Erikson of evading his Jewish identity. Had not Erikson changed his name from Homburger to Erikson as a way of repudiating and disguising his Jewishness? The father of identity was marked down by Berman as a shifty and fainthearted suppressor of his own ethnic identity. Extrapolating from Erikson's own work in identity psychology, Berman now made Jewishness—one's ethnicity—the litmus test of an authentic identity.[66]

Nevertheless it is important to stress that Erikson himself was not *directly* responsible for the exploitation of identity in the fields of ethnic and national history. He popularized the term; but we do not use it as Erikson used it. Indeed, by a further irony, Erikson himself denounced what might be called the extension of his identity concept into the sphere of ethnicity and nationhood. Erikson was a champion of "universal specieshood" and explicitly rejected the process of "pseudospeciation"—or what might be described as the manufacture of exclusive group identities—whereby differentiations between groups hardened into "dogmas and isms." Instead, in this sphere, Erikson championed a "universal identity" that embraced the various differences and divisions of the world. Curiously, this "universal identity" bore a stronger resemblance to the pre-Eriksonian usage of identity to signal mankind's shared origins and character and had much less affinity with the use—or abuse—in the sphere of ethnicity of Erikson's own deployment of "identity."[67]

Given this curious and surprising semantic history, what are the implications for the historiography of ethnicity and nationhood? The language of identity is not mentioned in the great constitutional documents that united the British nations. There were no provisions in the Anglo-Scottish Treaty of Union of 1707 for the preservation of Scottish "identity," expressed in exactly those terms. Of course, there were concrete guarantees regarding the peculiarities of the Scottish legal system and, in an accompanying Act, the particular privileges of the established Scottish church.[68] However, the term identity was not used. "Identity" has only seeped into constitutional documents in the very recent past in the wake of wider social currency. For instance, identity looms prominently in the Belfast Agreement of 1998. Here "parity of esteem" between the two communities in Northern Ireland was a central plank of the peace process. Parties to the agreement

> affirm that whatever choice is freely exercised by a majority of the people of Northern Ireland, the power of the sovereign government with jurisdiction there shall be exercised with rigorous impartiality on behalf of all people in the diversity of their identities and traditions and shall be founded on the principles of full respect for, and equality of, civil, political, social and cultural rights, of freedom for discrimination for all citizens, and of parity of esteem and of just and equal treatment for the identity, ethos, and aspirations of both communities.

In addition, the parties agree to "recognise the birthright of all the people of Northern Ireland to identify themselves and be accepted as Irish or British, or both, as they may so choose . . . "[69] Identity is linked to the psychological notion of "parity of esteem," a psycho-social concept unheard of, and possibly unimaginable, in 1707.

The Canadian political scientist and philosopher Charles Taylor has referred to this new phenomenon as the "politics of recognition." Although "parity of esteem" in Northern Ireland exemplifies the notion of "recognition" discussed by Taylor, as does the hyphenated multiculturalism of the United States, his insights are, of course, more immediately shaped by the modern Canadian predicament about identity. In fact, Taylor has been active in the intense identity politics of Canada, and Quebec in particular. Based for much of his career at McGill University in Montreal, Taylor served as national vice-president of the New Democratic Party (NDP) and as president of its Quebec branch, as well as running on several occasions for the federal parliament as an NDP candidate, on one occasion against Pierre Trudeau. In addition, Taylor has been prominent in debates over the Quebec language issue. Such activities endow Taylor's theories of recognition with a worldly dimension so often lacking in contemporary political philosophy. Taylor is concerned not only with communities, but also with the self, and his analysis of the politics of recognition runs in tandem with his genealogical approach to the formation of the modern "self." Taylor is equally interested to understand the flip side of the politics of recognition, namely a concern about non-recognition or misrecognition. As Taylor notes: "Nonrecognition or misrecognition can inflict harm, can be a form of oppression, imprisoning someone in a false, distorted, and reduced mode of being." But could misrecognition or nonrecognition inflict harm on ethnic and national groups in the past? And, if not, does this mean that they had a reduced—or minimal—sense of identity? Taylor notes that the premodern notion of honor has given way to a modern concern with dignity. Taylor traces the ultimate source of the politics of recognition to "the massive subjective turn of modern culture." We now look inward. Taylor's analysis explores the extent to which recognition has succeeded an emphasis on rights and liberties. Minorities and subaltern groups, it seems, do not want freedom alone; they want to be recognized for what they believe themselves to be. The former does not presuppose an identity, or rather it presupposes a very diminished sense of identity compared to its modern form.[70]

Nevertheless, Taylor assumes that identity must be a staple component of human culture, even if not always expressed in those terms or given the prominence that it enjoys today: "In premodern times, people didn't speak of 'identity' and 'recognition'—not because people didn't have (what we call) identities, or because these didn't depend on recognition, but rather because these were then too unproblematic to be thematized as such."[71] I remain to be convinced of this; and here I must part company from Taylor, on a number of grounds. Premodern conceptions of ethnicity were anything but "unproblematic." Research into early modern political argument finds Englishmen taking sides—Whig or Tory—on the question of whether parliament and the common law had their roots in the Anglo-Saxon period or whether the Norman Conquest created a caesura in English history, all institutions thereafter existing by grace of the conqueror. On the other hand, the very same generations of Englishmen tended to trace the origins of their ecclesiastical institutions back to the era of the ancient Britons. Do we have here a case of multiple identities, of Englishmen identifying both with Germanic Saxons and with Celtic Britons? Who did they really think were their ethnic ancestors? Or were Englishmen thinking juridically and not in terms of "identities"? Were Englishmen using the ethnic patchwork of English history to construct narratives of institutional continuity (or—in the case of royalists—disruption) within the bounds of a particular territory? Did early modern Englishmen think in an instrumental fashion about ethnicity, an approach alien to modern assumptions about identities?[72]

Early modern England is no singularity in this regard. Similar puzzles become apparent in the cases of Scotland and Ireland. In early modern Ireland, Protestants, most of whom descended from the New English settlers of the sixteenth and seventeenth centuries, traced their political privileges back to the arrival of the Old English in the twelfth century; however in the ecclesiastical sphere they celebrated the history of the ancient Celtic church of Ireland as if it were the direct institutional precursor of the Protestant Church of Ireland. Clearly, their primary concern was with the pedigree of their institutions, finding in distinguished and historic lineages a means of establishing the legitimacy of their political constitution and their embattled minority church. Otherwise, ethnologically speaking their sense of "identity" appears very confused. In Scotland the political nation of the Lowlands constructed political and ecclesiastical myths that drew upon the history of the ancient Gaelic Scots of Dalriada, while directing hostile barbs and directing reformist programs aimed at the assimilation of Highland Gaels to non-Gaelic Lowland norms. Again, the historian is presented with a very confused scene of confused ethnic identification, or with a culture in which ethnic identification is subordinated to the more immediate needs of political and religious ideologies. Did the early modern world have "identities" in any meaningful sense?[73]

The political arguments of the early modern British world were not expressive of identities; but rather they were concerned with other issues, with dignity, autonomy, and prescriptive rights. Character, for example, was a prominent concern of civic humanists.[74] Yet, despite this obsession, civic humanists did not emphasize the identities that distinguished different ethnic groups; rather they stressed the mutability of all peoples. Cassandra-like, they warned that every people was liable to the temptations of luxury and corruption. Institutions, laws, and morals determined the "character" of a people. Civic humanists were not concerned with the ethnic specifics of identity so much as the moral characteristics required to sustain constitutional self-rule. "Between the Roman people under the commonwealth, and the Roman people under the dominion of the emperors," claimed the eighteenth-century civic humanist Thomas Gordon, "the difference was as great as between different nations, and they only resembled each other in language and dress. They were indeed as different, or rather as opposite, as men uncorrupted and free are to debauched slaves." In civic humanist thinking, the gulf between freedom and slavery provided the key distinction, not the superficial ethnic differences to be found among ancient Romans, Athenians, and Spartans.[75]

The literati of the early modern world appear to display in their histories, treatises, and pamphlets, multiple senses of who they were. But were these senses of themselves, strictly speaking, "identities"? To describe an early modern allegiance or concern for jurisdictional autonomy as an identity suggests the importation of a psychological and subjective dimension into an outward and objective position. The ascription of identities to early modern figures is to gloss another kind of affiliation with an additional psychological coating unimaginable to the original. Their confessional adherence, allegiance to rulers, sense of status, obsession with pedigree, concern to preserve inherited privileges, and confident ascription of moral categories left little space for identities as we conceive them. The resilience of religious and humanistic discourses precluded quests for authentic identities. Indeed the notion of religious identities seems peculiarly problematic. Orthodoxy, conformity, and obligation—rather than identification—historically determined the relationships between individuals and their religion; though such relationships may well be different in a pluralistic society. Truth and status are external and objective; identity is internalized and subjective. As Kathleen Wilson notes, people of the eighteenth century "tended to assess themselves less through their internal lives (although their state of virtue, sin and morality was important to many) than through their behavior, social position and reputation"; therefore "in some ways, the notion of identity in its modern psychological sense may have been anachronistic." For Wilson, however, identity remains a necessary, albeit problematic, tool for investigating eighteenth-century experiences.[76]

Is "identity," perhaps, an avoidable anachronism? Does the existence of an identity depend upon the possession of a language of identity, which we have, I think, shown to be historically contingent? Does the existence of an alternative vocabulary for what we would call "identity" change the nature of premodern identity into something quite distinct and barely recognizable, into something different altogether? I remain to be convinced that a people without the concept of "identity" can hold an identity or identities. Did identities exist in the past, albeit expressed in a more muted way, or did they not exist at all, with group consciousness expressed in some other way entirely? Authenticity now exhibits a salience in political culture that it never formerly enjoyed.

The application of "identity" to other periods distorts understanding of the ways in which these earlier cultures saw themselves and articulated their values. In particular, an anachronistic emphasis on identity obscures other—more historically sensitive—priorities. There appear to be doubts about the validity of identity as a cross-cultural concept. The demands of past-centeredness lead the historian to inquire whether the previous invisibility of ethnocentric authenticity and identity in political culture was actually the result of a genuine absence in the mental and cultural equipment of past generations? One wonders whether identity was merely of secondary importance in the past, and hence a relatively submerged or latent feature of past discourse. Alternatively, it may have been present, but expressed in a very different idiom or register.

In what precise ways was past identity anchored in reality? How, for example, was the identity of an early modern harmed? Today, identity is harmed just as much by a denial of respect as by any denial of rights to a group. An identity in the modern sense is not a mere instrument; rather it exemplifies the authentic being of a people. Identities do seem to have become more visible with accelerated secularization. People whose grandparents adhered to "The Truth," as the religious communities in which they worshipped saw it, now began to talk of "values." Identities seem to constitute another element in this new lexicon. In this respect, the past differs widely from the present. What was once—if it existed at all—a matter of privilege and right, possibly dignity, is now a matter of respect and recognition.

This leads finally to the vexed subject of historical nominalism. Are the historian's categories mere terms of convenience, and, as such, used in altogether too cavalier a fashion? Yet genuine puzzlement—beyond historiographical resolution—continues to lurk behind the issue. If past generations did not use the term identity to mean what it means today, did they nevertheless still articulate sentiments that correspond in some reasonable measure with what would nowadays be recognized as identity? Or is this a mere dispute about words?[77]

Notes

1. See, e.g., Keith Jenkins, *Re-thinking History* (London: Routledge, 1991).
2. John Vincent, *An Intelligent Person's Guide to History* (1995; Rev. ed. London: Duckworth, 1996), 28–29.
3. For an overview of the problem and the debate, see John Hutchinson and Anthony D. Smith eds., *Nationalism* (Oxford: Oxford University Press, 1994).

4. Elie Kedourie, *Nationalism* (1960; New ed. with afterword, London: Hutchinson, 1985); Isaiah Berlin, "The Bent Twig: on the Rise of Nationalism," in *The Crooked Timber of Humanity* (London: Fontana, 1991); Eugene Kamenka, "Political Nationalism: the Evolution of the Idea," in *Nationalism: the Nature and Evolution of an Idea*, ed. Kamenka (London: Edward Arnold, 1976).
5. Ernest Gellner, *Nations and Nationalism* (Oxford: Blackwell, 1983).
6. Benedict Anderson, *Imagined Communities* (London: Verso, 1983).
7. See e.g. Eugen Weber, *Peasants into Frenchmen: the Modernisation of Rural France, 1870–1914* (London: Chatto and Windus, 1977).
8. Miroslav Hroch, *Social Preconditions of National Revival in Europe* (Cambridge: Cambridge University Press, 1985); Hroch, "From National Movement to the fully-formed Nation," *New Left Review* 198 (1993), 3–20; Eric Hobsbawm, *Nations and nationalism since 1780* (Cambridge: Cambridge University Press, 1990).
9. See, e.g., Neil Davidson, *The Origins of Scottish Nationhood* (London: Pluto, 2000).
10. See, e.g., Anthony D. Smith, *The Ethnic Origins of Nations* (Oxford: Blackwell, 1986); Smith, *The Nation in History* (Cambridge: Polity Press, 2000).
11. John A. Armstrong, *Nations before Nationalism* (Chapel Hill: University of North Carolina Press, 1982).
12. Samuel Johnson, *A Dictionary of the English Language* (1755; London, facsimile reprint, Times Books, 1979).
13. Raymond Williams, *Keywords* (1976; Rev. ed. London: Fontana, 1983), 213.
14. See, e.g., Peter Mandler, chap. 2, "Nationalist Origins 1800–1880" in *History and National Life* (London: Profile Books, 2002).

15. Michael Billig, *Banal Nationalism* (London: Sage Publications, 1995).

16. David M. Potter, "The Historian's Use of Nationalism and Vice Versa," *American Historical Review* 67, 4 (1961–62): 924–50, at 924 and 950.

17. D. H. Fischer, *Historians' Fallacies: Towards a Logic of Historical Thought* (New York: Harper and Row, 1970), 236–37.

18. R. R. Davies, "The Peoples of Britain and Ireland 110–1400. I. Identities," *Transactions of the Royal Historical Society* 6th ser. 4 (1994): 1–20, at 1, 3.

19. Patrick J. Geary, *The Myth of Nations: The Medieval Origins of Europe* (Princeton: Princeton University Press, 2002), 11–13, 15–16, 26–29, 33.

20. Patrick Amory, *People and Identity in Ostrogothic Italy 489–554* (Cambridge: Cambridge University Press, 1997), 33, 35–36, 326–27, 334.

21. Michael Biddiss, "Nationalism and the Moulding of Modern Europe," *History* 79, no. 257 (1994): 412–32, at p. 413.

22. Eric Hobsbawm and Terence Ranger eds., *The Invention of Tradition* (Cambridge: Cambridge University Press, 1983); Hobsbawm, "Outside and Inside History" and "Identity History is not Enough," both in Hobsbawm, *On History* (London: Abacus, 1997).

23. See, e.g., Dennis Deletant and Harry Hanak, eds., *Historians as Nation-Builders: Central and South-East Europe* (Houndmills: Macmillan, 1988); D. V. Schwartz and R. Panossian, eds., *Nationalism and History: The Politics of Nation Building in Post-Soviet Armenia, Azerbaijan and Georgia* (Toronto: University of Toronto Centre for Russian and East European Studies, 1994); S. Berger, M. Donovan and K. Passmore, eds., *Writing National Histories: Western Europe since 1800* (London: Routledge, 1999).

24. See, e.g., Peter Sahlins, *Boundaries: the Making of France and Spain in the Pyrenees* (Berkeley: University of California Press, 1989); Hugh F. Kearney, *The British Isles: A History of Four Nations* (Cambridge: Cambridge University Press, 1989); David Armitage and Michael Braddick, eds., *The British Atlantic World 1500–1800* (Basingstoke: Palgrave, 2002).

25. Roy Porter and Mikulas Teich, eds., *The Enlightenment in National Context* (Cambridge: Cambridge University Press, 1981); Porter and Teich eds., *Romanticism in National Context* (Cambridge: Cambridge University Press, 1988); Porter and Teich eds., *The Renaissance in National Context* (Cambridge: Cambridge University Press, 1992); etc.

26. Walker Connor, *Ethnonationalism* (Princeton: Princeton University Press, 1994), chaps. 4 and 9.

27. Susan Reynolds, *Kingdoms and Communities in Western Europe 900–1300* (Oxford: Oxford University Press, 1986), 252 fn. 254.

28. Smith, *Ethnic Origins of Nations*, 47.

29. Johnson, *Dictionary*.

30. Thomas Blount, *Glossographia* (1656; Menston: Scolar Press reprint, 1969).

31. Nathaniel Bailey, *Universal Etymological Dictionary* (6th edn., London, 1733).

32. Robert Gordon, "Encouragements for New Galloway in America," in *Royal Letters, Charters and Tracts, relating to the Colonization of New Scotland*, ed David Laing (Edinburgh, Bannatyne Club, 1867).

33. Edward, Lord Herbert of Cherbury, *The Antient Religion of the Gentiles* (1663: trans. from Latin, London, 1705), 3.

34. Sylvester O'Halloran, *A General History of Ireland* 2 vols. (London, 1778), II, 113.

35. *Oxford English Dictionary [OED]* 2nd edn., 20 vols (Oxford: Oxford University Press, 1989), V, 423.

36. For the problematics of ethnicity in the ancient Greek world, see Catherine Morgan, *Early Greek States beyond the Polis* (London: Routledge, 2003), chap. 1.

37. OED., V, 423.

38. *Ibid.*, VI, 448–49, 454–55.

39. Colin Kidd, *British Identities before Nationalism: Ethnicity and Nationhood in the Atlantic World, 1600–1800* (Cambridge: Cambridge University Press, 1999), chaps. 2 and 3.

40. Johnson, *Dictionary.*

41. See the illusionless self-awareness of Jim Dixon, a probationary history lecturer, in Kingsley Amis, *Lucky Jim* (1954; Harmondsworth: Penguin, 1992), 14.

42. Jenkins, *Re-thinking History*, 16.

43. R. Handler, "Is 'identity' a useful cross-cultural concept?" in *Commemorations: the politics of national identity*, ed. John R. Gillis (Princeton: Princeton University Press, 1994), 27.

44. OED, VII, 618, 620.

45. Johnson, *Dictionary; Encyclopedia Britannica* 3 vols. (Edinburgh, 1771), II, 830.

46. David Hume, *A Treatise of Human Nature* (Oxford: Oxford University Press, 1978), 252–53, 261.

47. *Ibid.*, 253.

48. *Ibid.*, 14–15.

49. Quoted OED, VII, 620.

50. Thomas Jefferson to John Adams, May 27, 1813, *Adams-Jefferson Letters*, ed. Lester J. Cappon (Chapel Hill: University of North Carolina Press, 2 vols., 1959), II, 323–24.

51. [W. B. Carpenter], "Ethnology, or the Science of Races," *Edinburgh Review* 88 (Oct. 1848): 429–87, at 432 and 471.

52. "The Physical History of Man," *North British Review* 4 (Nov. 1845): 177–201, at 179; [William Grove], Review of *Natural History of Man*, *Blackwood's Magazine* 56 (Sept. 1844): 312–30, at 330.

53. Robert Knox, *The Races of Men* (London: Renshaw, 1850), 126–27.

54. William Burns, *The Scottish War of Independence*, 2 vols. (Glasgow: Maclehose, 1874), I, 305–6.

55. Tudor Parfitt, *The Lost Tribes of Israel* (London: Weidenfeld and Nicolson, 2002); J. A. Aho, *The Politics of Righteousness: Idaho Christian Patriotism* (Seattle: University of Washington Press, 1990); Michael Barkun, *Religion and the Racist Right: The Origins of the Christian Identity Movement* (Revised ed. Chapel Hill: University of North Carolina Press, 1997).

56. John Gilder Shaw, *Israel Notwithstanding* (London, 1879), 77, 81, 87, 113, 117, 146–47; George Bullock, *The British not Gentiles* (London, n.d.), 1; J. M. Grant, *The British Nation Identical with the Stone Kingdom of Nebuchadnezzar's Dream* (London, [1880?]), 3; A. M. Rainey, *The Distribution of Ham, Shem, and Japheth* (London, [1881]), 9; Frederick Danvers, *The Covenant or Jacob's Heritage* (1877), 151, 155.

57. Edgar H. Brookes, *The History of Native policy in South Africa from 1830 to the present day* (2nd rev. ed. Pretoria: Van Schaik, 1927), 321, 449, 484, 499.

58. M. Perham, "The Politics of Emancipation," *The Listener* no. 1705 (Nov. 1961): 898.

59. *OED*, VII, p. 620.

60. Aldous Huxley, *Brave New World* (1932; London: Flamingo Modern Classics, 1994), 1, 5, 71–72.

61. Philip Gleason, "Identifying Identity: A Semantic History," *Journal of American History* 69, 4 (1982–83): 910–31.

62. Lawrence Friedman, *Identity's Architect: A Biography of Erik H. Erikson* (London: Free Association Books, 1999).

63. *Ibid.*, 149, 159–61, 171, 223–26, 266, 275; Erik Erikson, *Young Man Luther* (London: Faber and Faber, 1958), 12, 39, 49, 95, 176, 273.

64. Friedman, *Identity's Architect*, 103–4, 112, 162, 200, 238–41.

65. *Ibid.*, 304, 335.

66. *Ibid.*, 429–35.

67. *Ibid.*, 352, 380–81.

68. Gordon Donaldson ed., *Scottish Historical Documents* (1970; Reprinted Glasgow: Neil Wilson Publishing, 1997), 269–77.

69. The Agreement is on the Web at nio.gov.uk.

70. Charles Taylor, "The Politics of Recognition," in *Multiculturalism and the Politics of Recognition*, ed. Amy Gutmann (Princeton: Princeton University Press, 1992), 25, 27, 29; Ruth Abbey, *Charles Taylor* (Teddington: Acumen, 2000), 6.

71. Taylor, "Politics of Recognition," 35.

72. Kidd, *British Identities*, chs. 4, 5.

73. *Ibid.*, chaps. 6 and 7.

74. For civic humanism, see J. G. A. Pocock, *The Machiavellian Moment* (Princeton: Princeton University Press, 1975).

75. Thomas Gordon, "Discourses upon Tacitus," Discourse IX, "Of the People," in *The Works of Tacitus* vol. II, part 1 (Dublin, 1732), 159–66.

76. Kathleen Wilson, *The Island Race: Englishness, Empire and Gender in the Eighteenth Century* (London: Routledge, 2003), 2.

77. I should like to thank Dauvit Broun, Julia Rudolph, Brian Young, and Stephanie Larson for comments and suggestions.

Bibliography

Abbey, Ruth. *Charles Taylor*. Teddington: Acumen, 2000.

Aho, J. A. *The Politics of Righteousness: Idaho Christian Patriotism*. Seattle: University of Washington Press, 1990.

Amis, Kingsley. *Lucky Jim.* Harmondsworth: Penguin, 1992.

Amory, Patrick. *People and Identity in Ostrogothic Italy 489–554.* Cambridge: Cambridge University Press, 1997.

Anderson, Benedict. *Imagined Communities.* London: Verso, 1983.

Anon. "The Physical History of Man." *North British Review* 4 (Nov. 1845): 177–201.

Armitage, David, and Michael J. Braddick, eds. *The British Atlantic World 1500–1800.* Basingstoke: Palgrave, 2002.

Armstrong, John A. *Nations before Nationalism.* Chapel Hill: University of North Carolina Press, 1982.

Bailey, Nathan. *Universal Etymological Dictionary.* 6th ed. London, 1733.

Barkun, Michael. *Religion and the Racist Right: The Origins of the Christian Identity Movement.* rev. ed. Chapel Hill: University of North Carolina Press, 1997.

Berger, S. M. Donovan, and Kevin Passmore, eds. *Writing National Histories: Western Europe since 1800.* London: Routledge, 1999.

Berlin, Isaiah. "The Bent Twig: on the Rise of Nationalism." In *The Crooked Timber of Humanity,* Isaiah Berlin. London: Fontana, 1991.

Biddiss, Michael. "Nationalism and the Moulding of Modern Europe." *History* 79, no. 257 (1994): 412–32.

Billig, Michael. *Banal Nationalism.* London: Sage Publications, 1995.

Blount, Thomas. *Glossographia.* 1656. Reprinted Menston: Scolar Press,1969.

Brookes, Edgar H. *The History of Native policy in South Africa from 1830 to the present day.* 2nd rev. ed. Pretoria: Van Schaik, 1927.

Bullock, George, *The British not Gentiles.* London, n.d.

Burns, Williams. *The Scottish War of Independence.* 2 vols. Glasgow: Maclehose, 1874.

Cappon, Lester J., ed. *Adams-Jefferson Letters.* 2 vols. Chapel Hill: University of North Carolina Press, 1959.

Carpenter, W. B. "Ethnology, or the Science of Races." *Edinburgh Review* 88 (Oct. 1848): 429–87.

Connor, Walker. *Ethnonationalism.* Princeton: Princeton University Press, 1994.

Danvers, Frederick. *The Covenant or Jacob's Heritage.* n.p. 1877.

Davidson, Neil. *The Origins of Scottish Nationhood.* London: Pluto, 2000.

Davies, R. R. "The Peoples of Britain and Ireland 110–1400. I. Identities." *Transactions of the Royal Historical Society* 6th ser. 4 (1994): 1–20.

Deletant, Dennis, and Harry Hanak eds. *Historians as Nation-Builders: Central and South-East Europe.* Houndmills: Macmillan, 1988.

Donaldson, Gordon, ed. *Scottish Historical Documents.* 1970. Reprinted Glasgow: Neil Wilson Publishing, 1997.

Encyclopedia Britannica. 3 vols. Edinburgh, 1771.

Erikson, Erik. *Young Man Luther.* London: Faber and Faber, 1958.

Fischer, D. H. *Historians' Fallacies: Towards a Logic of Historical Thought.* New York: Harper and Row, 1970.

Friedman, Lawrence. *Identity's Architect: A Biography of Erik H. Erikson.* London: Free Association Books, 1999.

Geary, Patrick J. *The Myth of Nations: The Medieval Origins of Europe.* Princeton: Princeton University Press, 2002.

Gellner, Ernest. *Nations and Nationalism.* Oxford: Blackwell, 1983.

Gleason, Philip. "Identifying Identity: A Semantic History." *Journal of American History* 69, 4 (1982–83): 910–31.

Gordon, Robert. "Encouragements for New Galloway in America." In *Royal Letters, Charters and Tracts, relating to the Colonization of New Scotland,* ed. David Laing. Edinburgh: Bannatyne Club, 1867.

Gordon, Thomas. "Discourses upon Tacitus" Discourse IX, "Of the People." In *The Works of Tacitus.* Vol. 2, Part 1. Dublin, 1732.

Grant, J. M. *The British Nation Identical with the Stone Kingdom of Nebuchadnezzar's Dream.* London, [1880?].

Grove, W. Review of *Natural History of Man. Blackwood's Magazine* 56 (Sept. 1844): 312–30.

Handler, R. "Is 'identity' a useful cross-cultural concept?" In *Commemorations: the politics of national identity,* ed. John R. Gillis. Princeton: Princeton University Press, 1994.

Herbert of Cherbury, Edward, Lord. *The Antient Religion of the Gentiles.* 1663. Trans. from Latin, London, 1705.

Hobsbawm, Eric. *Nations and nationalism since 1780.* Cambridge: Cambridge University Press, 1990.

——. *On History.* London: Abacus, 1997.

Hobsbawm, Eric, and Terence Ranger, eds. *The Invention of Tradition.* Cambridge: Cambridge University Press, 1983.

Hroch, Miroslav. "From National Movement to the fully-formed Nation." *New Left Review* 198 (1993): 3–20.

——. *Social Preconditions of National Revival in Europe.* Cambridge: Cambridge University Press, 1985.

Hume, David. *A Treatise of Human Nature.* Oxford: Oxford University Press, 1978.

Hutchinson, John, and Anthony D. Smith, eds. *Nationalism.* Oxford: Oxford University Press, 1994.

Huxley, Aldous. *Brave New World.* 1932. London: Flamingo Modern Classics, 1994.

Jenkins, Keith. *Re-thinking History.* London: Routledge, 1991.

Johnson, Samuel. *A Dictionary of the English Language.* London, 1755; facsimile reprint, Times Books, 1979.

Kamenka, Eugene. "Political Nationalism: the Evolution of the Idea." In *Nationalism: the Nature and Evolution of an Idea,* ed. Eugene Kamenka. London: Edward Arnold, 1976.

Kearney, Hugh F. *The British Isles: A History of Four Nations.* Cambridge: Cambridge University Press, 1989.

Kedourie, Elie. *Nationalism.* 1960. New ed. with an afterword. London: Hutchinson, 1985.

Kidd, Colin. *British Identities before Nationalism: Ethnicity and Nationhood in the Atlantic World, 1600–1800.* Cambridge: Cambridge University Press, 1999.

Knox, Robert. *The Races of Men.* London: Renshaw, 1850.

Mandler, Peter. *History and National Life.* London: Profile Books, 2002.

Morgan, Catherine. *Early Greek States beyond the Polis.* London: Routledge, 2003.

O'Halloran, Sylvester. *A General History of Ireland.* 2 vols. London, 1778.

Oxford English Dictionary. 2nd ed., 20 vols. Oxford: Oxford University Press, 1989.

Parfitt, Tudor. *The Lost Tribes of Israel.* London: Weidenfeld and Nicolson, 2002.

Perham, M. "The Politics of Emancipation." *The Listener* no. 1705 (Nov. 1961).

Pocock, J. G. A. *The Machiavellian Moment.* Princeton: Princeton University Press, 1975.

Porter, Roy and Mikulas Teich eds. *The Enlightenment in National Context.* Cambridge: Cambridge University Press, 1981.

———. *The Renaissance in National Context.* Cambridge: Cambridge University Press, 1992.

———. *Romanticism in National Context.* Cambridge: Cambridge University Press, 1988.

Potter, David M. "The Historian's Use of Nationalism and Vice Versa." *American Historical Review* 67, 4 (1961–62): 924–50.

Rainey, A. M. *The Distribution of Ham, Shem, and Japheth.* London, 1881.

Reynolds, Susan. *Kingdoms and Communities in Western Europe 900–1300.* Oxford: Oxford University Press, 1986.

Sahlins, Peter. *Boundaries: the Making of France and Spain in the Pyrenees.* Berkeley: University of California Press, 1989.

Schwartz, D. V., and R. Panossian, eds. *Nationalism and History: The Politics of Nation Building in Post-Soviet Armenia, Azerbaijan and Georgia.* Toronto: University of Toronto Centre for Russian and East European Studies, 1994.

Shaw, John Gilder. *Israel Notwithstanding.* London, 1879.

Smith, Anthony D. *The Ethnic Origins of Nations.* Oxford: Blackwell, 1986.

———. *The Nation in History.* Cambridge: Polity Press, 2000.

Taylor, Charles. "The Politics of Recognition." In *Multiculturalism and the Politics of Recognition*, ed. Amy Guttmann. Princeton: Princeton University Press, 1992.

Vincent, John. *An Intelligent Person's Guide to History.* Rev. ed. London: Duckworth, 1996.

Weber, Eugen. *Peasants into Frenchmen: the Modernisation of Rural France, 1870–1914.* London: Chatto and Windus, 1977.

Williams, Raymond. *Keywords.* Rev. ed. London: Fontana, 1983.

Wilson, Kathleen. *The Island Race: Englishness, Empire and Gender in the Eighteenth Century.* London: Routledge, 2003.

Ann Moyer

"Without Passion or Partisanship": Florentine Historical Writing in the Age of Cosimo I

WRITINGS ON HISTORY HAD A HIGH PROFILE IN THE WORLD OF letters in sixteenth-century Europe. Rulers and governmental officials saw political value in recalling the past of their particular region. Historical works of all kinds found a wide individual readership as well. Publishers clearly expected historical publications to sell, for the presses of every region produced them in large numbers over the course of the century. History was among the principal fields of the studia humanitatis, and those with at least a smattering of humanistic education figured large among readers of history and even more so among its writers. Florence, with its reputation as a center for humanistic studies well established by the sixteenth century, had a particular and particularly important role in European historical studies. Florentine prominence in the field had been acknowledged already in the fifteenth century thanks to Leonardo Bruni (1369–1444), and had continued into the sixteenth with the great historians Niccolò Machiavelli (1469–1527) and Francesco Guicciardini (1483–1540).

These years saw great political changes in Florence as in the rest of Italy, many of them at the hands of foreign powers. The Holy Roman Emperor Charles V replaced Florence's republican government with a Medici duke in 1531 after a long siege, one more episode in the wars of

Italy that had racked the peninsula since the 1490s. The Florentines ratified the necessary change in their constitution the next year, in a political transition that marked for many twentieth-century historians the beginning of Florence's long decline. These modern historians tended to identify Florentine cultural creativity with its republican rule, so it was assumed that the loss of the latter led inevitably to the loss of the former as well. Yet that picture has begun to change significantly. Art historians have long taken a more positive view of sixteenth-century Florence; the administration of Cosimo I (1537–74) has come to find respect as well, with a greater appreciation of both his political leadership and his cultural programs. Indeed, Cosimo's men so excelled at organizing, planning, and managing major artistic projects as well as events such as court marriages and diplomatic visits, that many of the era's men of letters are known to modern historians solely in their roles as assistants to Cosimo's construction and presentation of a public Florentine image.

46 These sixteenth-century Florentines presented themselves and their city to an audience that was not only Italian but European. Their newly defined identity, as a duchy with its own laws but with its duke subject to the approval and oversight of the Holy Roman Empire, made a necessity of this broader horizon. The wide interest in history across Europe made historical references an effective choice in their programs, and in any case Florentines had an enviable recent past on which to draw. To plan these projects, Cosimo turned to men of letters who had by and large already established solid and distinguished reputations of their own, several of them in historical studies.

Florentines remained at the forefront of historical scholarship, both in producing important works of history and in advancing historical methods and use of sources. When they wrote works of history or involved themselves in studies of the past more generally, they certainly did not restrict themselves to Florentine subjects. Nonetheless, their pride and interest in the region gave their city a recurring place in their writings. Benedetto Varchi (1503–65), Pierfrancesco Giambullari (1495–1555), and Vincenzio Borghini (1515–80) may serve as examples of Florentines whose historical scholarship included work for Cosimo or involved them in commissioned work with a significant historical component. Their historical writings share several important features. First, they expanded further on innovations begun a generation before them in the use of written sources. Second, they broadened historical research into eras that had previously received little interest, notably the Middle Ages, and into aspects of life in the past not commonly treated in previous historical writing, features now often grouped under the umbrella of cultural history. Third, they promoted the use of new types of sources, from linguistic evidence to material artifacts we would call antiquarian studies, as well as writing and debating about historical methods. Finally, their level of source criticism of all types was very high, collectively among the best anywhere in Europe. No one of these features was unique to Florence. In composite, however, one may see Florence as a genuine center for innovation and high achievement in historical studies.

It has often been assumed that these Florentine scholars must have confined or modified their scholarship to conform to a particular ducal policy or desired image for the city. That is, because of Cosimo's interest in promoting Florence's image, he is often presumed to have developed a particular image of the city or scholarly program to which scholars then had to conform. In fact, an examination of Cosimo's support for historical research suggests the reverse. While Cosimo's artistic projects were highly programmatic, his support of scholars and scholarship, whether by accident or design, was much more open-ended. Cosimo did his best to promote excellence in Florentine letters and learning. Humanistic distinction itself served to enhance the city's image and prestige by providing tangible evidence of Florentine greatness and achievement. Far from attempting to shape historical research itself to conform to a particular political agenda, Cosimo modified some of his public programs when necessary to accommodate their findings.

History was a subject in which Cosimo held a particular interest. He enjoyed having historical works, old and new, read to him, and he took pleasure in conversing with experts. A notable expression of those interests was his support of the humanist Benedetto Varchi in writing a Florentine history intended to treat Florence's recent past, the years that followed those covered by Guicciardini. Varchi had not yet written any history when Cosimo persuaded him to return to Florence in 1543.

Nonetheless, by that time he enjoyed a reputation both as a man of letters, and as a man with long-term anti-Medicean and pro-republican views. His commission as a historian came some three years after his arrival in the city.

Varchi had begun his career as a notary after studying law at Pisa; he turned full-time to the study of letters with the receipt of an inheritance, though he always needed to supplement this income. He had supported the expulsion of the Medici and the return of the republican government in 1527. When that republic fell in turn, resulting in the exile of many fellow republicans, he was out of town on other business, and waited a year before returning to Florence.[1] During the 1530s he continued his literary studies, including both study and editorial work with the noted professor and textual editor Piero Vettori, and became known as a poet, critic, and classical scholar. When Alessandro was assassinated in 1537, resulting in the unexpected selection of Alessandro's distant cousin Cosimo as successor, Varchi left Florence and joined the exiles in an unsuccessful attack on the city, before abandoning military efforts and returning to scholarly ones. A former pupil, Filippo Strozzi, went on to help lead the exiles to a decisive defeat later that summer at Montemurlo.[2] The captured leaders of the revolt were executed, Cosimo consolidated his power, and by the early 1540s he began his efforts to rebuild Florence's intellectual and cultural life. Cosimo expanded the university, established the Accademia Fiorentina, and undertook an active campaign to attract major scholars to the city. Varchi initially remained in Padua and Venice. He finally returned with the offer of a small salary for contributing his linguistic, literary, and scholarly expertise to the city as a member of the Accademia Fiorentina, one of many former opponents now officially reconciled with Cosimo.[3]

In late 1546 or early 1547, Varchi undertook at Cosimo's request the task of researching and composing a history of Florence's recent past from 1527 until the advent of Alessandro.[4] The great size of the project left it prone to frequent interruptions. Some of the interruptions came from the Medici themselves, as when Varchi put the history aside to complete his translation of Boethius's *Consolation of Philosophy*, which Cosimo's wife Eleonora was especially anxious to see.[5] Despite such breaks, Varchi worked fairly steadily on the history for about six years, and sporadically thereafter. He kept widening the scope of the project, mainly pushing the end date forward to around 1538 to include Cosimo and Montemurlo, and perhaps intending to extend back into the fifteenth century as well. It remained unfinished at his death, and so was read for many years only in manuscript.

Not all Florentines agreed at the outset that Varchi was the right person for the task. In his proem, Varchi acknowledged the complaints in order to rebut them. Such a project as the writing of history lay far from his previous interests and writings, according to some.[6] Others had claimed that because he had not in fact participated in the political events of the 1520s, he was in no position to understand the complexities of the decisions and events as they had unfolded. Varchi asserted the merit of the stance of the neutral, detached observer, a stance that had been valued in antiquity for historical writing; the benefits that accrued from the wide-ranging, assiduous research he had conducted; and the fact that to a philosopher and lover of learning, no subject was alien. He even disclosed the amount of his stipend. His defense echoed the remarks of an early supporter, the exile Jacopo Nardi, who had written him early in 1547, praising his detached objectivity: "If I had to choose someone today . . . to write without passion, and who had the other qualities required for such a task, truly I would not know anyone else to select than you; among those who might be capable, none who would be so accomplished a writer; further, you have always appeared in the theater as a spectator and not as an actor in the drama of this crazy world."[7]

Varchi had written to Nardi as part of an effort to accumulate the broadest possible range of sources. Nardi had been involved both in the defense of the city and in the keeping of city records in 1527. He would go on to write his own history of Florentine politics.[8] Nardi replied to Varchi with information and suggestions for other persons outside Florence whom he might contact, mainly among the community of exiles. Few of the exiles retained official documents, but a number could add journals or diaries to their memories. Some, for example Annibale Caro in Rome, conducted interviews with exiles and others there and sent the results to Varchi.[9] Notes also survive of some of Varchi's own interviews with witnesses and participants. Though many Florentine state papers had been lost during and after the 1527 siege, Varchi was given full access to those that remained. Indeed, he found himself dunned and insulted as a pedant by the ducal archivist and his staff for having signed out several volumes of papers and kept them at home for a good three years.[10] The archivists preferred Filippo Nerli, who was busily at work on his own *Commentari* on the siege of Florence and wanted to consult the papers as well.[11]

In constructing the work, Varchi relied first upon some contemporary narrative accounts to assemble his own outline; then he filled in the contents with his more specific sources.[12] One of these narratives was in fact Filippo de' Nerli's *Commentari.* Despite the work's value in providing a chronology, contemporaries disparaged it for its pro-Medici bias.[13] In addition to several such Florentine sources, Varchi also availed himself of modern histories recently published across Europe; included among them were Johann Sleidan's Protestant history of the Reformation, translated and published by Torrentino in Florence in 1557, as well as texts circulating in manuscript.[14] One source Varchi did not have access to until late was Guicciardini's *History of Italy.* The work was still unpublished, and manuscript access was controlled by Guicciardini's nephew. He wanted to maximize the impact of its publication, and so he refused to allow most scholars to see it. Torrentino issued the first sixteen books in 1561, and a complete edition appeared in Venice with Gabriel Giolito in 1564.[15]

Varchi had long been friends with Paolo Giovio, who had spent some time in Florence working on his history of recent times. The work was published in Florence in Latin, and soon thereafter in Italian translation as well.[16] At a fairly early point Giovio took him aside after reading part of the work. He advised in no uncertain terms, as Varchi related in a letter, that Varchi be less direct in assessing recent events: ". . . he gave me his opinion at some length, like a brother, that I was truly mad to speak the truth so freely, because one can't do such things today; I would simply inspire hatred from many and favor from no one, and in the end would be cut to pieces."[17]

This warning might seem to suggest a reference to limits to political criticism in Florence and to official restrictions on scholarship. But a closer look complicates and alters such a reading. Giovio had received his copy of the work directly from Cosimo himself. Giovio was actually alluding to potential attacks not from Cosimo, but from the many surviving participants in the events discussed in Varchi's work. Varchi's criticisms of personal conduct during the tumultuous years of his study in fact spared no side, from the Medici to the republicans.

Giovio himself knew about both personal and political conflicts caused by writing histories of recent events. He had gone through several episodes of controversy, some of which resulted in his re-writing the section in question. One such notable case involved Charles V, and required Cosimo's intervention; it serves as a reminder that Cosimo established and maintained the relative independence of himself and of Florence by careful and constant negotiations with imperial authorities. Charles V became convinced at one point that Giovio's recent work had shown a pro-French bias; Giovio was then resident in Florence. He communicated to Cosimo a request that Cosimo either force Giovio to correct the "errors," or withdraw his support and prevent further printing. Behind the scenes, Cosimo reached a compromise based on Giovio's well-known scholarly need for documentation about imperial actions (in this case, in Tunis). Charles's staff offered to provide a body of sources; Giovio agreed to use the sources in revising the chapter, and the matter was dropped.[18] The challenge also elicited a statement from Cosimo to the imperial ambassador about his own goals and policies in the support of scholarship: "We have afforded Giovio the convenience of printing his histories here in Florence, to give this universal boon to the living and to posterity, and we lay no charge upon him unless it be to write without passion or partisanship, and we are confident that in so doing he cannot fail to satisfy His Majesty, whose actions have ever been beneficent and just."[19] For his part, Charles V expressed skepticism on receipt of the letter that Cosimo intended to exert any control over Giovio's work.[20]

Varchi did make use of Giovio's histories in his own writings, though sparingly, as his research convinced him that Giovio's reliability needed improvement. One reason, discovered by Annibale Caro in the course of interviewing Giovio in Rome, was Giovio's reliance solely on his own memory, rather than documentary evidence, in his treatment of the Florentine events relevant to Varchi. Another was this very willingness on Giovio's part to rewrite sections of the work to please or placate various political leaders; he had in fact done so on numerous occasions. To avoid a feud between himself and Giovio, Varchi waited to circulate his criticisms until after Giovio's death.[21]

Varchi's progress in the writing of his history was a matter of public knowledge. It was marked by frequent, lengthy trips to Pisa, given Cosimo's frequent presence there, to meet with him and read and discuss his most recent chapters. Varchi's sixteenth-century biographer, Silvano Razzi, offers a colorful (if perhaps apocryphal) description of Cosimo's rapt attention as Varchi read, and his frequent comment: "Miracoli, Varchi, miracoli!"[22] These visits were well known to contemporaries; at times they led to panicky and last-minute requests for assistance to complete unfinished sections by the deadline of the next scheduled reading. On one such occasion Baccio Valori wrote Piero Vettori at his country home in S. Casciano, saying that Varchi was due to read the section in which he discusses the origins of the city (in Book 10), and asking if Vettori could please contribute some information.[23]

The work itself thus held considerable interest to many. Numerous partial manuscript copies testify to the work's appeal for a variety of readers. Yet Varchi died before completing it, and it was only published in the eighteenth century. While this particular publication delay may have been extreme, the pattern itself was all too common, as the slow publication of Guicciardini attests. Florence was full of histories in process, histories in manuscript, and histories published only posthumously. Pierfrancesco Giambullari added his own history to the latter group. He left his longtime friend Cosimo Bartoli to edit several of his works, including his *History of Europe,* after Giambullari's unexpected death.[24]

Giambullari came from a family with Medicean ties, and he spent much of his career as a canon at S. Lorenzo. He was part of the group that became the Accademia Fiorentina from its earliest origins in 1540, and was involved in planning the elaborate public festivities that marked Cosimo's marriage to Eleonora di Toledo in 1539. Giambullari is best known for his theories about the origins of the Etruscan language, which he shared with his colleague Giovanni Battista Gelli and worked out in the 1540s. These theories took as their basis the writings of Annius of Viterbo, who had argued (based on evidence that he forged himself) that central Italy had been settled by Noah directly after the biblical Flood, and that ancient culture had had its earliest and most formative center in the area around Viterbo itself. Giambullari attempted to show, based on linguistic evidence that drew on his earlier studies of Hebrew and Chaldean, that the Etruscan language had developed from the language of Noah, Aramaic.[25] These claims were a matter of considerable debate in Florence and elsewhere, and Giambullari and his supporters came to be referred to as "Aramei."

Giambullari was able to name Cosimo among his supporters. Indeed, when Cosimo married Eleonora of Toledo in 1539, Giambullari took the opportunity to work some of his theories into the celebrations. After the couple's triumphal entrance into the city, they and their guests enjoyed a banquet and allegorical Trionfo in the courtyard of the Palazzo Medici. The Trionfo included a presentation of personifications of Tuscan cities who offered their blessings upon the wedding; their introductions, which incorporated descriptions of their origins, took as their basis the theories of Giambullari and the writings of Annius.[26] Later, Giambullari composed and published a description of the events.[27] Cosimo's interest in his language theories continued throughout Giambullari's career; Cosimo even offered some suggestions in the composition of *Il Gello.* Nonetheless, the theories were widely disputed, and most Florentine scholars ultimately rejected them. Later events sponsored by Cosimo, such as the wedding celebrations of his son Francesco to Joanna of Austria in 1565, ceased to feature or make allusions to Giambullari's ideas.[28]

At nearly the same time as Giambullari was developing these linguistic theories, he began work on his *History of Europe;* much of it was probably written about 1547. Unlike his writings on language, which focus mainly on Florence and the Florentine language, this work is particularly noteworthy for its breadth. It was one of the earliest modern pieces of historical writing to consider Europe as a single unit with a single, coherent history.[29] Yet given this lofty goal, the time period actually treated seems unexpected: it covers the years 887–947. The finished work would have had a much broader sweep, from 800–1200, according to his friend and colleague Cosimo Bartoli, who edited the manuscript for publication and gave Giambullari's funeral eulogy. Gelli also referred at one point to Giambullari's work on a history of the years 1000 to 1300, as if a further extension of the work had been planned.[30] On the other hand, a nineteenth-century scholar, Giuseppe Kirner, argued that a line in its first draft suggested that Giambullari had stopped a mere decade or so away from his original goal, about 957.[31] The author's plans for his project may well have changed over time.

These several dates, however, help give us a sense of some of the basic historical goals of Giambullari and his friends. First, the narrative is that of political history, as one might expect from humanists, whose sense of the appropriate subject matter for history came from the Greeks and Romans and hence centered upon public actions and events. Second, the narrative begins with the Carolingians, in fact the late Carolingians. Finally, if he had continued until about 1200 as Bartoli claimed he had intended, Giambullari would take the story to the rise of the communes and the development of the Italian city-states. Gelli's date of 1300 would include the strife among Guelfs and Ghibellines and the age of Dante—that is, extending to the very beginnings of the age his contemporaries would consider modern. Some collaboration may also have been intended; for example, Bartoli himself wrote a life of the twelfth-century emperor Frederick Barbarossa (c. 1123–1190), published in 1559.[32]

Giambullari's own comments at the beginning of his *History* help explain the apparently arbitrary dates of the surviving portion of the work. He noted that the events of the revival of empire under Charlemagne and his descendants, and the accompanying revival of ancient valor that had nearly vanished, are so well known that he does not need to repeat them. But from the rule of Arnolfo (the penultimate German Carolingian) for the next seventy years or so there is almost no information—for those years, until the rise to power of Otto I and his dynasty—the bare summaries are poor and the descriptions even worse. According to this smaller claim, Giambullari would be raising from obscurity the years often referred to later as the Dark Ages. Giambullari's introductory remarks emphasize both the importance of a broadly European focus (as opposed to merely Italian) and the desire to bring to light a unique set of events that had previously been hidden.[33]

These remarks serve as a reminder that the narrative and source-related issues facing Italian scholars differed in some important ways from those north of the Alps when they turned to the history of early medieval Europe. Many peoples of northern Europe had moved into the region only in late antiquity, and their written records began still later. Yet Italian historical records and narratives reached back centuries earlier, to the ancient Romans and Greeks. Florence's foundation as a late-republican military colony fell within this historical era. Further, Florence had been the subject of an impressive fourteenth-century chronicle, that of Giovanni Villani.[34] Villani's chronicle contained detailed information dating from as early as the twelfth century; in addition, it provided a continuous narrative from antiquity, one with which Renaissance historians might argue and disagree, but was (and is) nonetheless considered a valuable source of information. For the Florentines, the study of the "middle ages" or late antiquity did not involve a search for the origins of their people. Nor did it present the historiographic problems of studying pre-literate migrant groups, as it might for northern Europeans, many of whom were still attempting to displace the stories of their origins onto more dignified figures from classical or biblical antiquity. Rather, such studies involved an effort to assess and explain the events that distinguished the ancient world from their own.

Like Varchi, Giambullari and his colleagues emphasized the great number of sources he consulted.[35] Unlike Varchi's sources, however, all were historical narratives, some medieval and others of fairly recent composition. His main source was Liutprand of Cremona, whose text covers the same years and events. Liutprand was both a scholar and a participant in the events he narrated, having served both the Italian court in Pavia and that of Otto I. Liutprand's work was actually available to Giambullari in print; it had been edited and published, twice, in the first decades of the sixteenth century.[36] And in fact, so had nearly all of his sources. The presses of Paris, Lyon, Strassburg, and elsewhere had begun printing editions of the major medieval chronicles by the century's early decades; the book market and the collection-building at the Laurenziana Library helped bring these resources to Giambullari. He was making use, then, of the newest body of information available thanks to the print industry.

The *History of Europe* took Liutprand's work as the narrative foundation, but did not merely repeat its contents. Where the earlier Lombard scholar had centered his story on Italy, Giambullari used the German Carolingian regions that became the heart of the Holy Roman Empire to anchor his narrative. From there he moved outward to other European regions. The first book begins with a summary of the decline of the Roman Empire after the capital's move to Constantinople, the subsequent Carolingian revival, and the decline of the Carolingians in turn in their various regions. He then turns to a geographic description of Europe before picking up his political narrative. As he introduces particular regions into his story, he begins the discussion with a similar geographic survey. Each of the seven books begins with events in Germany (and often returns to them later as well), then moves on to consider a different region in which significant events occur in the time period in question. Book 2, for example, treats Germany; France; Germany; Italy; Bulgaria; Greece; Moravia; Italy; Spain; Germany; Saxony; England; and ends again with Germany.

Many of his sources dealt with a single region exclusively, for example, the Saxons and Saxony, and the sources varied widely in quality as well. Giambullari attempted to correlate various sources when they described the same events. Sometimes he followed the one that held for him the most verisimilitude; at other times he simply noted discrepancies in the sources and left readers to draw their own conclusions. For some regions, he could resort to good recent scholarship that had already evaluated these earlier sources, and Giambullari noted them with gratitude. For example, he seems to have relied on Polydore Vergil's *Anglicae historicae* (1534) for England; and he cites Beatus Rhenanus and his writings (notably the *Rerum Germanicarum Libri Tres,* 1531) often and with great respect.

Giambullari's critical collation of available narratives into a single, consistent one recalls Varchi's initial steps at assembling his own narrative. Unlike Varchi, Giambullari lacked documentary evidence for this early time period. In addition, his narrative task was far more complex; while Varchi centered his history on the events of a single city, Giambullari was attempting to correlate the major events across the entire continent. Giambullari also chose to insert speeches at key points in the narrative, in the style of Thucydides. To Giambullari, those tenth-century events whose memory was worth preserving, were worth preserving in the same style as ancient history. They held the requisite abilities to delight and to instruct that qualified them as events meriting the attentions of both historian and reader. Further, the work suggests a point of origin for a genuinely European, post-classical history; it locates that fundamental transformation in the heritage of the Carolingians. Giambullari's Florentine colleagues appreciated these innovations. Bartoli noted in his eulogy that the *History of Europe* alone would be sufficient to keep alive Giambullari's name and memory for years to come.

Vincenzio Borghini was twenty years Giambullari's junior. Borghini became a Benedictine and spent most of his life in Florence, acquiring a thorough education and a distinguished reputation as a scholar. He also had a noted administrative career; in 1552 he was given charge of the city's foundling hospital, and in 1570 was named part of a three-person committee in charge of instituting reforms in the region's nunneries. Borghini is best known now for his role as advisor to Giorgio Vasari in the composition of the *Lives of the Artists,* and he served as Duke Cosimo's representative to the Accademia del Disegno. He worked frequently for Cosimo as a consultant on major artistic projects and spectacles.

Borghini's scholarship covered a broad range of studies of the past, ranging from editorial scholarship to studies of the modern Tuscan language, to examinations of ancient dietary habits and Roman archaeology. His editorial work on Boccaccio was widely praised, despite its trouble with Reformation censors less fond than he of the writings of the fourteenth-century Florentine;[37] so too were his annotations on the chronicler Giovanni Villani.[38] His time-consuming administrative obligations, as well as his personal inclinations, kept him from involvement with the Accademia Fiorentina.[39] Those obligations also prevented his completing for publication his extensive writings on Florentine and Tuscan history and culture; a team of colleagues edited the bulk of them and brought them out as four volumes of *Discorsi* four years after his death in 1580.[40] His notebooks survive, and many of the remaining substantial works have been published in recent years.[41]

Borghini's editors described his unfinished task. He had planned a three-part work entitled *Dell'origine e nobiltà di Firenze.* The first part was to treat the city's origins. The second would cover events in the city from its early days as part of the Roman Empire, then continue through the changes in Italy to about the year 1200, from which point onward its history was already relatively well documented. The third was to focus on the Florentine language. The first part was finished but not revised, and it filled the first volume. It was bound with the second volume, which consisted of supplementary works. Volumes three and four included sections of what Borghini would have redacted into part two. Borghini had not yet really written the third part, his editors argued; most of his writings on language thus remained as drafts in his notebooks, to await modern editors. It is the cluster of writings intended for part two, published as volumes three and four of the *Discorsi,* that parallel most closely the historical writings of Varchi and Giambullari. They address a range of topics: the coats of arms of Florentine families; coinage and the minting of money; Florence's urban status at the time of the Lombards, Carolingians and the earlier Holy Roman Empire; the history of the bishopric and its bishops.

Borghini's contributions to medieval history writing are several. One is the breadth of his interest in the past. It extended far beyond the common subjects of humanist historians—public events and acts—into a fascination with customs, habits, and patterns of behavior. The other innovations are related. He broadened considerably the types of evidence considered useful for studying the past. His use of documents was far more extensive than most contemporaries, perhaps even more so than Varchi given the breadth of subject matter he studied. He was also at the forefront of the use of epigraphic evidence, and went still further in including archaeological evidence, building styles, place names, and any other available source of local information. Above all, he coupled that breadth of topics and sources with an extremely careful critical sense. Like Varchi, Borghini was part of the circle of humanists who worked with Piero Vettori, who himself carried on and extended the principles of text criticism and editing developed by the Florentine scholar Angelo Poliziano in the late fifteenth century. Borghini kept meticulous records of his descriptions of objects and locations, sketches (in color when necessary, as for coats of arms), and relevant textual references. So too his correspondence is filled with queries and replies to and from colleagues whom he has asked to consult and report on the time span, relative abundance and quality of records in various local archives, and on occasion to copy them for him as well.

During Borghini's lifetime, his unpublished writings were available to men of letters in Florence; some of them, in fact, had been written in response to particular queries and requests of various sorts. The writings on noble families and family trees had obvious modern applications in a world in which an elevated family lineage was ever more valuable.[42] His treatise on the dietary habits of ancient Romans aided physicians who were trying to make sense of the dietary regimens described in ancient medical texts.[43] Borghini continued to pursue a number of these subjects on his own, apparently far beyond the range of the original request.

Cosimo came to rely on Borghini for the programs of a large number of artistic projects. An especially noteworthy case is his planning of the elaborate imagery, symbolism, and artistic programs related to the extended wedding festivities of his son and heir, Francesco, to Giovanna of Austria in 1565.[44] One of these events included the performance of a play in the Great Hall (Salone dei Cinquecento) of the Palazzo Vecchio, which had just been redecorated with paintings by Giorgio Vasari on the history of Florence, its military victories, and the glories of the Medici family. Borghini had conducted the historical research and helped select the featured historical episodes. Cosimo's correspondence (from Pisa) with Borghini about the project shows the high value he continued to place on historical accuracy. Borghini's research had convinced him that a traditional scene featured in a number of earlier Florentine histories, the refoundation of the city by Charlemagne after its earlier destruction, had in fact never happened.[45]

Cosimo wrote Borghini to clarify his position on the commission, insisting on historical accuracy and supporting Borghini's research. Perhaps he had not been properly understood, he argued, but he had not wanted to suggest that Florence had never been subjugated, since that was obviously incorrect; rather, he agreed that it had never been destroyed. Thus it would not do to have a painting that represented its rebuilding, so the Carolingian scene certainly should go. Yet he did not want Borghini's labor to result in a loss, by debunking a topic only to leave nothing in its place. Therefore he proposed that the theme of the now-vacant spot be taken by a story from one of the authors Borghini had consulted in his efforts, Paulinus of Milan.[46] And so the story of the liberation of Florence from the siege of Radagasius in the early fifth century, hardly a mainstay of Florentine legend, found its place in the program.[47]

The decision to omit the Charlemagne story met with some scholarly resistance; Girolamo Mei, a Florentine then resident in Rome, even circulated a treatise in Florence proposing his own version of Florentine history in which the refoundation of the city featured prominently. Borghini was forced then to defend not only his own reputation, but that of Cosimo, who had requested the substitution in the name of historical accuracy and approved his version of the city's foundation as well. Happily for them both, Borghini was generally acknowledged the winner from the evidence presented in the voluminous exchange of letters. Cosimo nonetheless asked Borghini to write up his research for publication. It was that request, according to his editors, that had sent Borghini into his ever-widening project of regional historical research.[48]

Despite the unfinished nature of his writings and the necessity of publishing the surviving segments as distinct discourses, some issues and themes can be seen to recur. One is his sense of historical periodization. The region's political history had moved several times between order and disorder as it underwent its gradual transformation from the world of antiquity. Borghini concurred with the common opinion that the later years of the Roman Empire in the West had ushered in a long-lasting trough in terms of both political order and cultural achievement. Charlemagne had relieved but not transformed it. The real turning point came some time around the millennium. About that time, or perhaps a bit before, the Tuscan cities began to throw off the yoke of subjection to Goths and Lombards and to reassert their greatness and power. Borghini represents the era as a new age or rebirth; indeed, in his treatise on Florentine coinage he clearly applies to it the term "rinascimento": ". . . or as I call it, the new age, or Rebirth of new liberty in Tuscany, and of its greatness and power . . ."[49] It seems quite clear that for Borghini, this was the single most significant transition of the era. The Florentine focus of his studies meant that unlike Giambullari, he did not attempt to generalize or compare it to other European regions.

As important as political developments were to Borghini's studies, his interest in the past moved far beyond the public events of conventional history, to encompass topics now considered part of social or cultural history. Just how Borghini would have identified the genre in which he worked is unclear; the title of his planned work as reported by the deputies does not include the term "history," nor do the writings to which Borghini clearly gave a title. Rather, they are simply named by topic, as contemporaries titled other antiquarian works. These studies tend to proceed topically as well as chronologically; they are full of digressions that often constitute small treatises on their own on various topics, from discussions of architectural history to the presentation of manuscript evidence on word usage, to more general reflections on method.

Borghini's discourse on the church and Florentine bishops is a good example.[50] It is very much a document-based study; throughout the work Borghini maintains a running commentary on the quantity and quality of documentary evidence, and his need at various points to rely on collateral texts and documents. In some cases he needed to move beyond written sources altogether, and resort to the study of material culture. To support his claim that S. Lorenzo dated from the time of a visit by St. Ambrose, for example, Borghini included lengthy discussions of changes in church architecture over time in Florence and environs. He returned to the subject of architecture several times.

In other instances, his interest in customs and social behavior led him to explore a number of topics introduced by his sources, or for which they had presented incomplete or confusing information that he decided merited further investigation. In one example, his attention was drawn to the early ceremonies performed by newly installed bishops in the city. The new bishop walked in procession from S. Piero, barefoot, to the cathedral; he visited the tomb of S. Zenobius, the city's bishop in the days of the Emperor Constantine and one of the city's patron saints; then he repaired to the sacristy to wash, put on shoes, and continue with the service.[51]

Borghini recognized that such concerns were far from the ordinary expectations for subjects covered in historical writing. Indeed, at one point he warded off potential criticism of his interest in habits and customs: "It may seem to some that I expand too much about small and particular things, but among so many tasks I undertake for others, you may concede to me this small satisfaction of recalling, and insofar as I can, to represent to others who are interested, the habits, customs, and manner of life of past ages; and besides, as far as I know, no one will be forced to read more than he cares to."[52]

Borghini's attention also extended to matters of social behavior and organization. Particularly interesting is his discussion of the development of patterns of lordship, vassalage, and landholding in the countryside. As his narrative reaches the twelfth century and the complex political intrigues of the age of the Staufen, he pauses to discuss some curious changes in the countryside. Diocesan landholding at this time was expanding, he notes, though not by simple donations. Landowners seemed to be signing over lands to the church to avoid their being taken by the Emperor, yet nonetheless keeping control of them. The documents in which the practices are found, notably contracts, referred to these landowners with names like *fideli* and *uomini* of the bishop, and include terms like *omaggio*. Further, these contracts include references to farm workers called serfs that were tied to the land.

At this point, Borghini decides to digress in order to try to present a picture of these clusters of behaviors, as the terms in the documents, he notes, are no longer in use. He discusses the documentary evidence, with extensive quotations to define terminologies and practices. He compares these serfs to various types of unfree labor over time, such as Greek helots or Lombard aldii, as well as modern contadini or lavoratori; he sees his last reference to them around 1300. So too he goes over the terminology and practices of lordship.[53] Borghini seems not to know of the contemporary French legal scholars who had become interested in the history of feudalism; he worked out his discussion on his own.[54] Nor did his interests match those of the northern jurists, interests that had arisen out of ongoing legal practice. Far from relating to his experience, the world of serfs and lords seems to have been as far from Borghini and his presumed readers as it is from modern undergraduates. The topic began for him as a problem in understanding archdiocesan records, but expanded into an issue meriting investigation in its own right.

These examples serve only to introduce, not to exhaust, Florentine historical scholarship. They are sufficient to illustrate a number of prominent features. One is the quality of research practice exercised by writers of history, and expected by readers as well. Even minor figures like Nerli expect their work to meet a relatively high standard in use of evidence, sufficient for him to run off to the archivist complaining about access to city documents. Historians faced tough criticism in letters (circulated more or less widely among colleagues) and more if their work suffered from shoddy scholarship. Scholars made a point of criticizing one another's work on the basis of accuracy and thoroughness, as well as the author's relative level of passion versus detachment.

Further, all of these scholars were aware of the high level of interest in their findings on the part of those in Florence and elsewhere, and of the public relations uses to which their scholarship might contribute. Yet whatever the particular findings, they could be cast in a positive light as desired. Girolamo Mei argued, for example, that his version of the city's history offered its own advantages. Though it denied Florence the prestige of an ancient foundation, it presented Florence and Florentines as a self-made people who had brought themselves to greatness amid the ruins of barbarian disorder, an image reminiscent of the one Venice had crafted. He asked his readers which would be the more honorable beginning of a city—to trace Florence's origins from the base deeds of Augustus, or from the good intentions of Desiderius the king of the Lombards.[55] At the beginning of his treatise he criticized those who seemed to think they were doing the city a service by attributing to it grand Roman origins, as if Rome itself should have had cause for embarrassment about its own humble early settlers. Florence would seem more worthy of praise if it had the most modest origins, Mei continued, having brought itself up through its own efforts to its present standing among the first cities of Europe.[56] Florence's present greatness was not in doubt to these scholars or to their presumed readers; the new findings of its historians might give rise to variations on the specifics of the city's rise to prominence or its current eminence, but did not threaten that basic narrative.

For his part, Cosimo made a point of valuing history that seemed accurate and true. If he had a particular image to promote, it seems to have been one of evenhandedness and a commitment to scholarly excellence, rather than to a particular set of outcomes or results. He had witnessed the degree to which scholars in Florence were subject to critical commentary not only from other Florentines, but from writers and readers elsewhere. If he wished Florentines to maintain a reputation for excellence, their work could not appear to bend to this or that political whim, though particular topics or projects could be promoted. The Florentine historians saw themselves as continuing and expanding upon the traditions of humanistic scholarship developed by their predecessors of the previous century. The existence of such a community of scholars in fact did serve Cosimo's image. Their advances in historical scholarship met his goal of serving the good both of the present and of the future.

Notes

1. Richard Samuels, "Benedetto Varchi and Sixteenth-Century Florentine Humanism," PhD dissertation, University of Chicago, 1976, 80 ff.

2. Ibid., 156.
3. Ibid., 283.
4. Benedetto Varchi, *Storia Fiorentina,* ed. Silvano Razzi and Francesco Settimanni (Cologne: P. Martello, 1721).
5. Anicius Manlius Torquatus Severinus Boethius, *Severino Boezio della consolazione della filosofia,* trans. Benedetto Varchi (Firenze: Torrentino, 1551).
6. "facessero giudizio e dicessero apertamente prima, che io non vorrei, e poscia, che quando pure io volessi, non saprei nè potrei, non che fornire, cominciare così alra impresa, e tanto dagli studj miei passati lontana; . . . " Varchi, Proemio, *Storia Fiorentina,* 41. See Samuels, 350–52.
7. "Se io avessi ad eleggere oggi uno . . . che fusse per scrivere senza passione, e avesse appresso le altre qualità, che si richieggono a tale impresa, io veramente non saprei pigliare altra che voi, perchè niuno altro conosco; che quando pure lo trovassi atto, (che non so chi) dovesse errere così intero scrittore come voi; conciosia che sempre siate intervenuto nel teatro come spettatore e non come attore delle fabule di questo pazzo mondo." Jacopo Nardi, letter to Benedetto Varchi January 24, 1547, in A. Pieralli, *La vita e le opere di Jacopo Nardi. Vol 1.* (Florence, 1901), 182; see Samuels, 352–53.
8. Jacopo Nardi, *Le historie della citta di Fiorenza* (Lione: T. Ancelin, 1582).
9. Samuels, "Benedetto Varchi," 355.
10. Ibid., 355–58.
11. Ibid., 356–58.
12. Michele Lupo Gentile, *Sulle fonti della storia fiorentina di Benedetto Varchi* (Sarzana: E. Costa, 1906).
13. Giovanni Battista Busini, *Lettere . . . a Benedetto Varchi sugli avvenimenti dell'assedio di Firenze, estratte*

da un codice della Biblioteca Palatina (Pisa, 1822; Florence, 1860), 213, 247; Lupo Gentile, *Sulle fonti*, 25–26.

14. Johannes Sleidanus, *Commentarii, ò vero historie di Gio. Sleidano. Ne le quali si trata de lo stato de la repub. e di la religione christiana, e di tutte le guerre & altre cose notabili, che sono occorse ne l'Europa da l'anno MDXVII infino al LV. Tradotte nuovamente in lingua toscana* (Florence: Torrentino, 1557); Lupo Gentile, 55–56.

15. Samuels, "Benedetto Varchi," 361; Lupo Gentile, 37–39.

16. Paolo Giovio, *P. Jovii . . . Historiarum sui temporis tomus primus—secundus* (Florence: Lorenzo Torrentino, 1550); Paolo Giovio, *La prima [-seconda] parte dell'historie del suo tempo*, trans. Lodovico Domenichi (Florence: Lorenzo Torrentino, 1551–1553).

17. "avendomi come fratello, mi voleva dire laramente l'oppenion sua, che io era un gran pazzo a dire il vero così liberamente perchè hoggi non si può far così, che n'acquisterei odio da coloro e non grado da nessuno, e finalmente che sarei tagliato a pezzi." Florence, BNC, Magl. XXV, 570, fol. 36. In Lupo Gentile, 30.

18. Cosimo's letter to the imperial ambassador, Bernardo de' Medici (Bishop of Forlì), presents a carefully crafted image of negotiation. The public portion of the letter makes the general statement about his goals; the next section, in cipher, invites suggestions for any necessary emendations to the sections on Tunis, with an offer to continue to allow Charles to see chapters in advance of publication; and finally, a postscript in Cosimo's hand claims that Giovio had told him that he had originally forwarded the chapter specifically to invite such suggestions for revision. T. C. Price Zimmerman, *Paolo Giovio: The Historian and the Crisis of Sixteenth-Century Italy* (Princeton: Princeton University Press, 1995), 239–40.

19. "Ho data la commodità al Iovio di far stampare le historie sua in Fiorenza per far questo bene universale ai vivi et a' posteri, et con esso non fo altra opera se non che le scriva senza alcuna passione et affetto, et so che, faccendo questo, non può se non satisfare a Sua Mayestà, sendo le imprese sua state sempre giustissime et sante." Cosimo I, letter to Bernardo dei Medici, Bishop of Forlì, imperial ambassador, Nov. 18, 1550. In Cosimo I de' Medici, *Lettere*, ed. Giorgio Spini (Florence: Vallecchi, 1940), 116–18. Translation in Zimmerman, *Paolo Giovio*, 239–40.

20. Zimmerman, *Paolo Giovio*, 240.

21. Published only much later: Benedetto Varchi, *Errori di Paolo Giovio nella storia*, ed. Vincenzo Follini (Badia di Fiesole, 1821). See Zimmerman, *Paolo Giovio*, 263–64, 363 n.5; Eric W. Cochrane, *Historians and Historiography in the Italian Renaissance* (Chicago: University of Chicago Press, 1981), 375.

22. Silvano Razzi, "Vita di Messer Benedetto Varchi," in Benedetto Varchi, *Storia fiorentina*, ed. Gaetano Milanesi, 3 vols. (Florence: Le Monnier, 1857), 1.12–15.

23. Baccio Valori, letter to Piero Vettori, October 9, 1563, London, British Library, Add. 10278, fol. 131.

24. Pierfrancesco Giambullari, *Historia dell'Evropa di m. Pierfrancesco Giambvllari nella qvale ordinatamente si trattano le cose successe in questa parte del mondo dall'anno DCCC. sino al 913. di nostra salute . . .*, ed. Cosimo Bartoli (Venice: F. Senese, 1566).

25. Giovanni Nanni, *Commentaria super opera diversorum auctorum de antiquitatibus loquentium* (Rome: Eucharius Silber, 1498).

26. Andrew C. Minor and Bonner Mitchell, *A Renaissance Entertainment: Festivities for the Marriage of*

Cosimo I, Duke of Florence, in 1539. An Edition of the Music, Poetry, Comedy, and Descriptive Account, with Commentary (Columbia: University of Missouri Press, 1968), 169, 186. See also A. M. Nagler, *Theatre festivals of the Medici, 1539–1637* (New York: Da Capo Press, 1976).

27. Pierfrancesco Giambullari, Apparato e feste nelle noze dello illustrissimo Signor Duca di Firenze, e della Ducchessa sua Consorta con le sue stanze, madriali, comedia & intermedij in quelle recitati (Fiorenza: B. Giunta, 1539; rpt. Venice: Antonelli, 1854).

28. Randolph Starn and Loren Partridge, *Arts of Power: Three Halls of State in Italy, 1300–1600* (Berkeley: University of California Press, 1992), 149–212.

29. The main precedents would have been the writings of Aeneas Silvius Piccolomini (1405–1464, Pius II), *Historia rerum ubique gestarum* [to which *Europam* was frequently added] (Venice, 1477, republished several times during the sixteenth century), and the history of Paolo Giovio. Giovio was more interested in establishing the worldwide importance of the events under his purview than he was in developing a European historical narrative as such.

30. Judith Bryce, *Cosimo Bartoli (1503–1572): The Career of a Florentine Polymath*, Travaux d'Humanisme et Renaissance 191 (Geneva: Droz, 1983), 242–43; see also Giuseppe Kirner, *Sulla 'Storia dell'Europa' di P. F. Giambullari* (Pisa, 1889), 10.

31. Kirner, *Sulla 'Storia dell'Europa,'* 10–11.

32. Cosimo Bartoli, *La vita di Federigo Barbarossa* (Florence: Torrentino, 1559).

33. Kirner, *Sulla 'Storia dell'Europa,'* 8–9.

34. Giovanni Villani's chronicle was continued after his death in 1348 to 1410 by his brother Matteo and Matteo's son Filippo. Sixteenth-century scholars had more than one printed edition available, as well as an abundance of manuscripts: Giovanni Villani, *Croniche* (Venice: Bartholomeo Zanetti Casterzagense, 1537); Giovanni Villani, *Cronica universali de suoi tempi* (Florence: Torrentino, 1554).

35. For a discussion of Giambullari's sources see Kirner, *Sulla 'Storia dell'Europa,'* 18–35.

36. *Liutprandus Cremonensis, Rerum gestarum per Europam . . . libri 14 / cum variantibus mss. Codicis Frising. Saec. XI. per manum J. v. Delling* (Paris, 1514).

37. Giovanni Boccaccio, *Il Decameron di Messer Giovanni Boccacci cittadino fiorentino. Ricorretto in Roma, et emendato secondo l'ordine del Sacro Conc. di Trento, et riscontrato in Firenze con testi antichi & alla sua vera lezione ridotto da'deputati di loro Alt. Ser.* (Florence: Giunti, 1573); Vincenzio Borghini, *Annotationi et discorsi sopra alcuni luoghi del Decameron, di m. Giovanni Boccacci . . .* (Florence: Giunti, 1574). See J. R. Woodhouse, "Il Borghini e la rassettatura del *Decameron* del 1573: un documento inedito," *Studi sul Boccaccio* 7 (1973): 303–15.

38. Vincenzio Borghini, *Annotazioni sopra Giovanni Villani*, ed. Riccardo Drusi (Florence: Accademia della Crusca, 2001).

39. Rick Scorza, "Borghini and the Florentine Academies"; J. R. Woodhouse, "Borghini and the Foundation of the Accademia della Crusca," both in *Italian Academies of the Sixteenth Century*, ed. D. S. Chambers and F. Quiviger (London: Warburg Institute, University of London, 1995), 136–64, 165–74.

40. Vincenzio Borghini, *Discorsi* (Florence: Giunti, 1584–85); Vincenzio Borghini, *Discorsi*, Annotations by Domenico Maria Manni (Florence: Pietro Gaet. Viviani, 1755; rpt. Milan: Società tipografica de'Classici italiani, 1808–9). Pagination hereafter will refer to the 1808–9 edition.

41. For a discussion of the fortuna of Borghini's papers, see Borghini, *Annotazioni sopra Giovanni Villani*, 18–20.

42. Vincenzio Borghini, *Storia della nobiltà fiorentina: discorsi inediti o rari*, ed. J. R. Woodhouse (Pisa: Marlin, 1974).

43. Florence. Biblioteca Nazionale Centrale (BNC). Magl. XXVIII, cod. 52, Vincenzio Borghini, [De conviti delli Antichi].

44. For a detailed discussion of these events and their visual program, see Starn and Partridge, *Arts of Power*, 149–212.

45. Nicolai Rubinstein, "Vasari's Painting of The Foundation of Florence in the Palazzo Vecchio," *Essays in the History of Architecture Presented to Rudolf Wittkower*, ed. D. Fraser, D. H. Hibbard, and H. M. Lewine (London: Phaidon, 1967), 64–73; Henk Th. Van Veen, "Art and Propaganda in Late Renaissance and Baroque Florence: the Defeat of Radagasius, King of the Goths," *Journal of the Warburg and Courtauld Institutes* 47 (1984): 106–18; Ann E. Moyer, "Historians and Antiquarians in Sixteenth-Century Florence," *Journal of the History of Ideas* 642 (2003): 177–93.

46. "o che noi non fussemo bene intesi, o non ci sapessemo fare bene intendere, haverete da sapere che non èmai cascato in nostra consideratione il dire che Fiorenza non sia mai state soggiogata, perchè questo è pur troppo notorio, ma dicemmo che la non era mai stata desolata, trattandosi di dipingere la sua reedificatione, et che questo si avvertisse bene, acciò non si incorressi in qualche absurdo. Così ci parse di dire a Giorgio; ma non sarà stata però invano la fatica durata da voi in ritrovare dietro a questo errore la verità; perchè il successo descritto da San Paolino nella vita di Santo Ambrogio a Santo Augustino della liberatione di Fiorenza nello assedio di Radagasio, potrà d'alhora servirci per la historia istessa che manca, essendo pure assai notabile et pio: et sino a hora a noi sodisfa non poco. Però, parendo così a voi ancora, si potrà pigliare questo soggetto, concordando la pittura con la verità del fatto, come è condecente et come voi saperete mostare a Giorgio, et così sarà tolto via ogni dubio, nè occorrerà pensare a altro." Cosimo I, letter to Vincenzio Borghini, from Pisa, November 12, 1564, in Cosimo I de' Medici, *Lettere*, ed. Giorgio Spini, 197–98.

47. Paulinus of Milan, *Via Sancti Ambrosii*, ed. and trans. Sr. Mary Simplicia Kaniecka (Washington: Catholic University of America, 1928), par. 50, 94–95.

48. Deputati, dedication of Borghini, "Della chiesa e vescovi fiorentini, to Alessandro de' Medici, Cardinal and Archbishop of Florence, *Discorsi* 4.137–39, at 137–38.

49. Vincenzio Borghini, *Discorsi di monsignore d. Vincenzio Borghini*, with annotations by Domenico Maria Manni, 4 vols. in 2 (Florence, 1808), 4.221.

50. Vincenzio Borghini, "Della chiesa, e vescovi fiorentini," *Discorsi* 4.141–591.

51. Ibid., 4.160. Borghini follows especially a description of 1286.

52. "Forse parrà ad alcuno, ch'io troppo in cose particulari e minute mi allarghi, ma fra tante fatiche prese per altri, mi si conceda questa mia piccola satisfazione, di ricordarmi, e per quanto me lece, rappresentare agli altri, a cui fusse in piacere, l'usanze, i costumi, e la maniere della vita de' passati tempo per tempo; e tanto più, quanto nessuno (ch'io creda) sarà forzato a leggerlo più, che si voglia." Ibid., 4.260.

53. Ibid., 4.387–99.

54. Donald R. Kelley, *Foundations of Modern Historical Scholarship: Language, Law, and History in the French Renaissance* (New York: Columbia University Press, 1970), 183–300.

55. Girolamo Mei, letters, in *Prose fiorentine raccolte dallo smarrito academico della Crusca* (Florence: Stamperia della sua Altezza Reale per li Tartini e Franchi, 1734).

56. Girolamo Mei, [On the origins of the city of Florence], Florence, BNC, Magl. II.x.64, fol.1v-2r.

Bibliography

Manuscripts

Florence. Biblioteca Nazionale Centrale (BNC). Mag.. II.x.64, fol.1v–2r. Girolamo Mei [On the origins of the city of Florence].

Florence. BNC. Magl. XXVIII, cod. 52, Vincenzio Borghini, [De conviti delli Antichi].

London. British Library. Add. 10278, fol. 131. Baccio Valori, letter to Piero Vettori, October 9, 1563.

Printed Sources

Boethius, Anicius Manlius Torquatus Severinus. *Boezio Seuerino della consolazione della filosofia.* Trans. Benedetto Varchi. Firenze: Torrentino, 1551.

Borghini, Vincenzio. *Annotazioni sopra Giovanni Villani.* Ed. Riccardo Drusi. Florence: Accademia della Crusca, 2001.

———. *Discorsi.* Florence: Giunti, 1584–85.

———. *Discorsi* . . . Annotations by Domenico Maria Manni. Florence: Pietro Gaet. Viviani, 1755. Reprinted Milan: Società tipografica de'Classici italiani, 1808–9.

———. *Storia della nobiltŕ fiorentina: discorsi inediti o rari.* Ed. J. R. Woodhouse. Pisa: Marlin, 1974.

Bryce, Judith. *Cosimo Bartoli (1503–1572): The Career of a Florentine Polymath.* Travaux d'Humanisme et Renaissance 191. Geneva: Droz, 1983.

Busini, Giovanni Battista. *Lettere . . . a Benedetto Varchi sugli avvenimenti dell'assedio di Firenze, estratte da un codice della Biblioteca Palatina.* Pisa, 1822; Florence, 1860.

Chambers, D. S., and F. Quiviger, eds. *Italian Academies of the Sixteenth Century.* London: Warburg Institute, University of London, 1995.

Cochrane, Eric W. *Historians and Historiography in the Italian Renaissance.* Chicago: University of Chicago Press, 1981.

Cosimo I de' Medici. *Lettere.* Ed. Giorgio Spini. Florence: Vallecchi, 1940.

Giambullari, Pierfrancesco. *Historia dell'Evropa di m. Pierfrancesco Giambvllari . . .* Ed. Cosimo Bartoli. Venice: F. Senese, 1566.

Kelley, Donald R. *Foundations of Modern Historical Scholarship: Language, Law, and History in the French Renaissance.* New York: Columbia University Press, 1970.

Kirner, Giuseppe. *Sulla 'Storia dell'Europa' di P. F. Giambullari.* Pisa, 1889.

Lupo Gentile, Michele. *Sulle Fonti Della Storia Fiorentina Di Benedetto Varchi.* Sarzana: E. Costa, 1906.

Mei, Girolamo. "Lettere." *Prose fiorentine raccolte dallo smarrito academico della Crusca.* Florence: Stamperia della sua Altezza Reale per li Tartini e Franchi, 1734.

Minor, Andrew C., and Bonner Mitchell. *A Renaissance Entertainment: Festivities for the Marriage of Cosimo*

I, Duke of Florence, in 1539. An Edition of the Music, Poetry, Comedy, and Descriptive Account, with Commentary. Columbia: University of Missouri Press, 1968.

Moyer, Ann E. "Historians and Antiquarians in Sixteenth-Century Florence." *Journal of the History of Ideas* 642 (2003): 177–93.

Nagler, A. M. *Theatre Festivals of the Medici, 1539–1637.* New York: Da Capo Press, 1976.

Nardi, Jacopo. *Le historie della citta di Fiorenza.* Lyon: T. Ancelin, 1582.

Paulinus of Milan. *Via Sancti Ambrosi.* Ed. and trans. Sr. Mary Simplicia Kaniecka. Washington: Catholic University of America, 1928.

Pieralli, Alfredo. *La vita e le opere di Iacopo Nardi. Vol. 1.* Florence, 1901.

Razzi, Silvano. "Vita di Messer Benedetto Varchi." In Benedetto Varchi, *Storia fiorentina,* ed. Gaetano Milanesi. 3 vols. Florence: Le Monnier, 1857, 1.12–15.

Rubinstein, Nicolai. "Vasari's Painting of The Foundation of Florence in the Palazzo Vecchio," *Essays in the History of Architecture Presented to Rudolf Wittkower,* ed. D. Fraser, D. H. Hibbard, and H. M. Lewine. London: Phaidon 1967, 64–73.

Samuels, Richard. "Benedetto Varchi and Sixteenth-Century Florentine Humanism." PhD dissertation. University of Chicago, 1976.

Starn, Randolph and Loren Partridge. *Arts of Power: Three Halls of State in Italy, 1300–1600.* Berkeley: University of California Press, 1992.

Van Veen, Henk Th. "Art and Propaganda in Late Renaissance and Baroque Florence: the Defeat of Radagasius, King of the Goths." *Journal of the Warburg and Courtauld Institutes* 47 (1984): 106–18.

Varchi, Benedetto. *Errori di Paolo Giovio nella storia.* Ed. Vincenzo Follini. Badia di Fiesole, 1821.

———. *Storia Fiorentina.* Ed. Silvano Razzi and Francesco Settimanni. Colonia: P. Martello, 1721.

Woodhouse, J. R. "Il Borghini e la rassettatura del *Decameron* del 1573: un documento inedito." *Studi sul Boccaccio* 7 (1973): 303–15.

Zimmerman, T. C. Price. *Paolo Giovio: The Historian and the Crisis of Sixteenth-Century Italy.* Princeton: Princeton University Press, 1995.

Jorge Cañizares-Esguerra

Whose Centers and Peripheries? Eighteenth-Century Intellectual History in Atlantic Perspective

AROUND 1580, AS THE SPANISH DOMINICAN DIEGO DURÁN researched his history of the Aztecs,[1] he found himself confronted with two contradictory accounts of the death of Moctezuma. The traditional account from Spanish sources contended that the Aztecs themselves had stoned Moctezuma to death. Indigenous sources, however, told a dramatically different story; namely, that the emperor and several other Aztec nobles had been stabbed to death by the Spanish conquistadors. Although this account was an obvious challenge to Spanish official historiography, Durán himself saw no choice but to accept it, for the story was recounted in native documents recorded in indigenous scripts and texts (fig. 1). Despite the generalized doubt about the reliability of Amerindian informants, Durán, like most Spaniards, believed that indigenous documents in non-alphabetical scripts kept trustworthy historical records.[2]

European intellectuals in the eighteenth century, however, held strikingly different views on the accuracy of indigenous historical sources. For example, in 1787 an anonymous British reviewer argued that a history of the Aztecs recently published in Italy by the Mexican Jesuit Francisco Clavijero (1731–1787) made no sense; it was a book "stuffed with impossible facts [and] absurd exaggerations." The

1500
a
1502
1500
1464
1402

reviewer derided histories like Clavijero's because they drew most of their facts from Mexican indigenous records, which, the reviewer argued, were primitive paintings, not writings, and therefore utterly unreliable. "All the history, therefore, anterior to the conquest by Cortés [should be] receive[d] with very great distrust."[3]

To be sure, lack of belief in non-alphabetical scripts was part of the skeptical mood that characterized the Enlightenment. In the following pages I describe how the history of the New World was written on both sides of the Atlantic in the eighteenth century. The skepticism that dominated the "age of reason" took on different meanings in different places. In Western Europe it generated new forms of reading, assessing, and validating testimonies and new forms of writing history that drew upon non-literary, material evidence. In Spain it prompted scholars to create new, more reliable narratives based on primary documentation, which in turn led to the formation of one of the largest specialized repositories of primary sources in the world, the Archive of the Indies. Finally, in Spanish America, skepticism was turned against its most ardent European promoters. Spanish American scholars questioned the ability of European observers to ever comprehend the past and nature of the New World.

Figure 1. Entries recording events that took place in the Central Valley of Mexico around 1500 C.E.: (a) *Histoire mexicaine depuis 1221 jusu'en 1594*; (b) *Codex en Cruz*. The copies belonged to León y Gama, who used these entries to exemplify the ascending scale of complexity and accessibility of indigenous sources. Differences in narrative complexity and calendrical accuracy between (a) and (b) are apparent, an indication that they were intended for two different audiences. The entries in *Codex en Cruz* exemplify how Aztec script worked. In 1402 C.E. (1 Rabbit, signified by a rabbit's head and one circle), day 1 Deer (a day symbol linked to a deer's head and one circle), Nezahualcoyotl ("Fasting Coyote" = a coyote's head and the symbol of a priest's fasting circle) was born (cradle) in the town of Texcoco ("Place of Pot/Alabaster Stone" = pot on top of a mountain). In 1464 (11 lint) day 12 Snake, Nezahualpilli ("Fasting Lord" = head and fasting circle) was born (cradle) in Texcoco ("Place of Pot"). Collection Goupil-Aubin, (a) MS 89 (1–2), fol. 24 and (b) MS 88 (5), fols. 71–74, 77. Courtesy of the Bibliothèque Nationale, Paris.

The great intellectual, cultural movements of the modern world like the Renaissance, the Enlightenment, and Romanticism are often presented as European inventions, passively and derivatively consumed everywhere else. The story that follows demonstrates the problematic nature of such an approach. In the age of Enlightenment, when it came to new ideas on how to write the history of the New World, there was as much intellectual creativity in the colonial peripheries as in the metropolitan core.

In Western Europe, skeptics not only questioned the reliability of Amerindian sources, they also doubted the credibility of earlier European observers. In the 1781 edition of his widely read *Histoire philosophique des deux Indes*, for example, the Abbé Guillaume-Thomas Raynal (1713–96) argued that all Spanish accounts of the New World were "confusing, contradictory and full of the most absurd fables to which human credulity could ever be exposed."[4] For Raynal, the conquistadors were plunderers, not dispassionate observers. In an earlier edition, Raynal had suggested that the only way to save any surviving historical records from the destruction and oblivion to which they had been subjected was to allow philosophers like Locke, Buffon, or Montesquieu to visit the New World.[5] Clearly, by the third quarter of the eighteenth century, the sources that Europeans had traditionally used to interpret the past of the Americas—translations of documents recorded in indigenous scripts and travel accounts by conquistadors, missionaries, sailors, and colonial bureaucrats—were considered unreliable. Many intellectual and cultural developments help explain this curious burst of skepticism.

One problem presenting itself to historians of pre-Columbian America was the reliability of the Bible as a historical source. The scriptures had long been assumed to be the sole surviving, accurate historical record of the human race. Since the second half of the seventeenth century, however, skeptics had begun to question its authority and credibility. As humanist antiquarians unearthed ancient sources, including ancient Egyptian chronologies, and as the Jesuits made available Chinese classical texts in translation, it became clear that the chronologies of Hebrews and heathens could not be easily reconciled. Eighteenth-century conservative luminaries such as the Neapolitan scholar Giambattista Vico (1668–1744) and the Anglican Bishop of Gloucester William Warburton (1698–1779) pursued a defensive strategy to safeguard the Bible's authority. Chinese ideograms and Egyptian hieroglyphs, long considered the repositories of ancient historical knowledge, lost their luster and prestige. Vico and Warburton argued that non-alphabetical scripts represented a more primitive stage in the evolution of mental faculties. Thus, in the debates over the reliability of biblical chronologies, Chinese and Egyptian sources were discarded and Amerindian pictograms came to exemplify the first stage in the evolution of writing. The primitive Amerindian paintings were seen as products of a childlike mentality, the initial phase in the evolution of the mental faculties. No wonder, then, that in 1787 Warburton was so willing to dismiss documents recorded in Mesoamerican scripts.

If academic debates over biblical chronology account for the loss of credibility of Amerindian sources in the eighteenth century, the intellectual elitism that characterized the Enlightenment helps explain why earlier reports of the New World were also considered untrustworthy. When Raynal called on philosophers to visit and report on the New World in order to replace the unreliable testimony of earlier Spanish witnesses, he was simply following a convention of his time. In his groundbreaking 1755 study of the origins of social inequality, Rousseau characterized the so-called European "age of discovery" as one of lost opportunities. According to Rousseau, missionaries, traders, soldiers, and sailors had not truly studied the foreign societies they visited and conquered, for they had failed to go beyond appearances. A new category of travelers was needed, Rousseau insisted, one whose "eyes [are] made to see the true features that distinguish nations."[6] Rousseau, therefore, invited the leading intellectual luminaries of his age to set sail and become philosophical travelers.

When Rousseau and Raynal called into question the reliability of typical European accounts of foreign societies, they were simply echoing the learned consensus of their age that the observations of untrained individuals were not trustworthy: witnesses left to their own devices failed to make accurate observations. This was one of the tenets of the "age of reason," which divided the world into two unequal parts: on one hand, the fear-stricken, deluded majority; and on the other, the reasonable few, whose minds had been trained to understand the world accurately.

Cornelius de Pauw (1739–99) typifies the authors north of the Pyrenees who in the second half of the eighteenth century sought to write histories of the New World while dismissing earlier Amerindian and European testimonies. De Pauw was a prolific author from the Southern Netherlands, whose *Recherches philosophiques sur les américains* [Philosophical Inquiries on the Americans] (1768–69) proved extremely influential. The book was structured as a series of essays evaluating previous reports on the New World. Utterly skeptical of the power of the untrained mind to observe accurately, De Pauw set out to demonstrate that contradictions plagued the literature on the history of the Americas. Take for example his analysis of the Inca Garcilaso de la Vega's *History of the Incas* (1609). Owing to Garcilaso's dual heritage as the son of a Spanish conquistador and an Inca princess, which gave him access to the most learned and accurate contemporary testimonies from both European and indigenous sources, Garcilaso had enjoyed since the early seventeenth century a reputation as the foremost authority on the history of the Incas. In De Pauw's hands, however, Garcilaso's history appeared riddled with contradictions.

Garcilaso had maintained that the Inca kept their records in quipus (knotted strings), not alphabetical writing. He had also argued that the great legislator, founder of the Inca dynasty, Manco Capac had turned the savages of Cuzco into civilized agriculturists and that the eleven rulers who followed Manco Capac had all been sage and prudent, spreading civilization and a humanely religious solar cult throughout an Inca Empire that expanded through gentle conquest. Garcilaso, finally, had argued that the Inca had established palaces, cities, universities, and astronomical observatories, as well as pious and prudent laws. De Pauw read Garcilaso carefully and attacked many of his premises. According to De Pauw it was inherently contradictory to maintain that the Inca enjoyed wise laws while they lacked writing, for laws existed only when written and codified. According to De Pauw, unwritten rules were not laws because they changed according to the whim of the times and the imagination of tyrants. There were other serious logical flaws in Garcilaso's narrative. The claim that one man, Manco Capac, had single-handedly transformed highland savages into civilized creatures in one generation was outrageous. For evidence, De Pauw cited the Jesuit missions of Paraguay, the most recent example of a successful transformation of savages into settled civilized agriculturists. The achievement of civilization in Paraguay had required no less than fifty years and the imposition of harsh policies to prevent the Amerindians from escaping. Societies, De Pauw argued, are not transformed by leaps, but like nature evolve in sequential stage—evenly, harmoniously, and slowly.

Drawing upon this principle of slow social progress, De Pauw maintained that Garcilaso's chronology of the Inca did not make sense. Garcilaso had argued that forty years after the death of Manco Capac, astronomical observatories had been built in Cuzco to determine solstices and equinoxes. To evolve from a state of savagery to sophisticated astronomical knowledge required more than forty years. Finally, based on the notion of the harmoniously integrated evolution of social institutions, De Pauw insisted that the Inca could not have had an advanced agricultural society without having at the same time iron, money, and writing, which they all lacked. Garcilaso had presented Inca rulers as patriarchal yet prudent, preoccupied with the welfare of the majority. But how could rulers have been prudent and gentle, De Pauw wondered, when the Inca had never developed institutions to check and balance the power of their monarchs? A fair, gentle patriarch was a contradiction in terms. So too was the idea that the Inca fought "just wars" even as they engaged in conquest. Even if one conceded to Garcilaso that Manco Capac had in fact been fair, prudent, and gentle, what were the chances, De Pauw sardonically asked, that twelve such statesmen should appear in succession? De Pauw applied the same unrelenting critical techniques to tear apart previous versions of the history of the Americas.[7]

If the views of learned authors such as Garcilaso, who had ably synthesized the testimonies of both Amerindians and Europeans, proved untrustworthy, how then should scholars write the history of the New World? Western European authors were not merely content with dismissing as sources translations of records written in indigenous scripts. Nor were these scholars satisfied with demonstrating logical inconsistencies in the accounts of travelers, missionaries, sailors, and colonial bureaucrats. Some philosophers like the Frenchman Charles-Marie de La Condamine (1701–74) chose to go to the New World and study firsthand the land and its peoples, thus doing away with bothersome intermediary textual authorities. As the eighteenth century unfolded, witnesses trained in the new European sciences arrived in the Americas in ever greater numbers.

In addition to on-site research, however, another option existed for scholars who did not trust the older accounts. Some European authors set out to reconstruct the past of the New World conjecturally, using non-literary, material evidence. Rousseau, for example, tried to do away with all evidence from literary sources. Paying lip service to the reliability of the Bible as an accurate account of the past, Rousseau turned to nature for insights, drawing endlessly on evidence from animal behavior to fill in the gaps in his evolutionary narrative of society and the causes of inequality. In addition, authors like De Pauw, who found suspect all previous accounts of the past of the New World, turned to nature for evidence upon which to build alternative histories of the Americas.

De Pauw offered a new conjectural history of the lands and peoples of America based entirely on facts from geology, geography, animal distribution, and some old-fashioned medical theories. De Pauw found evidence pointing to an early geological catastrophe in America: fossil bones of gigantic animals; earthquakes and active volcanoes still rocking the earth; seashells strewn over all the low valleys; ores of heavy metals protruding on the surface of the land. According to De Pauw, there were also substantial indications that the New World was a humid, putrid environment: the lesser number, smaller size, and monstrous appearance of quadrupeds; the degeneration of foreign animals; the successful development of "watery" plants from the Old World such as rice, melons, citrus, and sugar cane; the proliferation of insects and reptiles; the abundance of poisonous plants like curare, whose virtues only the savage knew; the American origin of syphilis (humanity's scourge). De Pauw concluded that a flood had suddenly transformed a continent of big animals and ancient civilizations into a land enveloped by miasmas. America's coldness and humidity, in turn, had emasculated its fauna and peoples. Drawing on an ancient medical tradition that assumed that males were "drier" than females, De Pauw argued that the Amerindians were effete. The Amerindians were millenarian inhabitants of the continent who, as a consequence of the flood that destroyed the New World, had become humid and insensitive; incapable of feeling passion and sexual urges, which, in turn, explained why upon arrival Europeans had found an allegedly sparsely populated continent.[8]

The eighteenth century witnessed many other conjectural histories of the New World. One of the leading historians of the age, the presbyter William Robertson (1721–93), rector of the University of Edinburgh, published his *History of America* in 1777. Rather than drawing upon geology and geography, Robertson made use of the new science of political economy as he sought to cast Amerindians as the missing link in the history of the evolution of human societies.

By the eighteenth century Spain had become a weak imperial power, reviled and ridiculed in Europe. Criticism of Spain, to be sure, was not new. In the Middle Ages, Europeans had represented Spain as a threatening frontier where Jews and Muslims roamed undisturbed. In the sixteenth century, as it consolidated a formidable overseas empire at the outset of the Reformation, Spain came to be both admired and despised. The figure of the intolerant, greedy, cruel Spaniard, dedicated to killing Amerindians and Dutchmen, came to life in the hands of Protestant printers. In the seventeenth century, Spaniards were commonly represented not only as cruel bigots but also as ignoramuses, and Spain was depicted as a country firmly controlled by superstitious friars.[9] While resisting these cartoonish representations, Spanish authorities and intellectuals were concerned about Spain's decline. Efforts to reform the economy and open the empire to new ideas were first attempted as early as the 1620s under the aegis of the Count-Duke of Olivares (1587–1645), but gained momentum after the War of the Spanish Succession (1701–14) when a new dynasty, the Bourbons, replaced the Habsburgs on the throne.

Reforms also extended to historiography. In debates that lasted from the 1740s until well into the 1790s, intellectuals argued that previous accounts about the history of the Americas were utterly unreliable. Some authors like the Count of Campomanes (1723–1803) substituted the conjectural histories offered by Northern European authors like Robertson for all previous available narratives. Others, however, came up with alternatives deeply rooted in Spain's own intellectual traditions.

Juan Bautista Muñoz (1745–99) typifies the authors who in the eighteenth century turned to the scholarship of Spanish humanism for inspiration. Muñoz inherited a corpus of critical Valencian scholarship, including the writings of such luminaries as Juan Luis Vives (1492–1540) and Gregorio Mayans y Siscar (1699–1781), Muñoz's own mentor.[10] Drawing upon this tradition, Muñoz rejected all previous accounts of the history of the New World. Muñoz did not think that existing narratives of America were unreliable merely because they were translations of records in indigenous scripts. Nor did he limit himself to the argument that previous accounts were doubtful because ignorant travelers, missionaries, sailors, and bureaucrats had written them. The older narratives, Muñoz maintained, were untrustworthy because they lacked a solid foundation. Since archival sources had not been written with the intention of moving audiences to support specific political agendas—as most printed documents usually are—Muñoz advocated the writing of new histories that were largely based on unpublished, primary documentation. Much earlier than German historian Leopold von Ranke (1795–1886), Muñoz considered painstaking archival research a precondition for writing history.

Because no adequate archive existed, Muñoz set out to organize one. Over a period of twenty years, he carefully put together one of the greatest collections of documents and manuscripts on the Spanish colonization of the New World.[11] Muñoz also persuaded the minister of the Council of Indies, José de Gálvez, to create the Archivo de Indias (Archive of the Indies) in the early 1780s.[12]

Muñoz envisioned himself as a Descartes of American historiography, doing away with previous textual authorities through methodical doubt, and as a Bacon of historical method, reconstructing knowledge upon solid foundations based on the painstaking collection of facts. He thought that within the archives of Spain would be found the answer to each and every one of the charges leveled by foreigners against the nation. Muñoz was a patriot who thought that the truth about the deeds of Spain in the New World could only emerge after the exhaustive accumulation of new documentary evidence. According to Muñoz, the sheer amassing of sources would demonstrate that the negative European portrayal of Spain was simply innuendo, deliberate manipulation of the truth, and biased interpretation of the available information.

Although in his first forays into the archives Muñoz despaired of finding any logic behind the thousands of stored documents, he slowly began to find order. In the many documents and manuscripts lying unpublished on the shelves of archives and private libraries, he found evidence that Spain had transformed the history of navigation and commerce. The documents also seemed to reveal what the rest of Europe had most denied: the profound contributions that Spain had made to the store of universal knowledge. The many unpublished travel reports of the sixteenth and seventeenth centuries, the countless geographical surveys (particularly those sponsored in the later sixteenth century under Philip II), and the various manuscripts on natural history, demonstrated Spain's significant contributions to natural history and geography. The many letters, reports, and trials of colonial bureaucrats, and the prolonged and well-documented discussions addressing the issue of laws for the colonies, on the other hand, proved the prudence and philosophical depth of Spanish colonial legislation, "a precious monument of human wisdom." The numerous unpublished ethnological studies of indigenous peoples, Muñoz argued, indicated that colonial laws had been hammered on the anvil of sound anthropological knowledge. The many documents related to the Church demonstrated that the conquest had never been motivated merely by greed. According to Muñoz, these documents also revealed that the civilization created by Spain in the Indies was a harmonious whole in material and spiritual balance. This search for evidence of the wisdom of Spanish legislation and of natural history observations was the organizing principle behind the invaluable collection of primary documents that Muñoz gathered in some hundred and fifty stout volumes over the course of twenty years.[13]

As in Europe, there was much support in Spanish America for the writing of new historical narratives. Yet these new histories of America were significantly different from those that appeared on the other side of the Atlantic. Spanish Americans, to be sure, tried to offer alternative accounts in which the inhabitants of the New World did not appear as degenerate and effete as conjectural historians like De Pauw had presented them. In the process, Spanish American writers also articulated a powerful and creative critique of Eurocentric forms of knowledge. Spanish American authors, for example, exposed the shortcomings and limitations of the new European philosophical travelers, who had been arriving in ever increasing numbers to the New World. Spanish American intellectuals maintained that foreign travelers were unreliable sources because they tended to be ignorant of native languages, gullible, and easily manipulated by savvy local informants: so much for the boasted skepticism of the observers from Western Europe.

The work of Antonio León y Gama (1735–1802) exemplifies the distinctly patriotic scholarship that appeared in eighteenth-century Spanish America. León y Gama first articulated his views on the limited ability of outside observers to understand the past and the nature of the New World in a debate over the curative power of lizards. A flurry of speculation and clinical experimentation greeted the public of Mexico in 1782 when the leading physician of the Audiencia (high court and council) of Guatemala, José Flores, published a treatise claiming to have discovered that the raw meat of lizards cured cancer.[14] The discovery triggered a medical controversy in the capital of Mexico. Some physicians proved through clinical trials that the lizards were in fact poisonous, not curative. León y Gama, however, denounced these clinical trials as having either administered to patients the wrong lizards or mishandled the ones that were curative. Drawing on the works of Francisco Hernández, the sixteenth-century savant sent by Philip II to compile a natural history of the New World, León y Gama maintained that several distinct species of lizards, some of them indeed poisonous, existed in central Mexico. The physicians who conducted the trials that proved the lizards poisonous might have failed to identify the correct species or, worse, might have mishandled the right ones, turning them poisonous. Great care and great knowledge was needed to identify the correct species. Once the right lizard was caught, León y Gama argued, it had to be fed only with the appropriate local insects; all females, particularly those pregnant, had to be discarded; finally, the lizard had to be treated gently, for if irritated it could become poisonous. The amount of knowledge that these techniques demanded from physicians was extraordinary. Doctors needed to know the natural history of the area in order to identify, feed, and treat the curative lizards properly. The message behind León y Gama's treatise was that only those who knew the local fauna and flora in all its exquisite detail and intricacy were qualified to use the lizards. Those ignorant of the bewildering details of Amerindian lore would never be able to master their curative powers.[15]

In the 1790s, in a different debate, this time over how to read Mesoamerican scripts, León y Gama maintained that outsiders had failed to understand the meaning of Amerindian sources for the same reasons that they had failed to grasp the importance of the curative power of lizards, namely, superficial acquaintance with the great complexities of Amerindian knowledge. By demonstrating the difficulty of reading Aztec documents, León y Gama set out to show the degree of linguistic and scientific knowledge required to handle this material appropriately, knowledge that only insiders could ever hope to master. León y Gama used Nahuatl documents recorded in indigenous scripts to make his case.

Nahuatl historical sources, León y Gama argued, ranged from widely accessible historical documents to arcane records that stored secret knowledge. He offered a few examples. *Codex histoire mexicaine depuis 1221 jusqu'en 1594*, on the one hand, indicated that the flood of Tenochtitlan occurred in the year "eight flint" (1500 CE) (see fig 1a). Although it located this event in equally rough fashion in the same year, the *Codex en Cruz* (see fig. 1b), on the other hand, dated other events using a finer grid. It recorded, for example, the dates of birth of the monarch of Texcoco, Nezahualcoyotl (1402 CE), his son Nezahualpilzintli (1464 CE), and the ruler Quauhcaltzin (1502 CE).

Sources such as *Codex histoire mexicaine*, León y Gama maintained, had been written for the masses because they required only a superficial acquaintance with writing techniques and astronomical knowledge. Sources such as the *Codex en Cruz*, on the other hand, were addressed to more knowledgeable and sophisticated audiences, for they demanded familiarity with the hieroglyphs of deities and towns as well as an exquisite command of multiple calendrical counts. A third type of source, such as the ritual calendar *Tonalamtl Aubin,* could only be read by highly trained religious specialists (fig. 2). With hundreds of symbols and obscure references to celestial phenomena and deities, sources such as

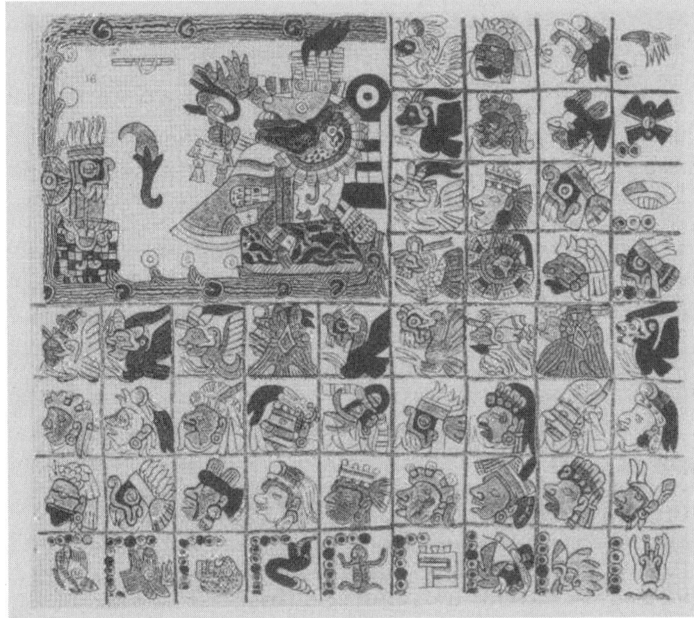

Figure 2. The dominant signs in the sixteenth week of the ritual calendar *Tonalamatl Aubin.* As in a typical ritual calendar, the dominant sign of the thirteen days of the "week" are located in the upper left corner. The thirteen day signs are located in the bottom line and in the upper four squares of the outer right column. The lines and columns in-between represent "accompanying" ritual cycles, including the cycle of the nine "lords of the night" that stand immediately to the left and above the squares that house the day signs. Leon y Gama used the *Tonalamatl Aubin* to recreate the many cycles of the calendar. Leon y Gama also used the image in the periphery of the upper left corner to argue that the sign "Ollin Tonatiuh" is frequently accompanied by the sign of the "Milky Way" as in the case of the Solar Stone. It also supported his thesis that most images in Mesoamerican sources referred to simplified hieroglyphic attributes of deities, as is the case of the figure of Tlaloc in the upper left corner and in the images of the lords of the night. Courtesy of the Bibliothèque Nationale, Paris.

Tonalamtl Aubin demanded from their intended audience complete command of both theological subtleties and astronomy.[16]

Complicating the picture of different documents for different audiences, there stood the additional problem of the nature of the logograms* and ideograms† used by Amerindians to record their annals. According to León y Gama, logograms and ideograms often alluded to local objects accessible only to a privileged few. An extensive knowledge of local natural history, León y Gama argued, was needed to understand the logograms of town names. The name of towns in such documents as the *Codex Cozcatzin* and the *Codex histoire mexicaine* could not be read without having first gained vast knowledge of the natural history of central Mexico (fig. 3a). The name of Cimatlan, Tulan, Papatztaca, and Huexotzinca in these codices used logograms with the images of local shrubs, trees, and flowers. According to León y Gama, some logograms were simply too idiosyncratic and undecipherable, as in the case of references in the *Codez Cozcatzin* to the town of "Teyahualco," whose rebus image León y Gama challenged anyone to explain (fig. 3b). Even more upsetting for those who sought a shortcut to the interpretation of Amerindian documents was the fact that some towns with similar Nahuatl names were identified with the same logograms in different documents. This, León y Gama argued, was the case of "Atempa" in the *Codex Cozcatzin* and "Atenco" in *Matrícula de Tributos* (fig. 3c).

But if to read the name of towns in Aztec sources required at times knowledge beyond the reach of common mortals, the reading of the name of rulers was even more difficult. According to León y Gama, the signs used to refer to rulers did not merely allude to the sound of their names but also to some aspects of their moral character. The fact that the logogram of the ruler Quauhcaltzin in *Codex en Cruz* was a caged eagle (see fig. 1 b), León y Gama argued, was of little use for those who knew that the logograms of the last Mexican monarch Quauhtemotsin, the Acolhua lord Quauhtletcohuatzin, and the lord of Coyuacan Quauhpocatzin were also represented as eagles in other sources. The eagles representing these rulers, however, showed subtle differences;

*A logogram is a symbol or letter representing an entire word (e.g., $ for dollar).

†An ideogram is a symbol or character representing an idea or thing.

Cimatlan.

Huexotzinca

Tulan.

Papatztaca.

a

Teyahualco.

b

c

their beaks appeared either shut, open, or giving off smoke, and their eyes were gazing up or down. According to León y Gama such subtle distinctions were allusions to some aspect of the moral character of these rulers that had been understood only by a handful of retainers. The logic behind these correlations, therefore, was now beyond the understanding of any mortal, including any late-colonial native elites.[17]

León y Gama's reading of Mesoamerican codices was subtle and sophisticated. Notwithstanding his faith in the curative power of lizards, León y Gama's insistence that there were different types of indigenous sources and that each required a vast amount of contextual information of linguistics and local natural history to be read, was unique for his age. León y Gama brought to bear learned humanist and antiquarian sensibilities to the reading and interpretation of sources in non-alphabetical scripts. His approach contrasts dramatically with the heavy-handed techniques of contemporary Western European conjectural historians. Radically different historiographical techniques seemed to have developed in each of the three areas of the Atlantic world discussed in this chapter, each paradoxically "modern" in its own way. Although Spanish America and Spain itself are traditionally considered peripheries to an eighteenth-century North Atlantic core, the

Figure 3. Pictograms for Mesoamerican towns in indigenous sources used by León y Gama to demonstrate the difficulty of establishing "general rules" for the reading of Mesoamerican scripts. (a) Ideograms of towns whose name in rebus refer to local plants. *Codex Cozcatzin* and *Codex Azcatitlan.* Collection Goupil-Aubin, MS 89 (3), fol. 34 (#4) and MS 89 (5), fol. 66, 68, 74. Courtesy of the Bibliothèque Nationale, Paris. (b) Ideogram of Teyahualco whose logic León y Gama could not make out. *Codex Cozcatzin.* Collection Goupil-Aubin, MS 89 (5), fol. 69. Courtesy of the Bibliotheque Nationale, Paris. (c) Two similar rebus signs that stand for two completely different towns. Some images show how phoneticism and pictography combined in Aztec script. The symbol for Huexotzinca (Codex Azcatitlan) is made up of a rump [tzin], which stands for the adjective "little," and a tree = "Little Tree." The teeth in the images for Atempa and Tenco (c) stand for *tlan,* also an adverbial particle ("near") = near water. *Codex Cozcatzin* (Collection Goupil-Aubin, MS 89 (5), fol. 64. Courtesy of the Bibliotheque Nationale, Paris.

scholarship produced by authors like Juan Bautista Muñoz and Antonio León y Gama are proof that the skepticism of the Enlightenment took on different meanings in different settings. Most studies of the Enlightenment, however, have failed to realize that the ideas produced by a handful of great French, British, and German writers were not simply "transmitted" to the rest of the world, where they allegedly were either vigorously consumed or forcefully rejected. We have seen in the preceding pages that the same intellectual tools were used in different ways in Europe north of the Pyrenees, Spain, and Spanish America. If in the skeptical "age of reason," non-Iberian authors created new and sophisticated forms of reading and invented the genre of conjectural history, Spanish writers anticipated the great insights of nineteenth-century German scholarship as they went about creating archives and histories based solely on primary sources. Scholars in Mexico took yet another route; they articulated a formidable critique of the limitations of knowledge that European skeptics were bound to face in the Americas. Oddly enough, it was colonial scholars like León y Gama who put together the most sophisticated historical monographs on the Americas created in the Enlightenment. When it came to affairs of the mind, there were no colonial peripheries and metropolitan cores in the "age of reason."

It is clear that the historiographical debate I have just sketched was intimately linked to the pursuit of diverse, often contradictory, political goals. Struggles over authority and reliability had clear political overtones. North of the Pyrenees, enlightened scholars called into question the reliability of all written sources because they were ultimately seeking to undermine the lasting cultural authority of traditional clerical bureaucracies, who had long had a purchase on power by claiming a sacred, privileged historiographical status for the Bible. Enlightened scholars also saw themselves actively contributing to the creation of a market driven "bourgeois public sphere." In it, a new breed of male critics asserted their authority and credibility by highlighting their independence from distorting feminine emotions and powerful patrons. In the process, the scholars of the Enlightenment went about creating new reading techniques and new conjectural reconstructions of the past that drew exclusively on new nonliterary sources. Peninsular Spanish historians, to be sure, had different motivations. Their epistemological and methodological contributions came about as they sought to restore Spain's authority to determine how the colonization of the New World was to be remembered. Scholars understood that empires are lost in the struggle over naming and remembering. It is not surprising therefore that along with the creation of a new academy of history, archives, and new historical narratives, the reforming agenda of the Bourbon crown also included sending dozens of cartographical and botanical expeditions to overseas territories. In addition to identifying new botanical resources for the empire, these expeditions primarily sought to challenge the power of the Dutch, English, and French to give names to new plants and old territories and to impose self-serving narratives of the history of European colonization in the New World, which had Spain as the villain. Finally historians in Spanish America had a political agenda of their own. Creoles there had long envisioned their territories as "kingdoms," loosely held parts of a much larger composite Iberian monarchy. But having kingdoms of their own, among other things, demanded scholars to endow these colonial territories with deep-rooted historical narratives and ancient dynastic genealogies. In places like Mexico, Creoles saw the ancient indigenous nobilities as their own biological ancestors, and intellectuals thus turned for inspiration to the rich store of native written and oral sources.[18]

Notes

1. Diego Durán, Nueva España *Historia de las Indias de Nueva España* [1581], ed. M. Garibay, 2 vols. (México: Porrua, 1967).

2. Ibid., 2:556.

3. *The London Review and Literary Journal* (August 1787): 16, 17.

4. Abbé Guillaume-Thomas Raynal, *Histoire philosophique et politique, des etablissemens et du commerce des Europeens dans les deux Indes,* 10 vols. (Genève: Jean Leonard Pellet, 1781): book 6, ch. xx, 3:255–56.

5. Abbé Guillaume-Thomas Raynal, *Histoire philosophique,* 7 vols. (Maestricht: Jean-Edme Dufour, 1774): book 6, ch. I, 3:3.

6. Jean-Jacques Rousseau, *Discourse on the origins and foundations of inequality among men* [1755], in *The Collected writings of Rousseau,* ed. Roger D. Masters and Christopher Kelly (Hanover, N.H.: University Press of New England, 1990–): vol. 3: note 8 in Rousseau's original, pp. 84–86.

7. Joannes Cornelius De Pauw, *Recherches philosophiques sur les américains, ou Mémoires intéressants pour servir à l'histoire de l'espèce humaine* [1768–69], 3 vols. (Berlin: G. J. Decker, 1770): 2:195–203.

8. Ibid., vol 1.

9. On European perceptions of Spain, see William S. Maltby, *The Black Legend in England: The Development of Anti-Spanish Sentiment, 1558–1660* (Durham, N. C.: Duke University Press, 1971); Julian Juderias, *La leyenda negra* (9th ed., Barcelona: Editorial Araluce, 1943); and Ricardo García Cárcel, *La leyenda negra. Historia y opinión* (Madrid: Alianza Editorial, 1992).

10. On this tradition in the Spanish Enlightenment, see Antonio Mestre, *Mayans y la España de la Ilustración* (Madrid: Instituto de España/Espasa Calpe, 1990).

11. For a partial description of the collection, see *Catálogo de la colección de Juan Bautista Muñoz*, 3 vols. (Madrid: Real Academia de Historia, 1954–56). The catalogue describes in detail the contents of seventy-six of ninety-five folio volumes of documentation collected by Muñoz now located at the Academy of History in Madrid. The remaining nineteen volumes can be found today at the Royal Library in Madrid. The catalogue also includes a short description of eighteen quarto volumes, most of which are located at the Royal Library as well. Muñoz was also responsible for pressing the Spanish authorities in Mexico to collect thirty-five additional volumes known as *Colección Memorias de Nueva España*, which is also housed at the Academy of History. The collection that Muñoz assembled totals 148 volumes.

12. On founding of the Archive of the Indies, see Margarita Gómez Gómez, "El Archivo General de Indias, génesis histórica de sus ordenanzas," *Archivo General de Indias. Ordenanzas* (Seville: Junta de Andalucia, 1986); and Francisco de Solano, "El Archivo de Indias y la promoción del americanismo científico," in *Carlos III y la ciencia de la Ilustración*, ed. Manuel Selles, José Luis Peset, and Antonio Lafuente (Madrid: Alianza, 1988): 277–96.

13. For the principles organizing Muñoz's collection and the Archive of the Indies, see Muñoz's "Idea de una obra cometida," Nov. 28, 1783. *[A]rchivo del [R]eal [J]ardín [B]otanico*, división 13, legajo 5, 8, # 9; and "Razón de una obra cometida," Nov 16, 1785, ARJB, división 13, legajo 5, 8, #10.

14. José Flores, *Específico nuevamente descubierto en el reino de Guatemala para la curación del horrible mal de cancro y otros más frecuentes (experimentado ya favorablemente en esta capital de Mexico)* (México: Felipe Zúñiga de Ontiveros, 1782).

15. Antonio León y Gama, *Instruccion sobre el remedio de las lagartijas. Nuevamente descubierto para la curacion del cancro y otras enfermedades* (México: Felipe de Zuñiga y Ontiveros, 1782).

16. Antonio León y Gama, *Descripción histórica y cronológica de las dos piedras que con ocasion del nuevo empedrado que se esta formando en la plaza principal de México se hallaron en ella en el año de 1790* [vol 1: 1792], ed. Carlos María de Bustamante, 2 vols. (México: Imprenta de Alejandro Valdés, 1832) 2:29–32 (par. 105–9). In the text, León y Gama never identified the provenance of the examples he cited. After a painstaking survey of the copies of codices he owned, I have identified the codices from which he drew most of his examples.

17. Ibid., 2:41–45 (par. 117–19).

18. For a more detailed account of the debates sketched here, see Jorge Cañizares-Esguerra, *How to Write the History of the New World. Histories, Epistemologies, and Identities in the Eighteenth-Century Atlantic World* (Stanford, Calif.: Stanford University Press, 2001).

Bibliography

Aldrige, A. Owen, ed. *The Ibero-American Enlightenment*. Urbana, Ill.: University of Illinois Press, 1971.

Anderson, Benedict. *Imagined Communities: Reflections on the Origins and Spread of Nationalism*. Second edition. London: Verso, 1991.

Armitage, David. "The New World and British Historical Thought: From Richard Hakluyt to William Robertson." In *America in European Consciousness*, ed. Karen Ordahl Kupperman. Chapel Hill: University of North Carolina Press, 1995.

Arnoldsson, Sverker. *La leyenda negra: Estudios sobre sus orígenes.* Goteborg: Acta Universitatis Gothoburgensis, 1960.

Ascher, Marcia, and Robert Ascher. *Code of the Quipu. A Study in Media, Mathematics, and Culture.* Ann Arbor: University of Michigan Press, 1981.

Barret-Kriegel, Blandine. *La defaite de l'erudition.* Paris: Presses Universitaires de France, 1988.

———. *Les Académies de l'histoire.* Paris: Presses Universitaires de France, 1988.

Batllori, Miguel. *La cultura hispano-italiana de los Jesuitas expulsos.* Madrid: Editorial Gredos, 1966.

Baudot, Georges. *Utopia and History in Mexico. The First Chroniclers of Mexican Civilization (1520–1569).* Trans. Bernard and Thelma Ortiz de Montellano. Niwot: University Press of Colorado, 1995.

Boone, Elizabeth Hill, and Walter D. Mignolo, eds. *Writing without Words: Alternative Literacies in Mesoamerica and the Andes.* Durham, N. C.: Duke University Press, 1994.

Brading, David. *First America.* Cambridge: Cambridge University Press, 1991.

———. *The Origins of Mexican Nationalism.* Cambridge: Centre of Latin American Studies, 1985.

Brotherston, Gordon. *Book of the Fourth World: Reading the Native Americas Through their Literature.* Cambridge: Cambridge University Press, 1992.

Cañizares-Esguerra, Jorge. *How to Write the History of the New World: Histories of Epistemologies and Identities* (Stanford, Calif: Stanford University Press, 2001).

Carbia, Rómulo. *La crónica oficial de las Indias Occidentales: Estudio histórico y crítico acerca de la historiografía mayor de Hispano América en los siglos XVI a XVIII.* Buenos Aires: Ediciones Buenos Aires, 1940.

Catálogo de la colección de Juan Bautista Muñoz. 3 vols. Madrid: Real Academia de Historia, 1954–1956.

Clavijero, Francisco. *Historia antigua de México.* Prólogo de Mariano Cuevas. Sepan Cuantos # 27. Mexico: Porrua, 1964.

———. *The History of Mexico Collected from Spanish and Mexican Historians, from Manuscripts, and Ancient Paintings of the Indians.* 2 vols. London: G. G. J. and J. Robinson, 1787.

———. *Storia antica del Messico cavata da' migliori storici spagnuoli, e da' manoscritti, e dalle pitture antiche degl' Indiani: divisa in dieci libri . . . e dissertazioni sulla terra, sugli animali, e sugli abitatori del Messico.* 4 vols. Cesena: G. Biasini, 1780–1781.

Cline, Howard, ed. *Handbook of Middle America Indians, vols. 12–15, Guide to the Ethnohistorical Sources.* Austin: University of Texas Press, 1972–1975.

Daston, Lorraine and Peter Galison. "The Image of Objectivity," *Representations* 40 (fall 1992), 81–128.

David, Madeleine V. *Le débat sur les écritures et l'hiéroglyphe aux XVIIe et XVIIIe siècles.* Paris: Ecole Pratique des Hautes Études, 1965.

De Pauw, Cornelius. "Amérique," in *Supplement à l'Encyclopédie*, vol. 1, pp. 344–54. Amsterdam: M. M. Rey, 1776–1777.

———. *Recherches philosophiques sur les Américains ou Mémoires intéressants pour servir à l'histoire de l'espece humaine.* 3 vols. Berlin: George Jacques Decker, 1770.

———. *Recherches philosophiques sur les Grecs.* 2 vols. Berlin, 1787.

Durán, Diego. *Historia de las Indias de Nueva España.* Ed. M. Garibay. 2 vols. México: Porrua, 1967.

Esteve Barba, Francisco. *Historiografía indiana.* Segunda edición. Madrid: Gredos, 1992.

Flores, José. *Específico nuevamente descubierto en el reino de Guatemala para la curación del horrible mal de cancro y otros más frecuentes (experimentado ya favorablemente en esta capital de Mexico).* México: Felipe Zúñiga de Ontiveros, 1782.

Florescano, Enrique. *Memory, Myth, and Time in Mexico: From the Aztecs to Independence.* Trans. Albert Bork and Kathryn R. Bork. Austin: University of Texas Press, 1994.

García Cárcel, Ricardo. *La leyenda negra. Historia y opinión.* Madrid: Alianza Editorial, 1992.

Garcilaso de la Vega, Inca. *Comentarios Reales de los Incas [1609].* Ed. José Durand. 3 vols., Lima: Universidad Nacional Mayor de San Marcos, 1959.

Gerbi, Antonello. *La disputa del nuevo mundo: Historia de una polémica 1750–1900.* Segunda edición en español corregida y aumentada. Mexico: Fondo de Cultura Económica, 1982.

Gibson, Charles. *Aztecs Under Spanish Rule: A History of the Indians of the Valley of Mexico, 1519–1810.* Stanford: Stanford University Press, 1964.

Gómez Gómez, Margarita. "El Archivo General de Indias, génesis histórica de sus ordenanzas." In *Archivo General de Indias. Ordenanzas,* 53–120. Sevilla: Junta de Andalucia, 1986.

Höpfl, H. M. "From Savage to Scotsman: Conjectural History in the Scottish Enlightenment," *Journal of British Studies* 17 (1978): 19–40.

Heikamp, Detlef. *Mexico and the Medici.* Florence: Editrice Edam, 1972.

Koenisberger, Helmut. "Spain." In *National Consciousness, History, and Political Culture in Early-Modern Europe,* ed. Orest Ranum, 144–72. Baltimore: The Johns Hopkins University Press, 1975.

Herr, Richard. *The Eighteenth-Century Revolution in Spain.* Princeton: Princeton University Press, 1958.

Hobsbawn, Eric, and Terence Ranger, eds. *The Invention of Tradition.* Cambridge: Cambridge University Press, 1983.

Hudson, Nicholas. *Writing and European Thought 1600–1830.* Cambridge: Cambridge University Press, 1994.

Iversen, Erik. *The Myth of Egypt and its Hieroglyphs in European Tradition.* Copenhagen: Gec Gad Publishers, 1961.

Juderias, Julian. *La leyenda negra.* Novena edición. Barcelona: Editorial Araluce, 1943.

Keen, Benjamin. *The Aztec Image in Western Thought.* New Brunswick, N. J.: Rutgers University Press, 1971.

Kohut, Karl, and Sonia V. Rose, eds. *Pensamiento europeo y cultura colonial.* Frankfurt and Madrid: Vervuert and Iberoamericana, 1997.

Kupperman, Karen Ordahl, ed. *America in European Consciousness 1493–1750.* Chapel Hill: University of North Carolina Press, 1995.

Lafaye, Jacques. *Quetzalcóatl et Guadalupe: La formation de la conscience nationale au Mexique.* Paris: Gallimard, 1974.

León y Gama, Antonio de. *Descripción histórica y cronológica de las dos piedras que con ocasión del nuevo empe-*

drado que se esta formando en la plaza principal de México se hallaron en ella en el año de 1790, 2 vols., ed. Carlos Maria de Bustamente. México: Imprenta de Alejandro Valdés, 1832.

——. *Disertación física sobre la materia y formación de las auroras boreales.* Mexico: Felipe de Zuñiga y Ontiveros, 1790.

——. *Instrucción sobre el remedio de las lagartijas: Nuevamente descubierto para la curacion del cancro y otras enfermedades.* Mexico: Felipe de Zúñiga y Ontiveros, 1782.

——. *Respuesta satisfactoria a la carta apologética que escribieron el Lic. Manuel Antonio Moreno y el Br. Alejo Ramon Sanchez. Y defensa contra la censura que en ella se hace de algunas proposiciones contenidas en la "Instrucción sobre el remedio de las lagartijas."* Mexico: Felipe de Zúñiga y Ontiveros, 1783.

Lockhart, James. *The Nahuas After the Conquest: A Social and Cultural History of the Indians of Central Mexico, Seventeenth Through Eighteenth Centuries.* Stanford, Calif.: Stanford University Press, 1992.

Lopez, François. *Juan Pablo Forner et la crise de la conscience espagnole au XVIIIe siècle.* Bordeaux: Bibliothèque de l'Ecole des Hautes Etudes Hispaniques, 1976.

Lynch, John. *Bourbon Spain 1700–1808.* Oxford: Basil Blackwell, 1989.

Macri, Marta J. "Maya and other Mesoamerican Scripts." In *The World's Writing Systems*, ed. Peter Daniels and William Bright. Oxford: Oxford University Press, 1996.

Maltby, William S. *The Black Legend in England: The Development of Anti-Spanish Sentiment, 1558–1660.* Durham, N. C.: Duke University Press, 1971.

Manuel, Frank. *The Eighteenth Century Confronts the Gods.* Cambridge: Harvard University Press, 1959.

Manzano, Juan. "Un compilador Indiano: Manuel Jose de Ayala," *Boletín del Instituto de Investigaciones Historicas*, vol. XVIII (1934–35), 61–63, 152–240.

Maravall, José Antonio. *Estudios de la historia del pensamiento español (siglo XVIII)*, Madrid: Biblioteca Mondadori, 1991.

Marcus, Joyce. *Mesoamerican Writing Systems: Propaganda, Myth, and History in Four Ancient Civilizations.* Princeton: Princeton University Press, 1992.

Méndez, Cecilia. "Incas Sí, Indios No: Notes on Peruvian Creole Nationalism and its Contemporary Crisis," *Journal of Latin American Studies*, 28 (1996): 197–225.

Mestre, Antonio. "La imagen de España en el siglo XVIII. Apologistas, críticos y detractores," *Arbor* 115 (1983): 49–73.

——. *Historia, fueros y actitudes políticas: Mayans y la historiografía del XVIII.* Valencia: Publicaciones del Ayuntamiento de Oliva, 1970.

——. *Mayans y la España de la Ilustración.* Madrid: Instituto de España/Espasa Calpe, 1990.

Mignolo, Walter D. *The Darker Side of the Renaissance. Literacy, Territoriality, and Colonization.* Ann Arbor: Michigan University Press, 1995.

Moreno de los Arcos, Roberto. "Ensayo biobibliográfico de Antonio de León y Gama," *Boletín del Instituto de Investigaciones Bibliográficas*, 3 (1970): 43–145.

——. "La Historia Antigua de México de Antonio León y Gama," *Estudios de Historia Novohispana* 7 (1981): 67–78.

Muñoz, Juan Bautista. *Historia del Nuevo Mundo.* Madrid: Viuda de Ibarra, 1793.

——. *Satisfacción a la carta crítica sobre las Historia del Nuevo Mundo.* Valencia: Joseph de Orga, 1798.

Muñoz Pérez, José. "La Idea de América en Campomanes," *Anuarios de Estudios Americanos,* 10 (1953): 209–65.

O'Brien, Karen. "Between Enlightenment and Stadial History: William Robertson on the History of Europe," *British Journal for Eighteenth-Century Studies,* 16 (1993): 53–63.

Pagden, Anthony. *Spanish Imperialism and the Political Imagination.* New Haven: Yale University Press, 1990.

Peset, José Luis. *Ciencia y libertad.* Madrid: CSIC, 1987.

Raynal, Guillaume-Thomas. *Histoire philosophique et politique, des etablissemens et du commerce des Europeens dans les deux Indes.* 6 vols. Amsterdam, n.p., 1770.

———. *Histoire philosophique et politique, des etablissemens et du commerce des Europeens dans les deux Indes.* 7 vols. Maestricht: Jean-Edme Dufour, 1774.

———. *Histoire philosophique et politique, des etablissemens et du commerce des Europeens dans les deux Indes.* 10 vols. Geneve: Jean Leonard Pellet, 1781.

Robertson, Donald. *Mexican Manuscript Painting of the Early Colonial Period: The Metropolitan School.* New Haven: Yale University Press, 1956.

Robertson, William. *The Works of William Robertson,* Ed. Alex Stewart. 12 vols., Edinburgh: P. Hill, 1818.

Rossi, Paolo. *The Dark Abyss of Time. The History of the Earth and the History of Nations from Hooke to Vico,* trans. Lydia G. Cocharane. Chicago: The University of Chicago Press, 1984.

Rousseau, Jean-Jacques. *Discourse on the origins and foundations of inequality among men.* In *The Collected Writings of Rousseau,* vol. 3., ed. Roger D. Masters and Christopher Kelly. Hanover, N. H.: University Press of New England, 1992.

Sánchez-Blanco Parody, Francisco. *Europa y el pensamiento español del siglo XVIII* Madrid: Alianza Editorial, 1991.

Sarrailh, Jean. *L'Espagne éclairée de la seconde moitié du XVIIIe siècle.* Paris: Impr. nationale, 1954.

Shapin, Steven. *A Social History of Truth: Civility and Science in Seventeenth-Century England.* Chicago: The University of Chicago Press, 1994.

Sher, Richard B. *Church and University in the Scottish Enlightenment: The Moderate Literati of Edinburgh.* Princeton, N.J.: Princeton University Press, 1985.

Smith, Anthony D. *Nationalism and Modernism: A Critical Survey of Recent Theories of Nations and Nationalism.* London: Routledge, 1998.

Smitten, Jeffrey. "Impartiality in Robertson's History of America," *Eighteenth-Century Studies* 19 (1985): 56–77.

Solano, Francisco de. "El Archivo de Indias y la promoción del americanismo científico." In *Carlos III y la ciencia de la Ilustración,* ed. Manuel Selles, José Luis Peset, and Antonio Lafuente. Madrid: Alianza, 1988: 277–96

———. "The Shaping of Moderation: William Robertson and Arminianism," *Studies in Eighteenth Century Culture* 22 (1992): 281–300.

Taylor, William. *Magistrates of the Sacred: Priests and Parishioners in Eighteenth Century Mexico.* Stanford, Calif.: Stanford University Press, 1998.

Thompson, I. A. A. "Castile, Spain and the monarchy: the political community from *patria natural* to *patria nacional*." In *Spain, Europe and the Atlantic World*, ed. Richard L. Kagan and Geoffrey Parker. Cambridge: Cambridge University Press, 1995.

Warburton, William. *Essai sur les hiéroglyphes des Egyptiens où l'on voit l'origine et les progrès du langage et de l'ecriture, l'antiquite des sciences en Egypte, et l'origine du culte des animaux—avec des observationes sur l'antiquité des hiéroglyphes scientifiques et des remarques sur la chronologie et sur la prière écriture des Chinois.* 2 vols. Paris: J. L. Guerin 1744.

——. *The Works of of the Right Reverend William Warburton.* 7 vols. London: John Nichols, 1788.

Widdifield, Stacie G. *The Embodiment of the National in Late Nineteenth-Century Mexican Painting.* Tucson: University of Arizona Press, 1996.

Whitaker, Arthur P., ed. *Latin America and the Enlightenment.* 2d ed. Ithaca: Cornell University Press, 1961.

Daniel Carey

Travel, Geography, and the Problem of Belief: Locke as a Reader of Travel Literature

IN A FAMOUS OUTBURST AGAINST THE PERNICIOUS EFFECTS OF John Locke's philosophy, the third Earl of Shaftesbury accused him of credulity for accepting travel reports as valid testimony of human nature. Locke's appetite for "Barbarian stories of wild Nations" was inconsistent with his ostensible caution in matters of assent.[1] Instead he was drawn in by an unreliable literary form, posing as history, which merely retailed stories of the monstrous to delight an audience captivated by romance. In Shaftesbury's disdainful estimation, "Histories of Incas or Iroquois, written by friars and missionaries, pirates and renegades, sea-captains and trusty travellers, pass for authentic records and are canonical with the virtuosi of this sort."[2] The philosophical motives for Shaftesbury's attack are complex, but his sharp-edged satire on the taste in travel invites us to consider how this form of writing was read and the way figures like Locke assessed its historical value.

Shaftesbury drew on a long tradition of complaint against the veracity of travel accounts in making his remarks. A much-quoted proverb held that "Travelers may lie by authority," suggesting that the obscurity of their exotic experience gave them a license to impose their fictions on readers unable (or unwilling) to authenticate what they had to say.[3] His complaint was prompted less by a global dissatisfaction with travel writing than by a specific antipathy to Locke's critique of innate ideas in Book I of the *Essay concerning Human Understanding* (1690). There Locke referred to a total of sixteen travel books in order to establish the absence of common agreement on basic matters of moral practice and religious belief.

Yet Shaftesbury encountered several problems by attempting to discredit the genre as a whole rather than by questioning the merits of the particular individuals whom Locke cited. Travel literature, despite the scope it offered for deception, nonetheless constituted a vital source of geographical information, and anyone who ignored it cut themselves off from striking and significant discoveries about the world. Participation in learned discussion was predicated to some extent on knowledge of this material and acceptance of it as offering historical testimony and insight. In the context of the new science, to take one important example, the reading of travel accounts and the control of travel played an important part in the development of natural history.[4]

We know that Locke had an unquenched appetite for travel literature. Indeed, a little over a month before he died, Locke was writing to his cousin Peter King requesting "the Turkie travels of your Exeter man."[5] We know also that his notebooks and journals are full of references to his reading that filtered into his published work in different ways. Elsewhere I have looked at the impact and philosophical deployment of travel by Locke.[6] In the present discussion I wish to consider some basic questions: how did Locke become aware of the travel books he read? On what authority did he accept them as trustworthy? What means, if any, did he have of checking their veracity? Shaftesbury parodied readers of travel as too wrapped up in narrative progression to make any effort to establish the truth of what they consumed. The reality, of course, was very different, even if the problems did not disappear.

This inquiry complements a larger investigation underway into patterns of reading in the early modern period, advanced by the work of Anthony Grafton, Ann Blair, and Adrian Johns, among others. We know from their investigations a great deal more about commonplacing, marginalia, and a range of other techniques and protocols of reading at this time in the context of humanist tradition and natural philosophy.[7]

But we have had little thus far that tells us about the way questions of truth were addressed and how authority functioned in the specific context of travel writing. Locke was part of a community of readers who attempted to make travel literature a useful and reliable resource.

I

Before looking in detail at Locke's notebooks, journals, and correspondence, we should set the discussion in a somewhat wider context. Interest in travel and geography, and reflection on the historical value of travel accounts was well established in the Oxford Locke entered in 1652. Christ Church, which elected him to a Studentship in May of that year, was the college of Richard Hakluyt[8] and, more recently, of Robert Burton. His encyclopaedic *Anatomy of Melancholy* (1621) led Burton to consider an array of travel books, and he donated his collection to the Bodleian Library and Christ Church in 1640.[9] Geographical study was strong throughout the university, represented by such figures as George Abbot, Robert Stafforde, Nathanael Carpenter, and Peter Heylyn.[10]

Commentators on the category of historical writing in Oxford took a rather contradictory line on travel books, by turns embracing the genre or consigning it to the realm of fiction. In 1648, Mathias Prideaux, a fellow of Exeter College, Oxford, produced *An Easy and Compendius Introduction for Reading all Sorts of Histories*, which contained an unfavorable assessment of travel relations. His thoughts on the subject occurred in a section largely devoted to condemning the pernicious taste in romances, a form he maligned as a "Bastard sort of histories." He included in this discredited category "All Journalls, Navigations, and Discoveries . . . All *Jesuiticall* and other *relations* of *strange things* done in *China* . . . "[11] Despite the negative conclusion, Prideaux rescued the compilations of Hakluyt and Purchas, together with Johannes de Laet's respected history of the West Indies, allocating them the modest role of recording matters such as "time & place." The conflicting assessment did not end there, however. Prideaux's text appears to have been largely written by his father, John Prideaux, Rector of Exeter College and later Bishop of Worcester.[12] The same John Prideaux had earlier supplied the substance of an another volume by an Exeter pupil, Robert Stafforde, who published a *Geographicall and Anthologicall Description of all the Empires and Kingdomes, both of Continent and Islands in this terrestriall Globe Relating their Scituations, Manners, Customs, Provinces, and Governments,* a study indebted to a range of travel writers for information.[13] The conjunction of the two works, both traceable to John Prideaux, suggests a complex and inconsistent outlook on the literature of travel.

In any case, not all commentators on the subject reiterated the worries evident in the *Compendius Introduction.* In 1663, Nicolas Horseman added an appendix to the English translation of Degory Wheare's widely circulated *De Ratione et Methodo Legendi Historias* (1623), which discussed the merit of histories devoted to particular nations. Like Prideaux, Horseman was Oxford educated (he became a fellow of Corpus Christi in 1659), but he treated travel writing unproblematically as a form of history, commending Christopher Columbus and a number of other authorities on the New World, including Gómara,

Acosta, Benzo (Benzoni), and Oviedo, as well as Jean de Léry, the Calvinist settler in Brazil. He went on to endorse travel writings about both Indies generally, including Jesuit relations, cautioning only against those authors who were "excessively taken up in setting forth the Miracles and Martyrdoms of their new Saints."[14]

Despite misgivings raised by some over the merit of travel accounts, an important group of Oxford-based geographers and historians accepted the conclusions offered by travelers and recirculated them in their work. Under the heading of "special geography," devoted to human custom, government, and religion, various figures relied on travel accounts as a documentary resource, and their work tells us much about how travel literature was read and accepted. In the first instance, geographers customarily adopted the moral conclusions made by travelers, supplying rapid, if highly unsympathetic summaries of human character. George Abbot, master of University College (and later Archbishop of Canterbury), composed one of the most popular summaries of the globe in his *Briefe Description of the Whole World,* which went through many editions after first appearing in 1599 (Locke purchased a copy while at Westminster School in 1649).[15] Abbot's text, produced for his Oxford students, was peppered with caustic summaries. For example, he described the Russians as "dull and uncapable of any high understanding; but very superstitious, having many ceremonies, and idolatrous solemnities." The case of the Laplanders was even worse, since "whatsoever living thing they do see in the morning at their going out of their doores, yea, if it be a bird, or a worm, or some such other creeping thing, they do yeeld a divine worship, & reverence thereunto for al that day . . . " Abbot's negative reports applied to marginal peoples in Europe as well as to distant Highlanders who had been so barbarous in former times "that they did not refuse to eate mans flesh."[16]

Similarly, Robert Stafforde refused to question the authority of European custom and affirmed that the residents of Europe "farre surpasse the residue of other parts, in Religion, Learning, Arts, valor and civility." His moral critique of various peoples accordingly lacked a self-reflexive moment, and he contented himself with cataloguing an array of faults and abuses, enlivened by the mention of occasional enclaves of civility. He agreed with Abbot in finding the Russians "very barbarous, perfidious, contentious, and most prone unto any contumelious behaviour," while their solemn rites could only be described as foolish and absurd. In Brazil, meanwhile, the inhabitants lacked faith, law, or king (as Léry had confirmed). Their excellent swimming impressed him, but he condemned them as "great dissemblers" who falsely shed tears on the approach of their friends.[17]

Peter Heylyn, who gave lectures on geography at Magdalen College, published a cosmographical survey in 1621 that was frequently reprinted and expanded.[18] He pursued something of a middle course, deploring images of human depravity but also delivering handsome compliments for civil attainments. He weaved through testimony supplied by travelers, compilers of accounts, and previous geographers, allocating praise and blame on the basis of humanist criteria. Thus he validated Persian practices that showed them to be "addicted to hospitality & poetry," proponents of learning, and magnificent in their expenditure. The Chinese shared many of these commendable customs and proved themselves "excellent artificers." By contrast, in the Niger delta local inhabitants virtually lacked the use of reason, and showed themselves "most alienate from dexterity of wit, and all arts and sciences."[19]

Locke's interest in travel and geography was therefore nurtured in favorable conditions in Oxford, even if the material was not free from controversy. His inclination to treat travel accounts as a historical resource had a number of important precedents, but Locke was not unaware of the larger problem of distinguishing true histories from false ones. This appears most clearly in his translation (dating from c. 1676–77) of an essay by the French Jansenist Pierre Nicole. In a pessimistic passage, Nicole worried about the inexactness of histories in their replication of truth. Since notice was never given when an author engaged in deception, it was impossible to avoid being imposed upon. In a notable sentence that Locke added to the original, he remarked: "In this Regard we are lesse abused, in the perusall of Romances; because one brings noe expectacion of Truth to the Reading of them: but tis that we aime at in the study of history, & yet we are scarce ever sure to finde it there."[20] Shaftesbury's inclination to regard travel accounts as romances solved the problem, but Locke did not take this course. He was left with the challenge of distinguishing the true from the false. The question is how he did so.

II

Over the course of his life, Locke compiled an impressive library of travel books. At the time of his death, he owned 195 volumes of travel writing, many of which were compendia produced between the sixteenth and early eighteenth centuries, such as those edited by Ramusio, Hakluyt, Purchas, Thévenot, and the Churchills, containing vast numbers of individual accounts within them.[21] Locke's method of commonplacing indicates that information drawn from travelers was relevant to him under a huge array of categories embracing the range of his interests: medicine, trade, coinage, government, religious belief, knowledge, opinion, as well as a variety of moral, social, and legal practices.[22] Of course Locke was also friendly with a number of prominent travelers, notably François Bernier, and in correspondence with others.[23] To assess his encounter with travel and travel writing, which covers the whole of his career, would require an intellectual biography. My objective here is more restricted—to consider the influences on Locke's reading habits, how he learned about texts and evaluated their authenticity and reliability.

One of the earliest and most significant figures for Locke was undoubtedly Robert Boyle. Boyle was an exceptionally avid reader of travel accounts and he often accompanied his scientific discussions, which covered a vast array of subjects, with reference to them. In fact he remarked on the unfortunate scarcity of copies of some works, such was their utility in his view.[24] Locke met Boyle sometime before May 1660 and they began a friendship which lasted until Boyle's death in 1691. Locke studied Boyle's works with great care and attention, noting his opinion of travelers in his journals and notebooks. Shortly after the appearance of Boyle's *Some Considerations Touching the Usefulnesse of Experimentall Natural Philosophy* (1663), a work that reads like a running commentary on Boyle's encounter with travel literature, Locke began studying the text closely. His notebooks frequently mention Boyle's opinion of the travelers he quoted and referenced. As Locke recorded, Boyle referred to "the famous Jesuit" Alvaro (Álvarez) Semedo, who had written on China;[25] "that great traveller" Vincent Le Blanc;[26] the Inca Garcilaso de la Vega, whom Boyle described as "a much applauded writer" on America;[27] and the "sober" Jesuit authority, José de Acosta.[28] Acosta and Garcilaso would later surface as authorities for Locke in his discussion of Amerindian society in the *Two Treatises of Government.*[29]

Remarks by Boyle in other writings similarly made their way into Locke's notebooks. From *Certain Physiological Essays* (1661), Locke noted the praise for the "bold & Illustrious" Captain Thomas James, who published his "strange and dangerous voyage" in search of a Northwest passage in 1633,[30] and the added endorsement of Acosta in the same work as a "learned" man who had "diligently" surveyed Peruvian mines and delivered "considerable and judicious Observations" about them.[31] Later, in the 1680s, when Locke was in exile in Holland, he read one of Boyle's "Hydrostatical discourses" and took note of the commendation of the "Intelligent" early natural historian of the New World, Gonzalo Fernández de Oviedo.[32] In addition, the two exchanged references personally. On one occasion, near the end of Boyle's life, Locke lent him his copy of Maurile de Saint Michel's *Voyage des Isles Camercanes* (1652). Locke later interpolated the comment: "he says there are some good things in it."[33]

Boyle's endorsements in his published work had a formulaic quality that may suggest he merely recommended what already appealed to his curiosity. Nonetheless, they serve an obvious rhetorical function of consolidating the authority of his sources, based either on Boyle's own assessment—of intelligence or learning, for example—or elsewhere of fame and reputation. He gestures toward an undefined circle of reception that accords an author applause and spreads his notoriety among the learned, and this reputation, as Boyle presents it, precedes his encounter with the texts that presumably earned them their esteem. Boyle's own reputation then becomes a guarantee of reliability for the texts he cited.

In Locke's case, Boyle's testimonials had a kind of cascading effect. After noting Boyle's reference to Adam Olearius as "that applauded writer" in the *Usefulness of Experimentall Natural Philosophy,*[34] Locke began reading a translation of the German diplomat's account of his travels as part of a mission to Muscovy, Tartary, and Persia.[35] This led to the recording of judgments on other travelers, including Olearius's view that Isaac de la Peyrère, in writing of Greenland, "hath published all that could be said of a country so unknowne."[36] The English translation of Olearius also included the travels of J. A. von Mandelslo, and Locke duly read this account. Not only did he learn of wife burning in India, as a reference (discussed below) in the early *Essays on the Law of Nature* indicates,[37] but also of Mandelslo's favorable view of the Jesuit authority Maffei, whom he cited as "the most learned & grave author that hath written of the affairs of the *Indies,*" and his judgment of the Venetian jeweller Gasparo Balbi as the author of a "handsom relation," also of India. He did not approve of Paulus Venetis on Madagascar, but sanctioned François Cauche's account of the island as more "exact" than any of the Dutch relations.[38] Copies of La Peyrère, Cauche, and Maffei ended up in Locke's library.[39]

The other great stimulus for Locke was the world of French learning, especially the contacts he made during his travels in France from 1675–79.[40] One of Locke's notebooks begun at this time contains long lists of books recommended by Henri Justel on a range of subjects including travel. Justel, a noted bibliophile, convened regular gatherings of learned individuals at his house during the 1660s and '70s, and he also edited the *Recueil de divers voyages faits en Afrique et en l'Amérique*

(1674).[41] The function of the lists produced for Locke was largely bibliographical, although there was an implied recommendation that came with them. One of them begins "Il faut avoir" and continues with numerous travel accounts, another starts "On peut avoir . . . "[42] On a far greater scale was Locke's correspondence with Nicolas Toinard (or Thoynard) whom he met at Justel's house sometime between June 1677 and April 1678.[43] In addition to his concerns with biblical interpretation and chronology, culminating in the posthumous publication of a harmony of Gospels,[44] Toinard had a keen interest in travel and exploration. In July 1679, after he had returned to London, Locke wrote to Toinard saying that he very much wanted to carry on a commerce in French books with him, above all in works of travel (*des bonnes relations des voyages*).[45] The flow of information from Toinard was consistent with this wish. Not long afterwards Toinard wrote to Locke correcting information in the Jesuit Alonso de Ovalle's account of Chile that misidentified a local creature (based on a manuscript that Toinard had obtained).[46] In the same letter he told Locke about another manuscript in his possession, this one in Portuguese, which recounted various "choses rares" concerning Angola. He wondered whether any English discussion existed of a local people said by Toinard to wage war against their enemies whom they then devoured. In addition these people refused to nourish their children but buried them alive.[47] Locke replied that there was indeed information regarding such a tribe from English sources. An Englishman who had lived a long time among the "Giagos" confirmed everything stated in the Portuguese manuscript and added many other things of note. Locke's source in this case was an account originally published in Purchas's *Hakluytus Posthumus* (1625).[48]

Toinard represented an exceptional source of information with whom Locke could correspond on matters of geographical and anthropological interest. For example, he asked Toinard whether he knew anything about an African people living near the river Gambra who were known as the Geloofs (i.e., Wolofs or Oulofs), a reference he had taken personally from Robert Boyle.[49] Later he asked him about the customs of inhabitants near the river Senegal, and followed up the gift of a travel book by François Froger, a friend of Toinard's, with inquiries concerning the natives and natural productions of Cayenne.[50] Locke sought references to various peoples who did not use the "nodus" or base of ten to count, which Toinard was able to supply.[51] Finally, when Locke learned of the Dominican friar Domingo Navarrete's account of China, published in Madrid in 1676,[52] he asked whether his friend would consider translating the text, as he had other Spanish travel relations, on the basis that it contained "des choses fort curieuses" which he wished to have published in a language he understood.[53] Locke later referred to Navarrete in the fifth edition of the *Essay* (1706) when he supplemented the evidence for his critique of innateness (I.iv.8).

Insofar as Toinard made his criteria explicit, he emphasized curiosity, rarity, and recentness in drawing Locke's attention to travel accounts, values that Locke evidently shared. Thus Toinard commended a Polish manuscript, which Mechisédec Thévenot had had translated, describing various routes from Moscow to Peking, as including "choses fort curieuses."[54] Although Toinard had not yet consulted the account, he had learned that Admiral Speelman, governor-general of the Dutch

possessions in the East Indies, had published a narrative which related "des choses surprenantes et admirables, et qui passent pour constants dans les Indes."[55] The work of Christoval de Acuña,[56] meanwhile, struck him as "fort curieux et rare," although it was surpassed by something even better and more recent, a description of a journey through the Straits of Magellan to California by Olenker which had come to his attention.[57] The preference for recent accounts suggests a straightforward attention to the most up-to-date sources, on the assumption, perhaps, that current travelers built on the work of their predecessors, checking their claims rather than repeating their errors—but this is only implicit.[58] What set these narratives apart was their inclusion of matters of surprise and wonder, appealing to the curiosity of someone with wide interests in natural history and anthropology. The risk here was of succumbing to the fabulous, but Toinard checked it, at least in the case of Speelman, by avowing that the unusual things he reported were subjects of "constant" observation in the East Indies, despite their novelty to readers in Europe.

Toinard's caution can be seen in his correspondence about the legendary *baranetz* or *agnus scythicus,* an extraordinary plant with a lamb growing out of it.[59] He notified Locke that he had written to Moscow for further information about this strange production of nature, said to exist in Tartary or Scythia, which many regarded as fabulous.[60] A couple of weeks later he added that he had come across an account of it in J. J. Struys's *Voyage*, a work that some held as fictive, and he was of the opinion that the *agnus tartaricus* discussion was an example of his impositions.[61] Nonetheless, Locke later studied Struys's volume with care.[62]

Locke indexed the letters he received from Toinard, marking certain passages for attention and adding cross-references on occasion in his notebooks. While responding wittily to his correspondent, particularly on the subject of an anatomized elephant,[63] he took the opportunity in one of his letters to make a recommendation of his own to Toinard. In August 1681 Locke sent him a copy of Robert Knox's *Historical Relation of the Island of Ceylon*, which had just appeared, despite the fact that Toinard did not read English. Knox had been held captive for nearly twenty years on the island by the king of Kandy, and when he returned to England he produced an important account of his observations and experience (with a preface by Robert Hooke). In his letter Locke said that he wished it had appeared in a language that Toinard could understand, but he sent it nonetheless in the hope that he would find someone to translate it for him. According to Locke, the book featured "bien de choses fort particulieres."[64] We know at least one aspect of it that caught Locke's eye. When addressing the claim that absolute power had a beneficial effect in correcting human nature in the *Second Treatise*, Locke referred his reader to Knox's discussion of the island's government, which showed "what kind of Fathers of their Countries it makes Princes to be, and to what a degree of Happiness and Security it carries Civil Society."[65]

In addition to discussing new works of travel, Toinard kept Locke in touch with various important figures, including François Bernier and Melchisédec Thévenot. He was also responsible for introducing Locke to Jean-Baptiste Du Bos, a young abbé of twenty-eight, whom Locke met in England in 1698.[66] They engaged in a regular correspondence for the rest of Locke's life, dominated by the discussion of new accounts of travel. Locke's letters have not survived, unfortunately, but the abbé Du Bos's include numerous references of interest. One exceptional letter from 1698/9 contains a virtual catalogue of travel literature with brief comments.[67] We can gain some insight into Du Bos's criteria of valuation from these remarks. On the subject of Henri de Tonti—whose account of La Salle's discoveries in America Locke later read—Du Bos noted that the manuscript had been polished by another hand, which contributed to his conclusion that at certain points it was evident the author had never been in the country he described.[68] Other publications he set aside as containing nothing new or as merely recounting adventures, presumably in contrast to observations.[69] Of the numerous works he mentioned enthusiastically, "curiosity" figured prominently as a term of praise, as it had for Toinard. The quality of a work therefore depended on its capacity to engage the intelligence with novel information, somehow striking and noteworthy. Truth, a difficult thing to ascertain, was necessarily deferred in the order of judgments. Nonetheless, Du Bos did cite the Portuguese Jesuit Gabriel de Magalhaes's relation of China as not merely "très curieux" but as adding many things to those known only by "raports imparfaits."[70] Similarly Sanson's account of

Persia featured a "quantité de choses curieuses et qui passé pour estre fort exact." In this case, the determination of authenticity devolved on others, notionally better informed as to matters of fact, who delivered a strongly favorable judgment.[71]

The same letter included a reading list on the kingdom of Siam, which had become the subject of numerous accounts following several French missionary and trading expeditions in the 1680s.[72] The terms of commendation are revealing once again. Du Bos cited the abbé Choisy's account of the country as "un peu plus circonstancieè" in comparison with Chaumont's relation of his embassy. However, he judged that the author's goal was to embellish what he recounted rather than to give "une just idee."[73] The Jesuit Guy Tachard's *Voyage de Siam* fared better in his estimation, with its descriptions and observations meriting the appellation "fort curieuses."[74] In Du Bos's judgment it was more attached to nature ("plus attaché a la nature") than the others. But the highest praise came for Simon de La Loubère's account, which he deemed "la plus exacte, la plus sincere et la plus juste," and Desfargues's discussion of the revolutions in the country, which was "plus sincere et mieux circonstanciee."[75] Exactness, justice, and "proximity" to nature are mimetic valuations, based on the quality of the works to capture ostensive matter of fact and narrate accurately. They therefore depend on a criterion of witness unavailable to Du Bos. The notion of a "circumstanciated" history is more difficult to understand, but it seems to imply that an account with a greater quantity of detail not only provides superior information but carries with it, rhetorically, greater conviction. Sincerity, of course, is a personal attribute, although the means of determining good faith are not immediately clear. Du Bos may have lacked personal experience, but he could at least organize his review of this literature by engaging in comparative analysis.

In any case, the impact of Du Bos's reports was considerable. The discussion of Siam and information he supplied on missionary controversies in China in subsequent letters made their way into Locke's elaboration of his case against innateness in later editions of Book I of Locke's *Essay*.[76] In his unfinished work "Of the Conduct of the Understanding" (intended as a long chapter for the *Essay*), Locke also referred to the Marian Islanders, following a discussion of this people by the Jesuit Charles Le Gobien. Once more, he was notified of the book by Du Bos.[77]

The analysis of Locke's benefit from French sources of opinion cannot be concluded, however, without emphasizing the importance of a published resource, the *Journal des Sçavans*. This learned periodical, which had certain parallels with the Royal Society's *Philosophical Transactions*, covered a wider ground in the world of polite and scientific discussion. Travel accounts fitted comfortably within its critical ambit, and Locke made note of works discussed in the periodical with exceptional frequency, many of which he then purchased and read.[78] On one occasion he also recorded a cautionary note. The Dutch traveler J. H. van Linschoten was cited for reporting "beaucoup de choses fausses" in an issue of May 1666.[79]

Although it was not on the same scale as his connections with France, Locke's exile in Holland also proved productive in terms of acquiring information on travel.[80] Here we can also see the relationship between his reading habits and the personal connections he formed with travelers and those in contact with travelers. He met Dr. Caspar Sibelius and spent twelve days with him in Deventer in 1684. Subsequently, Sibelius wrote to him and included in the letter some information he had received from the distinguished Dutch physician and naturalist Willem ten Rhyne, who had resided in the East Indies since 1674. Ten Rhyne answered Sibelius's inquiries regarding acupuncture, the Indian fig, and the use of moxa for cauterization. In addition he supplied some information on native practice in counting beyond the number ten, an inquiry that probably came from Locke (as indeed the others may have done). On the subject of poisons and the customs of various East Indian peoples, he deferred an answer until he had greater leisure.[81] It seems more than likely that Sibelius was the source of a manuscript of ten Rhyne's from which Locke made extensive transcriptions and translations in his journal for 1684. In these passages ten Rhyne described the customs of the Hottentots (i.e., the Khoi Khoi, residing near Saldanha Bay in South Africa, whom he met on his outward journey), notably their religious beliefs or lack thereof (a theme that arose in the *Essay*).[82]

As the same journal indicates, Locke made other interesting Dutch contacts. In Leiden he met Paul Hermann, a professor of botany who had lived for nine years in Ceylon (Sri Lanka). Locke recorded information from Hermann on the Sinhalese and his dubious view of the "snake stone" as an antidote against poison—he wondered whether it was not "for the most part if not wholy factitious"—and his skepticism about the merits of bezoar. Both remedies enjoyed adherents, and discussion of the subject had preoccupied the Royal Society from time to time.[83] Hermann had accumulated numerous rarities and observations during his travels, and he gave Locke "hopes the world should ere long see some of them."[84]

However, personal contact provided no guarantee that the informant either possessed or would tell the truth. At Sibelius's house, Locke met a "Mr Bremen" who had lived in Japan for eight years. The traveler had some portraits of Eastern people to show, including one of a Papua New Guinean with a tail a "little turning up crooked, it was not hayry. He said he knew not whether all the people of the place had such tayles but he had been assured by several credible Hollanders who have seen them, that severall of them had such tayles."[85] Locke later visited him again and confirmed that this story was beyond the man's witness, but Bremen did offer the story of the Kakerlaks, another "Eastern" people with very white skin dappled by coloured "slashes." Once a year these people "cast their skin," he reported, and returned to a pure white hue.[86]

III

From the world of learning and personal contacts we can turn to the world of travel accounts themselves, their editors and purveyors. In addition to the information such sources provided, they contained valuable bibliographical references and assessments of other authors. In some cases the judgments had added weight because they implicitly entailed a pattern of cross-checking that certified the veracity of what an earlier figure had reported. Thus Locke took note of the Italian nobleman Pietro della Valle's view of Pierre Belon, author of *Les observations des plusieurs singularitez & choses memorables trouvées en Grece, Asie, Iudée, Egypte, Arabies & autres pays estranges* (1554), observing that he was "much confirmed" by Valle who quoted him often.[87] In other instances the prestige of a traveler seems to have extended their entitlement to comment on other regions. Charles de Rochefort had no experience outside the Caribbean,[88] but Locke took note of his esteem for Jean de Léry, who wrote on Brazil, as "an author worthy of credit."[89] Both were French Protestant travelers in the territory of cannibals, but Rochefort had no personal witness to support his commendation. In a similar vein Locke took note of the opinion of Abraham Roger, a Dutch reformed minister who was sent to preach to the Christian community in Pulicat (Tamilnadu). Roger endorsed Gasparo Balbi as one who had written very well about the kingdom of Pegu (Lower Burma/Myanmar), in his *Viaggio dell'Indie orientali* (1590).[90]

In this respect, a parallel exists with the compilers of travel accounts who exercised editorial judgment in the absence of personal experience. Thus Locke recorded that Giovanni Battista Ramusio, the great Venetian editor, had endorsed the authority of Leo Africanus (whose work he was the first to publish) in the dedicatory epistle of his *Navigatione et Viaggi*. Ramusio described him as writing not only copiously, but also "con tanta certeza."[91] In 1685 Locke was reading the fourth volume of Thévenot's *Relations de divers voyages curieux* and he set down the editor's conclusion that the Jesuit traveler in Ethiopia,

Balthazar Tellez, had repaired the "injuries" perpetrated by Urreta and others against the interests of the public and of truth. Everything written before Tellez about the country was designated "fabuleux."[92] Similarly, Locke noted Samuel Purchas's opinion on numerous points, including his assessment of Urreta as "a very dunghill of lies."[93]

Locke also took recommendations on books of travel from other works he read. While visiting James Tyrrell at Oakley in 1682, Locke began reading Meric Casaubon's *Treastise of Use and Custom* (1638)—presumably making use of Tyrrell's copy, as none survives in Locke's own catalogue. Locke came across a reference in the text to the travels of the German nobleman Martin von Baumgarten, whom Casaubon commended as "no obscure man and of good credit every way," as Locke noted in his journal.[94] Later, Locke quoted Baumgarten in the *Essay*, recounting his narrative of dubious sexual customs practiced by Muslim holy men (I.iii.9).[95]

The notebook that provides us with the most intimate view of Locke's reading practices is Bodleian Library MS Locke c. 33, which he began using in the late 1670s. There he literally recorded his notes as he went along, creating indexes to subjects discussed and jotting topics and observations, filling the space available. This notebook deepens our sense of Locke's predicament as a reader as it reveals more about his own judgments on matters of veracity. In reading Chardin's *Journal du Voyage en Perse* (1686), for example, he thought the author wrote with "great negligence & not out of memoires carefully taken." Locke's basis for this view was not his own objective witness, of course, but internal inconsistencies in the account, particularly in relation to matters of location by latitude. He also remarked that Chardin always traveled by night from Tiflis (Tbilisi) to Isfahan and yet he somehow described "all the country as he goes."[96] But these reservations evidently did not compromise Locke's interest in what Chardin had to say on the religion of the Mingrelians, an ethnically Georgian people living near the Black Sea (whom he encountered at the start of his journey before arriving at Tiflis). Chardin made some vituperative comments suggesting that they were not only larcenous but deemed assassination, murder, and lying "belles actions." Among them adultery, bigamy, and incest passed as virtues.[97] Does Locke's continued reading of Chardin, despite reservations about him, indicate that he merely believed what he was predisposed to accept? The evidence is too limited to adopt such a conclusion. In any case there are two considerations that tell against it. Locke had already taken note of similar discussions of the moral failings of the Mingrelians from the Italian missionary Arcangelo Lamberti.[98] Second, when Locke mounted his evidence in the *Essay* against uniformity of moral belief, he cited Lamberti rather than Chardin when he mentioned the Mingrelians (I.iii.9).

Despite Locke's avid reading and reference to travel, we have little by way of a formal pronouncement from him on the genre. To the extent that he gave one, his most general assessment came near the end of his life. Locke was asked for his thoughts on reading and study for gentlemen and he dictated a short piece outlining his advice in 1703. The work as a whole was intended for those who, by virtue of their social standing, anticipated a life of public service and required suitable recommendations for advancing their knowledge of moral and political matters.[99] The study of history was crucial for pursuing the art of government, and this discipline in turn required attention to chronology and geography. It was in this context that Locke introduced his discussion of travel books, as an adjunct to geography and history, providing valuable information. In fact he mentioned writers and collections worth considering in this domain in more detail than any other area. Locke began with the compendia of "our countrey-men" Hakluyt and Purchas, which he described as "very good." Also "very good" were the collections edited by Thévenot and Ramusio's sixteenth-century *Navigatione et Viaggi*. He took occasion to note the collection of travels produced by Awnsham and John Churchill, then in press, which he mentioned would contain various works previously unavailable in English.[100] When he turned to individual travelers, Locke ranged them according to nationality. Among the English, he cited "good books" by George Sandys, who traveled in Turkey;[101] Sir Thomas Roe, the diplomat resident at the court of the Grand Moghul;[102] Edward Browne, son of the famous physician, who traveled in Eastern Europe;[103] Thomas Gage, who traveled in the West Indies;[104] and finally William Dampier.[105] Among French writers, he listed as "very good" the works of Pyrard,[106] Bergeron,[107] Sagard,[108] and Bernier,[109] whose writings he had read with great care. We know that Locke could have included many more—and the absence of some of his favorite travelers like Jean de Léry, the Inca Garcilaso de la Vega, and José de Acosta is surprising—but he stopped short, saying that to record the "vast number" would take too long and occupy too much space. Those he mentioned were enough to be getting on with. He closed by commending this form of writing as containing "a very good mixture of delight and usefulness."[110]

This brief account leaves us with as many questions as answers. Knowing that Locke found this material pleasurable confirms the sense we have that it fueled his imagination and produced a particular kind of delight. Whether this was close to the pleasure he gained from romances in his earlier days,[111] we cannot say with certainty, but it seems to have offered an imaginative outlet to Locke while complementing his disciplined and serious intellectual pursuits. Less clear is what we should make of his repeated use of "good" to describe such texts. Good in what sense? Presumably they were especially informative and engagingly written, but some ambiguity remains. To the extent that their quality depended on the accuracy of the information they contained, then goodness may also attest to their reliability.

IV

In other contexts I have discussed the impact of travel accounts on Locke's philosophy and the way he used such material to advance his arguments, especially in the critique of innateness in Book I of the *Essay*.[112] This was an ongoing process for more than forty years. The earliest evidence appears in Locke's discussion of natural law in a series of lectures delivered in Oxford in about1664, while he was a Student of Christ Church, but the accumulation of relevant testimony continued to the end of his life, aided in this case by his correspondence with Du Bos and Toinard.

In his early writings on the foundation of the law of nature, Locke was somewhat more explicit in his criteria for assessing travel accounts than in the *Essay* or the *Two Treatises*. In common with his later critique, Locke rejected innateness and common consent as bases for natural law, and he proved his case in part by citing cultural diversity. He dwelled on the lack of proper moral behavior by primitive peoples because they were closest to nature and should therefore have manifested pure moral principles, undistorted by the accretion of customs in more civil society. Instead, Locke remarked,

> anyone who consults the histories both of the old and the new world, or the itineraries of travellers [*veteris et novi orbis historias et peregrinantium itineraria*], will easily observe how far apart from virtue the morals of these people are, what strangers they are to any humane feelings, since nowhere else is there such doubtful honesty, so much treachery, such frightful cruelty in that they sacrifice to the gods and also to their tutelary spirit by killing people and offering kindred blood. And no one will believe that the law of nature is best known and observed among these primitive and untutored tribes, since among most of them there appears not the slightest trace or track of piety, merciful feeling, fidelity, chastity, and the rest of the virtues; but rather they spend their life wretchedly among robberies, thefts, debaucheries, and murders. . . . [They] live in such ignorance of every law, as though there were no principle of rightness and goodness to be had at all.[113]

Locke's remark suggests a distinction between "histories" written about the old and New World and a form he calls the "itinerary," but whether the taxonomic difference is important seems unlikely. Histories may have had greater scope and ambition, but the important thing for the purposes of his argument is that the two kinds of writing complement and reinforce one another by drawing the same conclusions about mankind. Eyewitness seems an implicit qualification in both cases, although again Locke does not spell this out. He focuses above all on what they report, and their findings tell a grim story about human nature unimproved by strenuous exercise of reason or by the teachings of Scripture.

Parallel with the strategy later adopted in the *Essay*, in this work Locke did not confine himself to "primitive" societies alone, however persuasive his examples in this context might be. He also remarked on "polite" societies, which gave added force to his argument. Even those improved by living in a civil manner adhered to unaccountable customs, demonstrating once more the nullity of common consent or innate principles. In showing the absence of common agreement over the law of nature, Locke cited the practice of sati in India. As Locke reported it: "[A]mong the Indians the weak and timid female sex dares to make light of dying and to hasten to rejoin departed husbands by passing through the flames and through the gate of death. They allow the nuptial torches to be extinguished only in the flames of the funeral pyre . . . Of this fact Mandelslo, in the recently published itinerary of Olearius, declares himself an eye-witness." Locke stresses the fact that Mandelslo observed these events himself and that the report itself had appeared recently. Yet, as the narrative continues, we can see that Locke has also responded to the story of wife-burning as romance, and he shapes the narrative in a way that heightens the drama of self-immolation, even as it contradicts the law of nature predicated on self-preservation: "As he himself relates, he saw a beautiful young woman who after the death of her husband could not be prevailed upon, or restrained from murdering herself, by the advice, entreaties, and tears of her friends. At length, after an involuntary delay of six months, with the permission of the magistrate, she dressed as if for a wedding, triumphantly and with a joyous face ascended a pyre set up in the middle of the market-place, and cheerfully perished in the flames."[114] Locke drew a philosophical conclusion. The episode provided strong evidence of the "power of custom and of opinion based on traditional ways of life." Yet his sensitive portrayal of the scene raises the question of whether at this transitional stage in his life travel books served a dual function. They possessed philosophical utility but they also gave pleasure, replacing his youthful reading of romance with something more estimable that nonetheless contained traces of romance in the inclusion of adventure, exoticism, and on this occasion, tales of enduring love.

Locke's "philosophical" reading of travel engaged with moral, religious, and more generally sociological and anthropological questions. His perspective was undoubtedly influenced by the rhetorical practices characteristic of many seventeenth-century narratives of exotic peoples in which a familiar refrain of barbarism, savagery, and incivility appeared. The issue of how his belief was engaged remains, at some level, undecidable: Locke may have formed a view of human nature that found confirmation in the reports of travelers or the reports themselves may have influenced the view he took of mankind. The question is complicated further by the rhetorical and logical requirements of the argument he made regarding natural law. In any case, these considerations complemented one another and led him to introduce the testimony of travelers in general without qualification.

V

We are now in a position to consider the moves Locke made to defend himself when his references to travelers in the *Essay* came under attack. Shaftesbury presumably kept his comments to himself during Locke's lifetime, but Locke still had to contend with Edward Stillingfleet, Bishop of Worcester. When Locke cited these materials in his critique of innateness, he was careful to provide page numbers to specific editions, which made it possible to follow up on his sources. This courtesy enabled readers to check the statements for themselves, but it left open the larger problem of veracity—how could Locke know the truth of his travelers' assertions?

Stillingfleet was particularly exercised not by Locke's testimony on moral depravity and variation but by his denial of universal belief in God. However, he pursued a somewhat different strategy to the one later adopted by Shaftesbury. There were points of convergence between them, but while Shaftesbury was ready, at some point, to consign the entire form to the oblivion of fiction, Stillingfleet wanted to rescue travel accounts for his own purposes.[115] Accordingly he did not question the genre as a whole but rather the qualifications of the specific individuals introduced by Locke. He complained that Locke's testimony on atheism among natives living near Saldanha Bay, Brazil, the Caribbean, and Paraguay came

> from such as were not sufficiently acquainted with the People and Language of the Country; or that their Testimony is contradicted by those who have been longer among them and understood them better; or lastly that the account given of them makes them not fit to be a standard for the Sense of Mankind, being a People so strangely bereft of common Sense, that they can hardly be reckoned among Mankind, as appears by the best accounts both of the *Cafres* of *Soldania*, and the *Caiguae of Pariquaria.*[116]

Stillingfleet mounts a range of objections: local languages have not been mastered nor the people properly understood.[117] Furthermore, better accounts of them exist, although he does not name them. More contentiously, Stillingfleet wanted to set aside certain peoples as unfit standards of humankind. Locke balked at this move, but he was left with an obligation to defend his sources of testimony. He did so in the next reply he published:

> I will crave leave to say that whom I relied on for his testimonies concerning the Hottentots of Soldania was no less than an Ambassador from the King of England [Sir Thomas Roe] to the great Mogul: of whose relation, monsieur Thevenot, no ill judge in the case, had so great an esteem, that he was at pains to translate it into French, and publish it in his (which is counted no unjudicious) collection of travels. But to intercede with your Lordship for a little more favourable allowance of credit to Sir Thomas Roe's relation: Coore, an inhabitant of the country, who could speak English, assured Mr Terry that they of Soldania have no God. But if he too have the ill luck to find no credit with you, I hope you will be a little more favourable to a divine of the Church of England [John Ovington], now living, and admit of his testimony in confirmation of Sir Thomas Roe's.[118]

Locke provided a thorough response: if the status of the witness is at issue, he introduces an ambassador (Roe); in the case of Roe's report, Locke could have relied on Samuel Purchas's redaction, but he chose instead Melchisédec Thévenot's French translation, which acquired added significance as the subject of a recent editor's judicious assessment.[119] But if the ambassador is not to be believed because he can no longer be consulted, then a living eyewitness will be produced (Ovington). If contradictions among the authorities are alleged, he demonstrates unanimity. If questions are raised about the ability of Europeans to interpret native languages, Locke finds a local inhabitant (in the person of Coore) who was fluent in English.[120] In a manner consistent with practices in natural history, Locke multiplies the number of witnesses while clarifying their social and professional status and their linguistic ability. Furthermore, he followed guidelines set out in his chapter on probability in the *Essay*, where he stressed the importance of evaluating testimony on the basis of the number of witnesses, their integrity, their skill, the consistency and circumstances of the report, and finally the existence of contrary testimonies.[121]

Locke addressed the issue of credibility more formally in a later reply to Stillingfleet. In this instance he rejoined the argument over conceptions of soul. If Stillingfleet reckoned that the immateriality of the soul was a universal or "common" notion, Locke introduced Cicero as someone who doubted it, and he followed this up with a reference to a contemporary account of Siam. The narrative in question was written by Simon de La Loubère, who served as Louis XIV's envoy-extraordinary to the King of Siam in 1688. On the basis of this journey La Loubère produced a two-volume work, *Du Royaume de Siam* (1691), in which, among other observations, he noted that the Siamese found it virtually impossible to conceptualize the idea of "pure spirit" in the sense of an immaterial soul. La Loubère referred to missionaries—presumably Jesuit—as his source, and extended this belief generally to "all the pagans of the east" who shared it with the ancient Greeks and Romans in his view.[122]

Anticipating Stillingfleet's response, Locke shored up his source's credibility. "This gentleman," he said, "was not a man that travelled into those parts for his pleasure, and to have the opportunity to tell strange stories, collected by chance, when he returned; but one chosen on purpose (and it seems well chosen for the purpose) to inquire into the singularities of Siam."[123] Locke demonstrates his familiarity with the standing attack on the veracity of travelers, but he catches himself in something of an inconsistency. La Loubère shuns strange stories, ostensibly, and yet his mission is expressly to investigate so-called "singularities." The distinction is a nice one, but it depends, as Locke presents it, on motive and commission. La Loubère was not an adventurer, someone prompted by the desire to accumulate stories as an end in itself, but rather someone appointed to a legitimate office.[124] Locke goes on to commend him further: "he has so well acquitted himself of the commission, which his epistle dedicatory tells us he had, to inform himself exactly of what was most remarkable there; that had we but such an account of other countries of the east . . . we should be much better acquainted than we are, with the manners, notions and religions of that part of the world." Again, the emphasis lies on the observation of what is remarkable and exceptional, the rare and unusual. Locke neglects to point out that the same dedicatory letter makes it clear that La Loubère only spent three months in Siam, nor does he clarify that we are at some remove from the original source by virtue of having La Loubère's testimony mediated through missionaries. Still, it is worth noting the opinion of D. K. Wyatt that the book is "univerally regarded as the finest work on seventeenth-century Thailand."[125] All this may be true, but Locke does not acknowledge that he has no way personally to determine the correctness of what La Loubère asserts about the Siamese. He lacks a solid criterion.

For Locke, travel literature had an undoubted documentary value and the information it contained was important and compelling. His reading was framed within moral terms that coincided with the language and interests of the work he read, and also by interests in natural history he shared with Boyle and others. Although he sought guidance

about individual authors deemed less than trustworthy, and may have avoided Linschoten and Thevet since he had encountered blanket negative judgments about them, he went ahead and engaged with the work of others even when he had been informed or concluded that they erred on particular points or more generally (like Struys). Locke does not seem to have regarded travel accounts as especially ripe sources of deception, suspect for their rhetorical conventions of exaggeration, and to that extent in need of singling out for greater caution. The form represented a useful historical resource and its credibility was certified by cumulative investigation, cross-checking, and by discourse among learned and sympathetic individuals. His reading habits emerged from a community of like-minded friends with avid curiosity who operated with shared conventions for evaluating testimony and investigating and understanding what no one could ignore.[126]

Where does this leave us with the genre of travel reportage? One option, pursued by Shaftesbury as much as by Swift, was to convert the whole of it into fiction or romance and to deny its truth-value altogether. But this was not a tenable position in practice. It was tantamount to rejecting all the texts of exotic anthropology or the geography of distant peoples in order to avoid the danger of being caught out by any fictive interlopers.

Locke, like Boyle, had worked out canons for evaluating testimony. Following these procedures, the knowledge gained remained probabilistic rather than certain. To that extent, occasional error represented an epistemological cost of doing business, remediable, ostensibly at least, through further observation. Locke's "trusty travellers," as Shaftesbury sarcastically described them, remained a vital if problematic resource.

Notes

I would like to thank the Irish Research Council for the Humanities and Social Sciences for the award of a Government of Ireland Fellowship, which allowed me to carry out the research for this essay.

1. Anthony Ashley Cooper, third Earl of Shaftesbury, *Several Letters Written by a Noble Lord to a Young Man at the University* (London, 1716), 39.

2. Anthony Ashley Cooper, third Earl of Shaftesbury, "Soliloquy, or Advice to an Author," in *Characteristics of Men, Manners, Opinions, Times, etc.*, 2 vols., ed. John M. Robertson (1900; rpt. Gloucester, Mass.: Peter Smith, 1963), 1: 222.

3. See Morris Palmer Tilley, *Dictionary of the Proverbs in England in the Sixteenth and Seventeenth Century* (Ann Arbor: University of Michigan Press, 1950), T476; see also Emanuel Strauss, *Dictionary of European Proverbs*, 3 vols. (London: Routledge, 1994), #576. For discussion of related issues, see Daniel Carey, "Henry Neville's *The Isle of Pines* (1668): Travel, Forgery and the Problem of Genre," *Angelaki* 1:2 (1993/4): 23–39; and Percy G. Adams, *Travelers and Travel Liars* (Berkeley: University of California Press, 1962).

4. See Daniel Carey, "Compiling Nature's History: Travellers and Travel Narratives in the Early Royal Society," *Annals of Science* 54 (1997): 269–92. More generally, see Steven Shapin, *A Social History of Truth: Civility and Science in Seventeenth-Century England* (Chicago: University of Chicago Press, 1994), 243–58.

5. Letter of September 16, 1704; *The Correspondence of John Locke*, 8 vols, ed. E. S. de Beer (Oxford: Clarendon Press, 1976–89), 8: 393. The text was Joseph Pitts, *A True and Faithful Account of the Religion and Manners of the Mohammetans* (Exeter, 1704).

6. Daniel Carey, *Locke, Shaftesbury, and Hutcheson: Contesting Diversity in the Enlightenment and Beyond* (forthcoming, Cambridge University Press).

7. Anthony Grafton, *Commerce with the Classics: Ancient Books and Renaissance Readers* (Ann Arbor: University of Michigan Press, 1997); Ann Blair, *The Theater of Nature: Jean Bodin and Renaissance Science* (Princeton: Princeton University Press, 1997); Blair; "Reading Strategies for Coping with Information Overload, ca. 1550–1700," *Journal of the History of Ideas* 64 (2003): 11–28; Adrian Johns, *The Nature of the Book: Print and Knowledge in the Making* (Chicago: University of Chicago Press, 1998), chap. 4; Johns, "Reading and Experiment in the Early Royal Society ," in *Reading, Society and Politics in Early Modern England*, ed. Kevin Sharpe and Steven N. Zwicker (Cambridge: Cambridge University Press, 2003), 244–71. For the study of reading in the context of politics, see Kevin Sharpe, *Reading Revolutions: The Politics of Reading in Early Modern England* (New Haven: Yale University Press, 2000); and more generally *A History of Reading in the West*, ed. Guglielmo Cavallo and Roger Chartier, trans. Lydia G. Cochrane (Cambridge: Polity Press, 1999); and *Books and Readers in Early Modern England: Material Studies*, ed. Jennifer Andersen and Elizabeth Sauer (Philadelphia: University of Pennsylvania Press, 2002).

8. Hakluyt, like Locke, attended Westminster School before matriculating at Christ Church.

9. Nicolas K. Kiessling, *The Library of Robert Burton* (Oxford: Oxford Bibliographical Society, 1988). Burton owned sixty-two travel titles. See appendix nine.

10. See J. N. L. Baker, *The History of Geography* (Oxford: Blackwell, 1963); Edmund W. Gilbert, *British Pioneers in Geography* (Newton Abbot, Devon: David & Charles, 1972); Margarita Bowen, *Empiricism and Geographical Thought: From Francis Bacon to Alexander von Humboldt* (Cambridge: Cambridge University Press, 1981).

11. Mathias Prideaux, *An Easy and Compendius Introduction for Reading all sorts of Histories* (Oxford, 1648), 343, 345.

12. John Prideaux donated an interleaved copy of *An Easy and Compendius Introduction* (1648) with his own annotations to the Bodleian Library, shelfmark 4° P 77 Th.

13. For the connection between Stafforde and John Prideaux, see Anthony à Wood's manuscript note on the Bodleian Library copy of the third edition (1634). Shelfmark Wood 386. See also Wood, *Athenae Oxoniensis*, 4 vols., ed. and rev. Philip Bliss (London, 1813–20), 2:291. In his preface to the reader, Stafforde reported: "The Methode I had from my Tutor, and so farre forth the rest, that I account it but the gleanings of his plentifull Harvest" (A2v).

14. Degoraeus Wheare, *The Method and Order of Reading Both Civil and Ecclesiastical Histories, To which is Added, An Appendix* [by Nicholas Horseman] *concerning Historians of particular Nations, as well Ancient as Modern*, trans. Edmund Bohun (London, 1685), 219.

15. Maurice Cranston, *John Locke: A Biography* (1957; Oxford: Oxford University Press, 1985), 23. Locke's copy of the 1635 edition is held in the Folger Shakespeare Library.

16. George Abbot, *A Briefe Description of the Whole World* [1599], 6th ed. (London, 1624), E1v, E2v, O3r. Abbot named Olaus Magnus and Peter Martyr as his sources, and elsewhere acknowledged Richard Hakluyt's compendium of voyages.

17. Robert Stafforde, *A Geographicall and Anthologicall Description of all the Empires and Kingdomes, both of Continent and Islands in this terrestriall Globe Relating their Scituations, Manners, Customs, Provinces, and Governments*, 3rd edn. (London, 1634), 5, 24, 54.

18. *Microcosmus, or A Little Description of the Great World. A Treatise Historicall, Geographicall, Politicall, Theologicall* (Oxford, 1621). Eight editions appeared by 1639. In 1652, he expanded the text under the title *Cosmographie*, and it went through eight editions before 1700. For discussion of Heylyn's sources and perspective, see Robert Markley, "Riches, Power, Trade and Religion: The Far East and the English Imagination, 1600–1720," in *Asian Travel in the Renaissance*, ed. Daniel Carey (Oxford: Blackwell, 2004), 169–91. A book list of Locke's dating from c.1667 includes "Peter Heylin All he writ." PRO/30/24/47/30, fol. 42r. This presumably expressed an aspiration rather than actual reading. In a late work of 1703, "Some Thoughts concerning Reading and Study for a Gentleman," Locke mentioned Heylyn's "general" geography but stated that he had not been "much conversant" with it. For an edition of "Some Thoughts" from the manuscript, see John Locke, *Some Thoughts concerning Education*, ed. John W. Yolton and Jean. S. Yolton (Oxford: Clarendon Press, 1989), appendix 3; for this reference, p. 323.

19. Heylyn, *Microcosmus*, 331, 357, 379. For an account of Heylyn' s citations (by nationality of author and continent of reference), see Robert Mayhew, "Mapping Science's Imagined Community: Geography as a Republic of Letters, 1600–1800," *British Journal for the History of Science* 38: 1 (2005): 73–92.

20. *John Locke as Translator: Three of the Essais of Pierre Nicole in French and English*, ed. Jean Yolton (Oxford: Voltaire Foundation, 2000), 71.

21. If volumes of "geography" are included, as they should be in all but the category of "general geography," the number of titles owned by Locke rises to nearly 275. See the subject analysis by John Harrison and Peter Laslett, *The Library of John Locke*, 2nd ed. (Oxford: Clarendon Press, 1971), 18. Hereafter abbreviated as *LL*. Locke also owned William Hacke, *A Collection of Original Voyages* (London, 1699), a single volume that contained four accounts. *LL* 1370b. In addition, he possessed various maps and atlases. Harrison and Laslett describe Locke's collection of books on travel, exploration, and geography the "great strength of his collection" (27). Richard Ashcraft's claim that he owned "one of the finest collections of voyage and travel books in the seventeenth century" may be somewhat exaggerated, but nonetheless highlights the significance of these holdings within his library. "John Locke's Library: Portrait of an Intellectual," in *John Locke: Critical Assessments*, 4 vols., ed. Richard Ashcraft (London: Routledge, 1991), 1: 23. Of course Locke also read many works of travel that he did not own or that did not survive in his final collection, as his journals and notebooks testify. It is also worth noting that Locke helped form the library of his patron, the first Earl of Shaftesbury, at Wimbourne St. Giles in Dorset, which included the purchase of numerous works of travel. A catalogue was produced for the third Earl in 1709. See PRO 30/24/23/12.

22. See for example MS Locke d. 10, known as "Lemmata Ethica," and MS Locke d. 11.

23. Locke's journal during his travels in France records the address of Jean Chardin. MS Locke f. 2, p. 177. A letter from Chardin has also survived (August 15, 1681, *Correspondence*, 2: 429–30). Through his acquaintance with Henri Justel, Locke was introduced to Melchisédec Thévenot, editor of the four-volume *Relations des divers voyages curieux* (Paris, 1663–72). François Bernier was a physician and traveler of great distinction who spent thirteen years in Mughal India, producing several accounts of the country. See Gabriel Bonno, *Les relations intellectuelles de Locke avec la France* (Berkeley: University of California Press, 1955).

24. *New Experiments and Observations Touching Cold, or an Experimental History of Cold, Begun* (London, 1665), C7r–v. *The Works of Robert Boyle*, 14 vols., ed. Michael Hunter and Edward B. Davis (London: Pickering & Chatto, 1999–2000), 4: 218.

25. MS Locke f. 14, p. 170. The English edition of Álvaro Semedo's *History of that Great and Renowned Monarchy of China* (London, 1655) was based on a translation of the Portuguese original into Italian as *Historica relatione del gran regno della Cina* (Rome, 1653).

26. MS Locke f. 14, p. 93. *Les Voyages Fameux du sieur Vincent Le Blanc Marseillois* (Paris, 1648). Le Blanc traveled extensively in Asia, Africa, and America in the latter part of the sixteenth century.

27. MS Locke d. 11, p. 3; MS Locke f. 14, p. 29.

28. MS Locke f. 14, p. 68. For Locke's notes on natural history, mining, and medical issues from José de Acosta, dating from c. 1667, see MS Locke f. 19, pp. 214–15, 253, 274–76, 280–83, 284–86, 290–91. See also MS Locke f. 27, p. 154. The latter reference is noted by J. R. Milton, "Dating Locke's *Second Treatise*," *History of Political Thought* 16:3 (1995): 368n.

29. He quoted José de Acosta in the Second Treatise §102, from the English translation published as *The Naturall and Morall Historie of the East and West Indies*, trans. Edward Grimeston (London, 1604); and Garcilaso in the First Treatise §57, citing the French translation published as *Le commentaire royal, ou L'histoire des Yncas, roys du Peru*, trans. Jean Baudoin (Paris, 1633). See also *Essay*, I.iii.9.

30. MS Locke f. 14, p. 102. Robert Boyle made extensive use of *The Strange and Dangerous Voyage of Captain Thomas Iames* (London, 1633) as a source in *New Experiments and Observations Touching Cold*.

31. MS Locke f. 14, p. 68.

32. MS Locke f. 8, p. 114. See *Tracts written by the Honourable Robert Boyle containing New experiments* (London, 1672), 99–100, where he quotes Oviedo as a "credible eye-witness" on the subject of pearl divers in Cuba and the effect of air in creating buoyancy. Locke also had an intimate familiarity with Boyle's *General History of the Air* (London, 1692) which he was responsible for publishing after Boyle's death. This work contained numerous references to the testimony of travelers gathered in person by Boyle, together with references and quotations from published accounts, including the insertion of thirteen pages discussing the Peak of Tenerife. On Tenerife, see 171–84; for travel references generally, 150–202. *Works of Robert Boyle*, 12: 100–33.

33. MS Locke f. 10, fol. 107 (entry for October 5, 1691). In MS Locke d. 10, p. 101, Locke recorded a title that came from Boyle, identifiable as Nicolas Gervaise, *Description historique du Royaume de Macaçar* (Paris, 1688). See also a reference to a history of Cochin China in Italian, noted from Boyle. MS Locke f. 28, p. 176 (identifiable as Cristoforo Borri, *Relatione della nouva missione delli P.P. della compagnia di giesu al regno della Cocincina* [Rome, 1631]; Locke obtained a copy of this edition, *LL* 395b, and an English translation of 1633, *LL* 137). The connection with Boyle on the subject of travel is part of a wider pattern of participation by Locke in the aims and practices of the new science. Locke owned a number of travel books reviewed in the *Philosophical Transactions*, the Society's journal, although we cannot be sure this was the source that led directly to his purchases. It is striking that of the twenty-four works of travel identified by Michael Hunter as investigated by the Royal Society's committee of correspondence, beginning in 1664, Locke owned all but one. See the list in Michael Hunter, *Establishing the New Science* (Woodbridge, Suffolk: Boydell, 1989), 118–19. Locke's library of travel books was almost identical to Isaac Newton's, and there are considerable overlaps with Robert Hooke's collection. See John R. Harrison, *The Library of Isaac Newton* (Cambridge: Cambridge University Press, 1978). Harrison and Laslett note "the really remarkable resemblance, or, in this case, near identity" of Locke's collection of travel books with those of Isaac Newton (13). See also Leona Rostenberg, *The Library of Robert Hooke: The Scientific Book Trade of Restoration England* (Santa Monica: Modoc Press, 1989). This reproduces the sale catalogue of Hooke's library. For a discussion of his holdings in geography, exploration and travel, see 135–40.

34. MS Locke f. 14, p. 140.

35. *The Voyages and Travels of the Ambassadors sent by Frederick Duke of Holstein to the Great Duke of Muscovy, and the King of Persia . . . whereto are added The Travels of John Albert de Mandelslo . . . into the East-Indies*, trans. John Davies (London, 1662).

36. MS Locke, f. 14, p. 172.

37. John Locke, *Essays on the Law of Nature*, ed. and trans. W. von Leyden (Oxford: Clarendon Press, 1954), 172–73. J. R. Milton concludes that Locke's reading of travel literature in the period from 1658 to March 1667 (when he began living in London) was prompted by interests "that seem generally to have been medical or botanical rather than ethnographical." "Locke at Oxford," in *Locke's Philosophy: Content and Context*, ed. G. A. J. Rogers (Oxford: Clarendon Press, 1994), 36. This is certainly true of his extant note taking, but we should remember this ethnographic reference as well as his remarks in the same group of "essays" on atheism in the Bay of Saldanha and Brazil (without citation), pp. 173–75, and to barbarous and unaccountable customs reported by travelers generally, p. 141.

38. MS Locke f. 14, p. 112, 139, 138.

39. Isaac de La Peyrère, *Relation du Groenland* (Paris, 1647), *LL* 1328; François Cauche in *Relations Veritables et curieuses de l'Isle de Madagascar et de Bresil* (Paris, 1651), *LL* 642a; Giovanni Pietro Maffei, *Historiarum Indicarum* (Cologne, 1593), *LL* 1864.

40. For Locke's reading generally at this time, which included a significant amount of travel writing, see John Lough, "Locke's Reading during His Stay in France," *The Library*, 5th ser., 8 (1953): 229–58.

41. Henri Justel inherited the office of secretary to Louis XIV from his father who had purchased it. As a Protestant he fled France in 1681 and settled in England, where he became keeper of the royal library at St. James's Palace.

42. MS Locke f. 15, p. 19, 21. See also a letter of July 9, 1680 from Henri Justel that mentions news of two travel accounts. *Correspondence*, 2:210.

43. For a discussion of their friendship and shared interests, see Bonno, 116–56.

44. Nicolas Toinard, *Evangeliorum harmonia Graeco-Latina* (Paris, 1707).

45. Locke, *Correspondence*, 2: 56.

46. Letter of 30 August/9 September 1679, Locke, *Correspondence*, 2: 85.

47. Ibid.

48. Letter of September 20 and October 13, 1679, Locke, *Correspondence*, 2:116–17. See Andrew Battel's account of Angola, printed in Samuel Purchas, *Hakluytus Posthumus or Purchas his Pilgrimes*, 20 vols. (Glasgow: J. Maclehose and Sons, 1905–7), 6: 377–87.

49. Locke, *Correspondence*, 2:117. For the reference from Boyle, see BL Add MS 15642, p. 161. Printed in Kenneth Dewhurst, *John Locke (1632–1704) Physician and Philosopher: A Medical Biography. With an Edition of the Medical Notes in his Journals* (London: Welcome Historical Medical Library, 1963), 176.

50. On Senegal see Locke's letter of March 25, 1698 (*Correspondence*, 6: 361), and Toinard's letter of July 6, 1698 (*Correspondence*, 6:445). On Froger, see Locke to Toinard March 25, 1698 (*Correspondence*, 6:358).

51. For discussion of counting, see Toinard's letter of November 26/December 6, 1697, *Correspondence*, 6:265; and his letter of October 16/26, 1698, *Correspondence*, 6:492. This letter refers to the Tupinamba. Locke cited their practices in relation to numeration in the *Essay*, II.xvi.6, by reference to Léry. For other expressions of Locke's interest, see MS Locke f. 2, p. 292, and MS Locke c. 33, f. 11, note dated March 28, 1679 (both referenced to François Bernier); BL Add MSS 15642, pp. 86–87 (entry for April 25, 1679).

52. Domingo Navarrete, *Tratados historicos, politicos, ethicos y religiosos de la monarchia de China* (Madrid, 1676).

53. Letter of May 1, 1699, Locke, *Correspondence*, 6:615. See also earlier letters referring to Navarrete: September 2, 1698, *Correspondence*, 6:463; February 20, 1699, *Correspondence*, 6:569; and April 18/28, 1699, *Correspondence*, 6:603.

54. June 16/26, 1680, Locke, *Correspondence*, 2:200.

55. January 15/25, 1681, Locke, *Correspondence*, 2:347.

56. Christoval de Acuña, *Nuevo descubrimiento del gran rio de las Amazonas* (Madrid, 1641). The work was translated into French as *Relation de la Rivière des Amazones* (Paris, 1682). *LL* 16.

57. February 23/March 5, 1681, Locke, *Correspondence*, 2:386–87. Olenker (his name was spelled variously) took part in Sir John Narbrough's voyage in the *Sweepstakes* from 1669–71. See de Beer's discussion in 2:387n.

58. Although this was the pattern in the correspondence with Toinard, Locke was happy to use a very wide array of travel accounts, ranging in date of publication from 1530 to 1700, in his critique of innateness in Book I of the *Essay*.

59. For a valuable discussion, see Michel Mervaud, "Diderot et l'*Agnus Scythicus*: le mythe et son histoire," *Studies on Voltaire and the Eighteenth Century* (2003:01): 65–103.

60. June 22/July 2, 1681, Locke, *Correspondence*, 2:412.

61. July 6/16 or 7/17, 1681, Locke, *Correspondence*, 2:423.

62. MS Locke f. 28, p. 8, lists twenty-nine pages for attention in Struys's *Voyages* (Amsterdam, 1681). See also notes on the English translation (London, 1683), MS Locke f. 7, p. 146.

63. Letter of February 20, 1681, Locke, *Correspondence*, 2:381. Locke alluded to the Cartesian theory of the pineal gland as the locus of the soul and conjectured that the elephant must be "une beste d'une grande ame" if the gland was proportionate to its body. He also wittily commented on the Cartesian assessment of animals as machines without souls. He hoped that elephants would not be given paper and ink in case they wrote their memoirs and described human beings as the ones who were machines and themselves alone with understanding.

64. August 30, 1681, Locke, *Correspondence* 2:437. I have retained the original orthography of the letters throughout.

65. Locke, Second Treatise §92.

66. He was elected to the Académie française in 1720.

67. December 31, 1698/January 10, 1699, Locke, *Correspondence*, 6:531–38. Locke marked it with the heading "Voyages" and "A list of Voyages latterly published in France sent me by Mr du Bos." MS Locke c. 7, fol. 223.

68. Locke, *Correspondence*, 6:535. The text is Henri de Tonti, *Dernières decouvertes dans l'Amérique septentrionale de M. de La Sale* (Paris, 1697). *LL* 2960. For Locke's list of page notes on the rear fly-leaf of his copy, see his copy retained in the Bodleian Library, shelfmark Locke 7.80b. The front flyleaf was signed Du Bos.

69. Locke, *Correspondence*, 6:536, referring to J. J. Le Maire, *Les Voyages du Sieur Le Maire aux îles Canaries, Cap-Verd, Senegal et Gambie* (Paris, 1695), and Philippe Avril, *Voyages en divers états d'Europe et d'Asie, entrepris pour découvrir un nouveau chemin à la Chine* (Paris, 1692), as containing nothing new, and Charles Dellon, *Relation d'un voyage des Indes Orientales*, 2 vols (Paris, 1685) as an account of adventures. Nonetheless, Locke acquired copies of all these works in various editions, *LL* 1874, 2028, 942.

70. Locke, *Correspondence*, 6:536; a French edition appeared as *Nouvelle relation de la Chine* (Paris, 1688).

71. Locke, *Correspondence*, 6:536, referring to Sanson, *Estat present du royaume de Perse* (Paris, 1694). Locke owned the second edition published as *Voyage ou Relation de l'état present du Royaume de Perse* (Paris, 1695). *LL* 2554.

72. See Dirk Van Der Cruysse, *Siam and the West 1500–1700*, trans. Michael Smithies (Chiang Mai: Silkworm, 2002).

73. The abbé de Choisy accompanied the Chevalier de Chaumont on an embassy to Siam in 1685 to convert Phra Naraï to Christianity and published his *Journal du voyage de Siam* (Paris, 1686). Locke had referred to Choisy's account in relation to Siamese theology in the first edition of the *Essay* (I.iv.15). Chaumont returned to France in June 1686 and published his *Relation* in the same year.

74. Locke, *Correspondence*, 6:537. Tachard took part in the same embassy and published his *Voyage de Siam des Pères Jésuites* in 1686.

75. Locke, *Correspondence*, 6:537. La Loubère travelled in a subsequent embassy to Siam as envoy-extraordinary of Louis XIV in 1687. He later published *Du Royaume de Siam*, 2 vols. (Paris, 1691). For Desfargues or de Farges, see *Relation des Revolutions Arrivées a Siam dans l'Année 1688* (Amsterdam, 1691).

76. In the fourth edition (1700), Locke referred to La Loubère on the subject of Siamese and Chinese atheism (I.iv.8) and in the fifth edition (1706) he referred to the anonymous *Historia cultus Sinensium* (1700). Du Bos kept Locke informed about developments in the Chinese rites controversy and referred to this text in a letter of June 27/July 7, 1699, *Correspondence*, 6:647.

77. John Locke, *Of the Conduct of the Understanding* (Bristol, 1993), 10–11, drawing on Charles Le Gobien, *Histoire des Isles Marianes nouvellement converties à la Religion Chrestienne* (Paris, 1700). Locke owned a copy of the second edition (1701), *LL* 1275. Du Bos drew his attention to this work in a letter of February 14/24, 1700, *Correspondence*, 7:11.

78. See references to travel books drawn from the *Journal des Sçavans* in MS Locke d. 10, p. 1, 3, 11, 75, 83, 86, 103, 133, 157, 169, 179; MS Locke f. 15 (dating from c. 1677), p. 48, 52, 65, 74; MS Locke f. 8, pp. 85–86.

79. MS Locke f. 1, p. 262. He had earlier remarked this from the Latin translation: *Le Journal des Scavants hoc est: Ephemerides Eruditorum*, trans. M. F. Nitzschius (Leipsig, 1667), MS Locke f. 19, p. 271 (a note dating from 1667). Boyle had identified Linschoten as "that sober Relator of his Voyages" in *The Sceptical Chymist* (1661). *Works*, 2:347.

80. For his travels generally, see C. D. van Strien, *British Travellers in Holland during the Stuart Period: Edward Browne and John Locke as Tourists in the United Provinces* (Leiden: Brill, 1993).

81. Letter of August 4, 1686, Locke, *Correspondence*, 3:23. In a letter of September 1687, Sibelius said that he had heard again from ten Rhyne who reported further on medical practice in the Indies. Sibelius invited Locke's opinion on these matters and asked him for any further inquiries for ten Rhyne (*Correspondence*, 3:266–67).

82. MS Locke f. 8, pp. 193–94. Willem Ten Rhyne's account was published as *Schediasma de Promontorio Bonae Speï* (Schaffhausen, 1686). *LL* 2477. A translation appeared in the Churchills' *Collection of Voyages and Travels*, 4 vols (London, 1704), 1: 829–45, conceivably on Locke's suggestion.

83. Martha Baldwin, "The Snakestone Experiments: An Early Modern Medical Debate," *Isis* 86 (1995): 394–418.

84. MS Locke f. 8, p. 218.

85. MS Locke f. 8, pp. 59. Printed in Dewhurst, 241. Six months earlier, Locke had recorded a passage from W. Glanius, *A New Voyage to the East Indies* (London, 1682), 184, reporting the existence of men with tails in Formosa, based on Glanius's ostensible eyewitness. MS Locke f. 7, pp. 131–33.

86. MS Locke f. 8, pp. 63–65. Printed in Dewhurst, 242. The entry cites a location "towards Ternate, to the south east of Batavia [Jakarta]."

87. MS Locke f. 2, p. 4. Quoted in Lough, 235. Locke's source was Pietro della Valle, *Viaggi* (Venice, 1667). Locke also noted that Valle said João de Lucena "seems to speake thereof with good ground" in his life of Francis Xavier, although Valle added, in Locke's words, that "if I mistake not,

he is capable of a little correction" (MS Locke, f. 14, p. 31), and his good opinion of Ottaviano Bon, a Venetian diplomat, who had written a description of the Turkish court and seraglio. MS d. 10, p. 155. Valle owned a copy of Bon's manuscript account, which appeared in English translation as *A Description of the Grand Signor's Seraglio, or Turkish Emperours Court* (London, 1650).

88. Charles de Rochefort was sent to the Caribbean by the congregation of La Rochelle. He returned in 1650 and later established himself in Rotterdam where his *Histoire naturelle et morale des Iles Antilles de l'Amérique* appeared in 1658. See Régis Antoine, *Les écrivains français et les Antilles: des premiers Pères blancs aux surréalistes noirs* (Paris: Maisonneuve et Larose, 1978), 26–27, 34–37. Locke seems to have learned of the text from Boyle who referred to "the ingenious French Publisher of the natural and moral History of those *American* islands, commonly call'd by the French *Les Isles Antilles* and by us the *Caribe* Islands" in *Certain Physiological Essays* (London, 1661), 231–32, which Locke noted in MS Locke d. 10, p. 20. (We know Locke was reading this volume in the early 1660s from a reference to the text in MS Locke f. 14, p. 68. See J. R. Milton, "The Date and Significance of Two of Locke's Early Manuscripts," *The Locke Newsletter* no. 19 (1988): 47–89.)

89. MS Locke f. 14, p. 198. Locke was reading the English translation, *The History of the Caribby-Islands*, trans. John Davies (London, 1666). For this reference, see p. 342.

90. MS Locke d. 10, p. 133.

91. Giovanni Battista Ramusio, *Viaggi et Navigatio*, 3rd ed., part 1 (Venice, 1563), a2v. Noted in MS Locke f. 3, p. 66.

92. MS Locke f. 8, p. 277. Thévenot refers to Balthazar Tellez, *Historia geral de Ethiopia* (Coimbra, 1660), and Luis de Urreta, *Historia eclesiastica, politica, natural, y moral, de los grandes y remotos reynos de la Etiopia* (Valencia, 1610). Specifically, Thévenot complained about mistakes by Urreta and others in the country's geographical placement, errors about the source of the Nile and the reasons for its flooding, and the fact that the name Prester John was a title unknown among Ethiopian princes. The public waited with impatience "de bons & de seurs memoires" on these subjects, having existed on the "chimeres de scavans & gens d'esprit, faites sur de fausses informations" up to this point. Thévenot, 4: 1 (the volumes were printed in separate fascicles, with separate signatures and pagination). At another remove was the great Portuguese chronicler João de Barros, cited by Thévenot as "d'ailleurs tres exact" (that is, other than on Ethiopia). Barros had traveled no further than western Africa and relied on various primary sources. See C. R. Boxer, *João de Barros: Portuguese Humanist and Historian of Asia* (New Delhi: Concept Publishing Co., 1981). In this case Locke quickly followed up the note with another supporting comment from the distinguished classicist Isaac Vossius who termed Barros's treatment of geography "diligentius & exactius" in *De Nili et aliorum fluminum origine* (The Hague, 1666), 51. Noted in MS Locke f. 8, p. 277. Elsewhere Locke noted from Toinard that Barros and Diogo do Couto, who continued his chronicle, were "both excellent hist[orians] of the Portugals acting in the East Indies but Baros is the better" (MS Locke f. 28, p. 134).

93. MS Locke f. 7, p. 34.

94. MS Locke f. 6, p. 50, quoting Meric Casaubon, *A Treatise of Use and Custom* (London, 1638), 34. I am grateful to Henry Schankula for clarifying the circumstances of Locke's reading.

95. Introducing the passage, Locke said he quoted it because the book was "not every Day to be met with" (I.iii.9). Here he drew on Casaubon who also quoted the text on the grounds that the book was "not very common to bee had, nor perchance very commonly knowne" (34).

96. MS Locke c. 33, fol. 21r. The same notebook also mentions negative judgments on the truthfulness of certain travelers, including Francois Bernier's conclusion, confirming what Locke noted

from the *Journal des Sçavans*, that Linschoten was a "liar." He also noted Léry's view that the Catholic cosmographer André Thevet was a "menteur." Whether he knew the full background of the dispute between Thevet and Léry in Brazil is not clear.

97. MS Locke c. 33, fol. 21v. Mingrelia (Samegrelo) is an historic province of Georgia, though not all of its people accept the attribution of Georgian ethnicity.

98. MS Locke f. 2, p. 253 (September 4, 1677). His source was the translation in Thévenot, 1: 31–52.

99. The work was published under the title "Some Thoughts concerning Reading and Study for a Gentleman" in *A Collection of Several Pieces of Mr. John Locke*, ed. Pierre Desmaizeaux (London, 1720). The shape of study advocated by Locke can be seen by appreciating that he begins with rhetoric and oratory. In relation to morality Locke recommended, above all, the Gospel, and for anyone wishing to see to the heights to which the subject had been taken in "heathen" science, he endorsed Cicero's *De Officiis*. In relation to politics he mentioned his own treatises of government, as well as the work of Pufendorf, Algernon Sidney, and Hooker. In a related letter, written to the Countess of Peterborough in 1697, Locke endorses the reading of history for her son, Lord Mordaunt, together with the study of geography, maps, and chronology, but does not mention travel writing. *Correspondence*, 6:211–17.

100. Locke seems to have provided some editorial advice on this collection. In March 1701, Awnsham Churchill thanked Locke for his help. *Correspondence*, 7:586. For recruiting of material, see Locke's letter to Dr. John Covel (*Correspondence*, 7:172–73). Locke does not appear to have written the preliminary history of navigation or the long account of existing books of travel, despite the fact that he was named in the third edition (1744) on the title page. These works were included in the ninth edition of Locke's *Works* as his own. For a de-attribution, see G. R. Crone and R. A. Skelton, "English Collections of Voyages and Travels, 1625–1846," in *Richard Hakluyt and His Successors*, ed. Edmund Lynam (London: Hakluyt Society, 1946), 81–84; and E. S. de Beer, "Bishop Law's List of Books Attributed to Locke," *The Locke Newsletter* no. 7 (1976): 50–51. Bonno attributed them to Locke, on the basis of Locke's marginal notes to letters received from the abbé Du Bos, but without addressing Crone and Skelton (83, 215–16).

101. George Sandys, *A Relation of a Journey Begun A: Dom: 1610 . . . Containing a Description of the Turkish Empire* (London, 1615). Locke owned the seventh edition (1673). *LL* 2553.

102. Locke referred to Roe's attribution of atheism to the Hottentots in the *Essay*, I.iv.8 (from Thévenot's redaction, 1:2).

103. Edward Browne, *A Brief Account of Some Travels in Hungary, Servia, Bulgaria* (London, 1673). *LL* 498.

104. Locke had a long-standing interest in Thomas Gage who published *The English-American His Travail by Sea and Land, or A New Survey of the West India's* in 1648. For his earliest notes, see BL Add MS 32554, p. 124, 230; Locke later bought the third edition published as *A New Survey of the West Indies* (1677). For his notes see his journal from 1680, MS Locke f. 4, p. 155, 162, and page lists noted p. 160 and 176 (see also MS Locke f. 28, p. 68, from 1678); and MS Locke d. 10, p. 83, and 61 (where he discusses different editions).

105. In January and February 1699, Locke wrote to Toinard about the latest instalments of Dampier's travels. *Correspondence*, 6: 567.

106. François Pyrard, *Discours du Voyage des François aux Indes orientales* (Paris, 1611). Locke recorded a judgment on him as providing "a faithful relation of things he himself observed"; his account of Goa and the management of it by the Portuguese was "exact." It is not clear whether this is

Locke's own assessment or someone else's. MS Locke c. 33, fol. 6r. For Locke's notes on Pyrard, see MS Locke c. 33, fol. 5r–64, and MS Locke f. 3, p. 92, 94, 95, 96, 103–4, 108, 121, 129.

107. Pierre Bergeron was not actually a traveler but an editor best known for his *Relations des Voyages en Tartarie* (1634). *LL* 280. For some discussion, see Robert O. Lindsay, "Pierre Bergeron: A Forgotten Editor of French Travel Literature," *Terrae Incognitae* 7 (1976): 31–38.

108. Gabriel Sagard was author of *Le Grand voyage du pays des Hurons* (Paris, 1632), and *Histoire du Canada* (Paris, 1636). For Locke's notes on the work of Sagard, see MS Locke c. 33, fols 9r–11r; MS Locke d. 1, p. 1, 9, 89, 93; MS Locke f. 3, pp. 281–82.

109. Locke's reading of Bernier's several travel books appears in various journal references and cross-references: MS Locke f. 1, pp. 230–32, 248, 256, 257; MS Locke f. 6, pp. 20–25; MS Locke d. 1, p. 149, 173; MS Locke c. 33, fol. 14r; MS Locke d. 10, p. 13, 41, 105, 145; MS Locke f. 28, p. 60.

110. *Some Thoughts concerning Education*, appendix, 324.

111. Milton, "Locke at Oxford," 35.

112. See especially Carey, *Locke, Shaftesbury, and Hutcheson*, chaps. 1–3.

113. Locke, *Essays*, 141.

114. Ibid., 173. See *Voyages and Travels of . . . Mandelslo*, Bk 1: 40–41 (sig. Ffff4v–Gggg1r).

115. See Edward Stillingfleet, *A Defence of the Discourse Concerning the Idolatry Practised in the Church of Rome* (London, 1676), esp. 112–61. Locke was reading this volume during his time in France. MS Locke f. 1, p. 514, 515. MS Locke f. 2, p. 2, 3. See also Stillingfleet's *Origines Sacrae* and additions to the posthumous, seventh edition (Cambridge, 1702), 73–86. My attention was drawn to this by Ann Talbot.

116. Edward Stillingfleet, *The Bishop of Worcester's Answer to Mr. Locke's Letter* (London, 1697), 89–90.

117. Shaftesbury made the same point about the imperfect grasp of local languages by travelers in *Several Letters*, 40.

118. John Locke, *Mr. Locke's Reply to the Right Reverend The Lord Bishop of Worcester's Answer to His Second Letter*, in *The Works of John Locke*, 9th ed., 9 vols. (1794; rpt. London: Routledge/Thoemmes Press, 1997), 3:496. This statement was incorporated into the fifth edition of the *Essay* (1706), 39n. See Edward Terry, *A Voyage to East India* (London, 1655), 17; and John Ovington, *A Voyage to Suratt* (London, 1696), 489. Terry traveled as Sir Thomas Roe's chaplain; John Ovington, another Anglican divine, stopped at the Cape on his way to India. After the exchange with Stillingfleet, Locke incorporated these references into the next edition of the *Essay*, the fourth (1700).

119. Purchas, 4: 311. Thévenot's version appeared in *Relations*, 1:1–80. Locke's preference for Thévenot's edition, despite the fact that it was a translation from Purchas, may have been motivated not only by his friendship with him but also by the fact that Thévenot included in his edition a preliminary "Discours sur les Memoires de Thomas Rhoë," 7–12. In his preface to the first volume, Thévenot had remarked that "Hawkins, Rhoë, Terry, Methold, ont demeure long-temps, avec autorité, dans les Pays qu'ils decrivent, & par cette raison, leurs Relations en sont plus exactes & plus croyables" (a3v).

120. On Coore, or Coree, a Khoi Khoi chieftain of the Kora clan—from which the English version of his name was derived—see Kenneth Parker, "Telling Tales: Early Modern English Voyagers and the Cape of Good Hope," *The Seventeenth Century* 10:1 (1995): 141–44.

121. *Essay*, Iv.xv.4.

122. Locke, *Works*, 3:485.

123. Ibid., 3:486. G. W. Leibniz praised La Loubère as a "vir doctrina et judico." Leibniz, *Sämtliche Schriften und Briefe*, ed. by the Deutsche Akademie der Wissenschaften, erste Reihe, Band 7 (Berlin: Akademie Verlag, 1964), 620. Quoted in Sven Trakulhun, "The Widening of the World and the Realm of History: Early European Approaches to the Beginnings of Siamese History, c.1500–1700," in *Asian Travel in the Renaissance*, 89.

124. To that extent, he occupied a role similar to the individual travelers to whom Locke directed inquiries. See for example *Correspondence*, 1: 424–26, 431–33; 2: 591; 7: 735–37.

125. D. K. Wyatt, "Introduction" to Simon de La Loubère, *The Kingdom of Siam* (Kuala Lumpur: Oxford University Press, 1969), viii.

126. The circulation of travel books among friends is part of this pattern, including figures such as Dr. Daniel Coxe (MS Locke f. 5, p. 150; BL Add MS 15642, p. 119, 124), James Tyrrell (BL Add MS 15642, p. 132, 188); George Wall (BL Add MS 15642, p. 189); Martha Lockhart (MS Locke f. 10, fol. 187), and Damaris Masham (MS Locke f. 7, p. 13), as well as the giving of travel accounts as gifts (e.g., Dampier given to Peter Guenellon—MS Locke f. 10, fol. 368), and Garcilaso given to Furly in 1688 (MS Locke f. 29, p. 101), as noted by Milton, "Dating Locke's *Second Treatise*," 367n.

Bibliography

Primary Sources

Abbot, George. *A Briefe Description of the Whole World*. 1599. 6th ed. London, 1624.

Acosta, José de. *The Naturall and Morall Historie of the East and West Indies*. Trans. Edward Grimeston. London, 1604.

Acuña, Christoval de. *Nuevo descubrimiento del gran rio de las Amazonas*. Madrid, 1641. Translated as *Relation de la rivière des Amazones*. Paris, 1682.

Avril, Philippe. *Voyages en divers états d'Europe et d'Asie, entrepris pour découvrir un nouveau chemin à la Chine*. Paris, 1692.

Bergeron, Pierre. *Relations des Voyages en Tartarie*. Paris, 1634.

Bon, Ottaviano. *A Description of the Grand Signor's Seraglio, or Turkish Emperours Court*. London, 1650.

Boyle, Robert. *General History of the Air*. London, 1692.

———. *New Experiments and Observations Touching Cold, or an Experimental History of Cold, Begun*. London, 1665.

———. *Some Considerations Touching the Usefulnesse of Experimentall Natural Philosophy*. London, 1663.

———. *Tracts written by the Honourable Robert Boyle containing New experiments*. London, 1672.

———. *The Works of Robert Boyle*. 14 vols. Ed. Michael Hunter and Edward B. Davis. London: Pickering & Chatto, 1999–2000.

Browne, Edward. *A Brief Account of Some Travels in Hungary, Servia, Bulgaria*. London, 1673.

Cauche, François. *Relation du voyage que François Cauche de Rouen a fait à Madagascar*. Paris, 1651.

[Charmot, Nicolas and Charles Maigrot]. *Historia cultus Sinensium.* Cologne, 1700.

Chaumont, Alexandre de. *Relation de l'ambassade de Mr le Chevalier de Chaumont à la cour du roi de Siam.* Paris, 1686.

Choisy, François-Timoléon, abbé de. *Journal du voyage de Siam.* Paris, 1686.

A Collection of Voyages and Travels. [Published by Awnsham and John Churchill] 4 vols. London, 1704.

Dellon, Charles. *Relation d'un voyage des Indes Orientales.* 2 vols. Paris, 1685.

Desfargues. *Relation des Revolutions Arrivées a Siam dans l'Année 1688.* Amsterdam, 1691.

Gage, Thomas. *The English-American His Travail by Sea and Land, or A New Survey of the West India's.* London, 1648. Third edition published as *A New Survey of the West Indies.* London, 1677.

Gervaise, Nicolas. *Description historique du Royaume de Macaçar.* Paris, 1688.

Glanius, W. *A New Voyage to the East Indies.* London, 1682.

Hacke, William. *A Collection of Original Voyages.* London, 1699.

Heylyn, Peter. *Microcosmus, or A Little Description of the Great World. A Treatise Historicall, Geographicall, Politicall, Theologicall.* Oxford, 1621.

Justel, Henri. *Recueil de divers voyages faits en Afrique et en l'Amérique.* Paris, 1674.

Knox, Robert. *Historical Relation of the Island of Ceylon.* London, 1681.

La Loubère, Simon de. *Du Royaume de Siam.* 2 vols. Paris, 1691.

La Peyrère, Isaac de. *Relation du Groenland.* Paris, 1647.

Le Blanc, Vincent. *Les Voyages Fameux du sieur Vincent Le Blanc Marseillois.* Paris, 1648.

Le Gobien, Charles. *Histoire des Isles Marianes nouvellement converties à la Religion Chrestienne.* Paris, 1700.

Leibniz, G. W. *Sämtliche Schriften und Briefe.* Ed. the Deutsche Akademie der Wissenschaften. Erste Reihe, Band 7. Berlin: Akademie Verlag, 1964.

Le Maire, J. J. *Les Voyages du Sieur Le Maire aux îles Canaries, Cap-Verd, Senegal et Gambie.* Paris, 1695.

Locke, John. *A Collection of Several Pieces of Mr. John Locke.* Ed. Pierre Desmaizeaux. London, 1720.

———. *The Correspondence of John Locke.* 8 vols. Ed. E. S. de Beer. Oxford: Clarendon Press, 1976–89.

———. *An Essay concerning Human Understanding.* Ed. Peter H. Nidditch. Oxford: Clarendon Press, 1975.

———. *Essays on the Law of Nature.* Ed. and trans. W. von Leyden. Oxford: Clarendon Press, 1954.

———. *John Locke as Translator: Three of the Essais of Pierre Nicole in French and English.* Ed. Jean Yolton. Oxford: Voltaire Foundation, 2000.

———. *Of the Conduct of the Understanding.* 1706. Reprint Bristol, 1993.

———. *Some Thoughts Concerning Education.* Ed. John W. and Jean S. Yolton. Oxford: Clarendon Press, 1989.

———. *Two Treatises of Government.* Ed. Peter Laslett. 2nd. ed. Cambridge: Cambridge University Press, 1967.

———. *The Works of John Locke.* 9 vols. 12th ed. Reprinted London: Routledge/Thoemmes Press, 1997.

Maffei, Giovanni Pietro. *Historiarum Indicarum.* Florence, 1588.

Magalhaes, Gabriel de. *Nouvelle relation de la Chine.* Paris, 1688.

Mandelslo, J. A. von. *The Voyages and Travels of the Ambassadors sent by Frederick Duke of Holstein to the Great Duke of Muscovy, and the King of Persia . . . whereto are added The Travels of John Albert de Mandelslo . . . into the East-Indies.* Trans. John Davies. London, 1662.

Navarrete, Domingo Fernández de. *Tratados historicos, politicos, ethicos y religiosos de la monarchia de China.* Madrid, 1676.

Olearius, Adam. *The Voyages and Travels of the Ambassadors sent by Frederick Duke of Holstein to the Great Duke of Muscovy, and the King of Persia . . . whereto are added The Travels of John Albert de Mandelslo . . . into the East-Indies.* Trans. John Davies. London, 1662.

Pitts, Joseph. *A True and Faithful Account of the Religion and Manners of the Mohammetans.* Exeter, 1704.

Prideaux, Mathias. *An Easy and Compendius Introduction for Reading all sorts of Histories.* Oxford, 1648.

Purchas, Samuel. *Hakluytus Posthumus or Purchas his Pilgrimes.* 20 vols. 1625. Glasgow: J. Maclehose and Sons, 1905–7.

Pyrard, François. *Discours du voyage des François aux Indes orientales.* Paris, 1611.

Ramusio, Giovanni Battista. *Viaggi et Navigatio.* 3rd ed., part 1. Venice, 1563.

Rochefort, Charles de. *Histoire naturelle et morale des Iles Antilles de l'Amérique.* Rotterdam, 1658. Translated as *The History of the Caribby-Islands.* Trans. John Davies. London, 1666.

Sagard, Gabriel. *Le Grand voyage du pays des Hurons.* Paris, 1632.

———. *Histoire du Canada.* Paris, 1636.

Sandys, George. *A Relation of a Journey Begun A: Dom: 1610 . . . Containing a Description of the Turkish Empire.* London, 1615.

Sanson. *Estat present du royaume de Perse.* Paris, 1694.

Semedo, Álvaro. *The History of that Great and Renowned Monarchy of China.* London, 1655.

Shaftesbury, Anthony Ashley Cooper, Third Earl of. *Characteristics of Men, Manners, Opinions, Times, etc.* 2 vols. Ed. John M. Robertson. 1900. Reprint Gloucester, Mass.: Peter Smith, 1963.

———. *Several Letters Written by a Noble Lord to a Young Man at the University.* London, 1716.

Stafforde, Robert. *A Geographicall and Anthologicall Description of all the Empires and Kingdomes, both of Continent and Islands in this terrestriall Globe Relating their Scituations, Manners, Customs, Provinces, and Governments.* 3rd ed. London, 1634.

Stillingfleet, Edward. *The Bishop of Worcester's Answer to Mr. Locke's Letter.* London, 1697.

———. *A Defence of the Discourse Concerning the Idolatry Practised in the Church of Rome.* London, 1676.

———. *Origines Sacrae.* 7th edn. Cambridge, 1702.

Tachard, Guy. *Voyage de Siam des Pères Jésuites.* Paris, 1686.

Tellez, Balthazar. *Historia geral de Ethiopia.* Coimbra, 1660.

Ten Rhyne, Willem. *Schediasma de Promontorio Bonae Speï.* Schaffhausen, 1686.

Thévenot, Melchisédec, ed. *Relations des divers voyages curieux.* Paris, 1663–72.

Tonti, Henri de. *Dernières decouvertes dans l'Amérique septentrionale de M. de La Sale.* Paris, 1697.

Urreta, Luis de. *Historia eclesiastica, politica, natural, y moral, de los grandes y remotos reynos de la Etiopia.* Valencia, 1610.

Vega, Garcilaso de la. *Le commentaire royal, ou L'histoire des Yncas, roys du Peru.* Trans. Jean Baudoin. Paris, 1633.

Vossius, Isaac. *De Nili et aliorum fluminum origine.* The Hague, 1666.

Wheare, Degoraeus. *The Method and Order of Reading Both Civil and Ecclesiastical Histories, To which is Added, An Appendix* [by Nicholas Horseman] *concerning Historians of particular Nations, as well Ancient as Modern.* Trans. Edmund Bohun (London, 1685).

Wood, Anthony à. *Athenae Oxoniensis,* 4 vols. Ed. and rev. Philip Bliss. London, 1813–20.

Secondary Sources

Adams, Percy G. *Travelers and Travel Liars.* Berkeley: University of California Press, 1962.

Andersen, Jennifer, and Elizabeth Sauer, eds. *Books and Readers in Early Modern England: Material Studies.* Philadelphia: University of Pennsylvania Press, 2002.

Antoine, Régis. *Les écrivains français et les Antilles: des premiers Pères blancs aux surréalistes noirs.* Paris: Maisonneuve et Larose, 1978.

Ashcraft, Richard. "John Locke's Library: Portrait of an Intellectual." In *John Locke: Critical Assessments,* ed. Richard Ashcraft. 4 vols. London: Routledge, 1991.

Baker, J. N. L. *The History of Geography.* Oxford: Blackwell, 1963.

Baldwin, Martha. "The Snakestone Experiments: An Early Modern Medical Debate." *Isis* 86 (1995): 394–418.

Blair, Ann. "Reading Strategies for Coping for Information Overload, ca. 1550–1700." *Journal of the History of Ideas* 64 (2003): 11–28.

——. *The Theater of Nature: Jean Bodin and Renaissance Science.* Princeton: Princeton University Press, 1997.

Bonno, Gabriel. *Les relations intellectuelles de Locke avec la France.* Berkeley: University of California Press, 1955.

Bowen, Margarita. *Empiricism and Geographical Thought: From Francis Bacon to Alexander von Humboldt.* Cambridge: Cambridge University Press, 1981.

Boxer, C. R. *João de Barros: Portuguese Humanist and Historian of Asia.* New Delhi: Concept Publishing Co., 1981.

Carey, Daniel. "Compiling Nature's History: Travellers and Travel Narratives in the Early Royal Society." *Annals of Science* 54 (1997): 269–92.

——. "Henry Neville's *The Isle of Pines* (1668): Travel, Forgery and the Problem of Genre." *Angelaki* 1:2 (1993/4): 23–39.

——. *Locke, Shaftesbury, and Hutcheson: Contesting Diversity in the Enlightenment and Beyond.* Forthcoming, Cambridge: Cambridge University Press.

Cavallo, Guglielmo, and Roger Chartier, eds. *A History of Reading in the West,* trans. Lydia G. Cochrane. Cambridge: Polity Press, 1999.

Cranston, Maurice. *John Locke: A Biography.* 1957. Reprinted Oxford: Oxford University Press, 1985.

Crone, G. R., and R. A. Skelton, "English Collections of Voyages and Travels, 1625–1846." In *Richard Hakluyt and His Successors,* ed. Edmund Lynam. London: Hakluyt Society, 1946.

Cruysse, Dirk Van Der. *Siam and the West 1500–1700.* Trans. Michael Smithies. Chiang Mai: Silkworm, 2002.

Dewhurst, Kenneth. *John Locke (1632–1704) Physician and Philosopher: A Medical Biography. With an Edition of the Medical Notes in his Journals.* London: Welcome Historical Medical Library, 1963.

Gilbert, Edmund W. *British Pioneers in Geography.* Newton Abbot, Devon: David & Charles, 1972.

Grafton, Anthony. *Commerce with the Classics: Ancient Books and Renaissance Readers.* Ann Arbor: University of Michigan Press, 1997.

Harrison, John R. *The Library of Isaac Newton.* Cambridge: Cambridge University Press, 1978.

Harrison, John, and Peter Laslett. *The Library of John Locke.* 2nd ed. Oxford: Clarendon Press, 1971.

Hunter, Michael. *Establishing the New Science.* Woodbridge, Suffolk: Boydell, 1989.

Johns, Adrian. *The Nature of the Book: Print and Knowledge in the Making* (Chicago: University of Chicago Press, 1998), chap. 4.

———. "Reading and Experiment in the Early Royal Society." In *Reading, Society and Politics in Early Modern England,* ed. Kevin Sharpe and Steven N. Zwicker. Cambridge: Cambridge University Press, 2003.

Kiessling, Nicolas K. *The Library of Robert Burton.* Oxford: Oxford Bibliographical Society, 1988.

Lindsay, Robert O. "Pierre Bergeron: A Forgotten Editor of French Travel Literature." *Terrae Incognitae* 7 (1976): 31–38.

Lough, John. "Locke's Reading during His Stay in France." *The Library,* 5th ser., 8 (1953): 229–58.

Markley, Robert. "Riches, Power, Trade and Religion: The Far East and the English Imagination, 1600–1720." In *Asian Travel in the Renaissance,* ed. Daniel Carey. Oxford: Blackwell, 2004.

Mayhew, Robert. "Mapping Science's Imagined Community: Geography as a Republic of Letters, 1600–1800." *British Journal for the History of Science* 38:1 (2005): 73–92.

Mervaud, Michel. "Diderot et l'*Agnus Scythicus:* le mythe et son histoire." *Studies on Voltaire and the Eighteenth Century* (2003:01): 65–103.

Milton, J. R. "Dating Locke's *Second Treatise.*" *History of Political Thought* 16:3 (1995): 356–90.

———. "Locke at Oxford." In *Locke's Philosophy: Content and Context,* ed. G. A. J. Rogers. Oxford: Clarendon Press, 1994.

Parker, Kenneth. "Telling Tales: Early Modern English Voyagers and the Cape of Good Hope." *The Seventeenth Century* 10:1 (1995): 121–49.

Rostenberg, Leona. *The Library of Robert Hooke: The Scientific Book Trade of Restoration England.* Santa Monica: Modoc Press, 1989.

Shapin, Steven. *A Social History of Truth: Civility and Science in Seventeenth-Century England.* Chicago: University of Chicago Press, 1994.

Sharpe, Kevin. *Reading Revolutions: The Politics of Reading in Early Modern England.* New Haven: Yale University Press, 2000.

Strauss, Emanuel. *Dictionary of European Proverbs.* 3 vols. London: Routledge, 1994.

Tilley, Morris Palmer. *Dictionary of the Proverbs in England in the Sixteenth and Seventeenth Century.* Ann Arbor: University of Michigan Press, 1950.

Trakulhun, Sven. "The Widening of the World and the Realm of History: Early European Approaches to the Beginnings of Siamese History, c.1500–1700." In *Asian Travel in the Renaissance,* ed. Daniel Carey. Oxford: Blackwell, 2004.

Van Strien, C. D. *British Travellers in Holland during the Stuart Period: Edward Browne and John Locke as Tourists in the United Provinces.* Leiden: Brill, 1993.

J. G. A. Pocock

The Treaty Between Histories

I

This essay is written by an expatriate New Zealander who lives elsewhere and works on other histories but finds one of the starting points of his historical imagination in the New Zealand of the early middle twentieth century; specifically in the 1940s and the imagery of "island and time . . . not in narrow seas" then being presented. From this point and from others, he has developed a concern with the formation of histories—"formation" rather than "construction" or "invention," in the belief that highly complex patterns of experience are involved in their making—and the role of these histories in the formation of peoples, particularly the oceanic and island-inhabiting. At one level, this essay is part of a project of constructing a politics of historiography: that is, an enquiry into what it may mean to say of a political society and its people that it possesses a history, and that it contains the activity of writing and rewriting it.[1] At another level this essay is concerned with the writing and rewriting, and the articulation by means antecedent to writing, of histories in Aotearoa New Zealand, those which have been consequent on the reactivation of the Treaty of Waitangi.[2] Originally signed by Maori chiefs (*rangatira*) and representatives of the British Crown in

1840, this Treaty has become the basis for claims by Maori against the Crown (now identified with the government of New Zealand as a sovereign state), heard by a Tribunal whose judgments do not bind parliament or the courts of law but are read as morally obliging them. This essay originally appeared in a volume exploring the re-writing of history—both Pakeha and Maori—that now became necessary.

This reactivation is in itself an extraordinary process. In Canada and the United States—but not, it would seem, in Australia—indigenous peoples (first nations, aborigines, *tangata whenua*) are able to allege treaty rights formed by treaty with a self-creating federal authority and to claim "sovereignty" in some sense of that word on the grounds that their occupation of the land, and so their existence as "nations" or "peoples" antedates the formation of the state, and the now-dominant settler people, or Pakeha, with whom they entered into treaty. What is certainly unusual and apparently unique about the situation in Aotearoa New Zealand is that the Treaty of Waitangi was entered into by certain *hapu*—and by subsequent extension nearly all others—before there existed a settler majority, and that the *hapu* contracted with the British Crown as part of the process by which that Crown established its sovereignty over Te Ika a Maui and Te Wai Pounamu[3] and set about the organization of those islands as what became the sovereign state of New Zealand. The instrument by which that sovereignty was established taking the form of a treaty, it is now possible to allege breaches or failures to fulfill that treaty as claims against the sovereign itself and even against the legitimacy of its sovereignty, once the latter is acknowledged as conditional on observance of the Treaty as drawn up in 1840 and as now interpreted. In seeking to satisfy the justifiable claims of the *tangata whenua* (now a numerical minority), New Zealand—a unitary state and not a federation—has reached the brink of proclaiming its own sovereignty conditional upon a treaty that now approaches the stature of a fundamental law, contract of government, and ancient constitution. These are acts of conceptualisation that a professional student of English and British history in the seventeenth century and after cannot fail to find interesting.

On the one hand a treaty is a process of discussion and negotiation by which an agreement among or between those entitled to act for themselves is reached or subsequently modified. On the other hand—as for instance the names Treaty of Westphalia and Treaty of Waitangi illustrate—it is the product of that process. A treaty implies the presence of contracting parties; and if such a treaty is to be recognized as valid in a universe of law among states, the parties must be in possession of sovereignty, or enough of what is conveyed by the multiple and fluid meanings of that term, to make the treaty intelligible and binding in the eyes of both parties, of their posterity, and of other actors in the universe of international law. At Waitangi there occurred an encounter between inhabitants of two cultures, one possessed of a complex and sophisticated language of law, sovereignty and state, the other of a language no less sophisticated but ordering its moral universe in very different terms.[4] Since the former believed itself to possess, and afterwards acquired, a politically and morally dominant position, it felt entitled—but was at the same time necessitated—to determine the degree and character of the other's possession of the sovereignty necessary to a treaty-making capacity. It can plausibly be argued that the British actions of 1840 pursued a double and deceptive strategy: on the one hand attributing to Maori enough sovereignty to make them capable of entering into a treaty, on the other denying them—what indeed they did not possess—the sovereignty of a fully formed state, so that the Treaty could subsequently be denied the binding force of law. The revalidation of the Treaty can be seen as the liquidation of this strategy. It is important to realize, however, that the statements in which the strategy seems to consist—those made by Lord Glenelg on the one hand (recognizing Maori capacity), and Chief Justice Prendergast on the other (denying it)—are not only juridical and normative statements, but historical; they entail statements by the British about where the Maori stand in a historical process constructed by the British, and about where the British themselves stand in the same process.[5]

These statements are in an obvious way self-serving, but like most statements made in the complex and devious history of political discourse, they are not simple. They are not fully at the command of those who make them; our language is produced by history, and contains tensions, ambivalences, and contradictions deposited in it by processes occurring in the past. This is an anti-postmodernist statement; the proposition that language refers to nothing but itself is dismissed as an ignoble dream of subjectivity, and countered by the proposition that things have happened in the past, have been experienced and registered in language, and that the historical intelligence can scrutinize language in search of processes and events that have gone toward making it what it is. Without the proposition that things have happened and are still happening, with which we attempt to deal through the medium of speech, the Treaty debate in Aotearoa New Zealand of course makes no sense.

It is a cardinal rule of historical interpretation that any document will reveal more than its author intended it to convey. There are, broadly speaking, two reasons for this. One is that the author's language was molded by the conditions of the world it was shaped in—both with and without the author's knowledge—and can be made to yield information about those circumstances that it may or may not have been the author's intention to convey. Another is the inherent contestability and ambivalence of language itself, and of public language in particular. Political speech is a language in which past conflicts have been partially resolved; it contains the history of past conflicts and the possibility of future conflicts. Politicians and lawyers know this, and so do rhetoricians and poets: they are highly capable and often aware of speaking with forked tongues, of being read and heard in ways that convey more than one set of factual and value judgments. To discover that political speech is like this may lead to the making of historical statements, but may also oblige one to make decisions and judgments in the present. We may exploit the ambivalence of past language either to discover what its past users may have meant in their time, or to determine what we find it practically expedient to interpret them as having meant. It is probably inexpedient politically, as it certainly is morally, to disregard the discipline of history to the point of making them have meant what it is historically impossible that they could have meant.[6] However, the history of what a past statement meant is not altogether incompatible with the political decision that it shall be interpreted in a certain way in the present. Thus we interpret the Treaty of Waitangi as entailing obligations to do things that were not done, and we rewrite the history of Aotearoa New Zealand as a history of the nonperformance of these obligations. We cannot write history—including that of the making of the Treaty itself—exclusively as the record of how that was not done which ought to have been done, and that done which ought not to have been done; but by proceeding in this way we rediscover many grievances that did arise, and were perceived as arising, from nonperformance described in these terms, as well as occasions on which some actors knew very well that they were transgressing what could be considered obligations.[7] There are such people as scoundrels, and there are scoundrelly actions performed by those who did not acknowledge that they were scoundrels. The historical interpretation of documents is one way of uncovering such actions and their performers.

It is therefore important to possess means of exploring the language—both the language of enactment and the language of apologetics and ideology—employed by Pakeha both before and in 1840, and down to and past 2000, in search of what it could have meant, what it was made to mean, and made its users mean, and what it may now be held to have meant as we rehearse the past for legislative purposes. There will be differences between what the historian says about past statements and actions, and what the tribunal, or more perfectly the legislator, thinks it just or expedient to say about them; but these differences may not be incompatible and are acceptable so long as they are recognized for what they are. If a statute of the New Zealand Parliament declares—not in a preamble but in an enacting clause—that the invasion of the Waikato was unjustified, a historian who wishes to complicate or contest the statement is required only to recognize that it is the policy of the state to proceed on that contestable assumption.[8] The contestability of history is not denied; we have to live in it.

In the preceding paragraph, attention has been focused on the English language as employed for governmental purposes by Pakeha in New Zealand over the last two centuries, and two assumptions have been made about it. One is that it was and is highly, self-consciously, and methodically contestable, so that much history consists in the exploration of its ambivalences; the other, so far less explicit but very much present, is that it has contained and relied upon a tissue of historical statements and narratives concerning its own history, the history of the British, and that of the Pakeha state and people, and—though this we have hardly seen yet—the history of human society as those using this language have chosen to perceive it. The question may—or rather might—next be asked whether these assumptions, or others like them, should be applied to the study of *te reo Maori* (the Maori language) as it existed in 1840 or exists in 2001: was, or is, it a language formed to contest its own premises, or a language organized to construct what may be meant by a history? For a Pakeha writer like the present one, it may be more important to ask these questions than to attempt answers to them. Those who use *te reo Maori*—for that matter, those who use English as an instrument of Maori culture—are not only the best qualified to expound their own language; they have a good claim to prior authority when speaking in or about it, and expecting others to attend to what they are saying. Subject to that, Pakeha are going to hear language used by Maori; they are going to be affected by it and obliged to respond to it; they are entitled to ask for assistance in knowing what they hear and how they may and may not reply. The questions outlined are therefore worth asking; but before pursuing them, it is important to be clear about the roles of both language and history in a relation between peoples such as that set up by our modern understanding of the Treaty of Waitangi.

II

A treaty, in the European language of the law of nations—*jus gentium*—is drawn up between sovereigns encountering one another in a universe governed by no state or superstate. This universe used to be called "the state of nature" and in it the relation between sovereigns must be that of either peace or war; as the Declaration of Independence of 1776 put it, they were "enemies in war" (a condition that the Declaration proclaimed current), "in peace friends" (a condition to which it looked in future). A treaty was a *foedus*, and might be no more than a temporary accommodation; or it might establish a more permanent relationship, a confederacy, confederation, or federation, in which case there arose the question whether the public law of such an association was enforceable by a treaty-generated authority superior to the sovereign authorities entering into it, or by their conjoint sovereign wills alone. At this point, the treaty between sovereigns in international law resembles the contract of government in natural law, whereby autonomous individuals transfer authority to a sovereign civil government. The Treaty of Waitangi combines elements of both compacts, which is how it has come to be seen as constituting a sovereign political community in which Maori possess (as Australian Aboriginals do not) claims deriving from a *jus gentium* to which they were admitted in order to draw up a treaty and enter on a civil society.

There is a role for history implicit in any concept of sovereignty. A sovereign community will normally—at least in Euro-international perceptions of what constitutes normality—possess and deploy a history of what its sovereignty is, how it has come to be, and what explains and legitimizes its existence. If it sees itself as one among a number of sovereign communities, there will be a history of its encounters with others of its kind, and there may be a general or "universal" history of human political society in which the formation and fortunes of such sovereign communities is held to be a normal or a dominant feature of a historical process. At the same time, the "sovereignty" of such a community will begin to appear identical with its power to manage and indeed create its "history": to initiate and maintain its existence and to construct a record and narrative of how it has done so. This narrative is not at all likely to be one of undisturbed normality and satisfaction; it is likely to record various contestations and conflicts that may have been accommodated but are still going on—between the community itself and others adjacent to it, and between the members of the community and those included in its society but excluded from its citizenship or a share in its authority. Such a political history will be agonistic; to be excluded from the community is to be excluded from the *agoneia* and its history; but conflicts entail other conflicts, and citizenship, with its history, may be enlarged and transformed in the attempt to resolve them.

If two sovereigns enter into a treaty, including one by which the two sovereignties are modified or transformed by entering into a durable association, each will bring to the treaty, and retain after it, a history of its own that recounts and justifies the sovereignty by which it has entered into the treaty, and that it must continue to relate and enact if it is to survive as a sovereign (that is a self-affirming) entity or community after entering into the association. There will be at least two such histories—almost certainly more, taking into account the probable complexity of each historic community, the recorded conflicts among its members, and the imperfectly repressed or silenced histories of those excluded from membership—and each must be recorded and must be perceived as still being enacted. We must find room for the concept of a treaty between histories, each being recognized as performed by sovereigns in an increasingly complex and problematic associative sovereignty; and the exercise of sovereignty will entail the narrating and performing of histories in an intimate negotiation with one another. A treaty such as that at Waitangi is now considered to have become a device for the continuation of histories in a contested association; and if history be defined as the exercise of sovereignty, the sovereignty instituted by such a treaty is perpetually contested in a history of contestation.

In these circumstances it is both useful and important to look at the parties to the Treaty in 1840, and ask the questions: what kinds of sovereignty did they possess, and in what kinds of history did they enact the signing of the Treaty? There is an obvious danger of ethnocentricity; "sovereignty" and "history" are both Pakeha words, and we have noted a strategy by which the former was ascribed to Maori with one hand and denied to them with the other. We need to be cautious about the employment of the latter term as well as the former. Nevertheless there is a family of words—*kawanatanga, rangatiratanga, tikanga, mana*—used to assert a Maori capacity to manage their own affairs and to exist in a universe that explains and legitimizes Maori identity as a people possessing that capacity; and these words are used in claiming "sovereignty" as a term in some of its English-language meanings, which they heavily reinforce and modify. It is therefore possible to enquire after the "history" inherent in the Maori universe, both before and after contact, Treaty, dispossession, recovery and the other constituents of their "history" since 1769; meaning by the former usage (a) the temporal extensions of that universe, (b) the ways of performing, recording, and narrating actions authoritative in that universe, of which the Treaty as Maori saw and enacted it will have been one. We must warn ourselves, however, that "history" is a heavily freighted Pakeha term that we may never be able to separate from its Pakeha meanings, and that to include Maori in it may be no less an attempt at domination than to exclude them from it.

Our question, therefore, must be open to answer in Maori terms, which may not be compatible with the terms in which it is put. It is a consequence of "the treaty between histories" that "history" becomes not only negotiable but contestable; and negotiation is often conducted by competitive exclusion of items from negotiation.

III

For a Pakeha writer, it is easiest to elaborate upon Pakeha perceptions of history, to deal with them first and proceed from them to other perceptions that one understands less immediately. This of course incurs, and may not altogether avoid, the danger that one will find oneself using them as the norm by which other perceptions are to be understood and judged, or otherwise placing them in a position of dominance. Indeed, so long as there persist significant inequalities of power between Pakeha and Maori, this danger cannot be eliminated, since the conditions necessary for placing the opposed sets of perceptions on a footing of even academic and theoretical equality may not exist and cannot be taken for granted. It may be best to proceed in the order of one's understanding, to incur the risks, and look for ways out of the dilemma.

The Anglo-European culture that reached Aotearoa and began settling New Zealand between 1769 and 1840 was well equipped with historiographies that operated in a number of ways. There was, as has already appeared, a common-law jurisprudence that looked to the past for authoritative precedents, evidence of ancient usage, and the identity of the persons primarily wronged or dispossessed. This was an extremely powerful tool for ordering the past to the requirements of the Crown and its courts seeking to detect and remedy grievances and claims, but it differed from a historical method that from early modern times was built up in Europe from sources of which common-law jurisprudence was only one. The European historical method may be described as one of contextualization. It consisted in compiling evidence, predominantly philological and archaeological in character, suggesting states of language, culture, and society existing at various points in the past, and offering to show how words, actions, beliefs, and behaviour recorded in the past might be reinterpreted in the contexts thus reconstructed.[9] Because this method had developed its own techniques of falsification and verification, and because its objectives differed from those of the common law, it could lay claim to autonomy and perhaps objectivity, meaning independence from the practical purposes for which the past was studied in the present. The method of contextualization itself revealed, however, that this independence of practice was easier to claim than to achieve, and might never be attained in absolute purity. Historians sometimes knew this when philosophers were accusing them of not knowing or disregarding it. The Waitangi Tribunal and professional historians have been known to differ along this line of cleavage between jurisprudence and history; Maori claimants have been known to differ from them both, and from each other. All perceptions of history have political consequences, and the claim that historical method is indifferent to its consequences in practice has consequences for that practice.

The common-law mind (as the present writer once perhaps rashly called it) had played a part in building up a narrative of English constitutional history of sovereign importance (the adjective is more than an emphatic) to Pakeha settlers and the history they imposed on Aotearoa in the course of making it New Zealand. Now known as "the Whig interpretation of history," this narrative recounted how a parliament called into being by the Crown had used its final authority in declaring or altering the common law by statute to achieve an absolute incorporation of Crown and Parliament with one another.[10] By 1840 this incorporation had attained a sovereignty almost independent of the common-law jurisprudence whose version of history it presupposed and continued to recount. Law and its history could only be what the Crown in Parliament (or in its courts) declared them to be, and the authority of Crown in Parliament could be limited by neither fundamental law nor historical precedent. It was this view of history on which Chief Justice Prendergast relied in denying that the Treaty was a treaty or that it set limits to the Crown's authority to interpret or recognize it.[11]

Subsequent to 1840, Pakeha settlers became a majority of the population, and affirmed a further chapter of the "Whig interpretation," which remains of central importance to them. In this narrative the incorporation of Crown and Parliament has been repeated under New

Zealand conditions, so that the authority of the Crown and the authority of a majority in a democratically elected Parliament have become one and the same, each being exercised with the consent and by the authority of the other. This is not a Lockean formula. There has never occurred a moment at which the government of the Crown has been dissolved and power has reverted to the people, who have then exercised their prerogative to retain the Crown in being. The legislative sovereignty of the Crown has become the legislative sovereignty of Parliament (and perhaps the people embodied in it), and in Prendergast's mind—as Paul McHugh has shown—this sovereignty is not bound by anything occurring in its past history; history is nothing more than the record of its assumption of its sovereignty.[12] This narrative has been, and to all appearances must remain, of great significance to *te iwi Pakeha;* it is their *waka,* their record of how they came to be where and who they are, their narrative of how they came to be a parliamentary democracy; and they have been reluctant to admit that their autonomy, their government of themselves, is limited by obligations the Crown incurred before they existed as a people or the Crown became incorporate with them.[13] The Treaty narrative, however, affirms that the Crown was present in Aotearoa before they were and before it became New Zealand, and that at that time the Crown entered into a treaty with Maori, conveying obligations valid by the law of nations, that have been incurred by them as the Crown has become indistinguishable from their democratic will. Against the confident positivism of Prendergast, this narrative affirms a history that sovereignty cannot undo. This history is Tory in the sense that Crown precedes people—before Abraham was, I am—and it could hardly be undone by the proclamation of a republic in the twenty-first century. A dissolution of government entails a reversion of power to the people, but would confront Aotearoa New Zealand with the fact of itself as two peoples, associated in a Treaty relationship in which the Crown is a necessary mediator. Maori entered into a treaty with the Crown before there was a parliament or a people; whatever has been the history of that relationship, it is easy to understand why Maori republicans are thin on the ground. The Treaty commits the Pakeha to a history that is theirs, but not theirs to rewrite.

IV

In 1769, the year of Cook's landfall, Europeans were possessed of a complex set of understandings of human society as they knew it, which they employed both to dominate others and to understand themselves.[14] Since their culture was expanding through oceanic navigation to encounter and initially to rule most others on the planet—and is still doing so—these two objectives cannot be separated, but they are in a complex relationship and modify one another. Recent writings have examined the role of an Enlightened "stadial theory" of the history of human society, in which, in distinguishable stages, hunter-gatherers were succeeded by shepherds and then by agriculturalists and merchants. It has been explained that this theory was founded on Eurasian evidence, and failed to apply in the Americas and Oceania, where neither the domestication of hoofed mammals on pasture, nor the cultivation of grains on arable soil, had played a dominant part. The theory was nevertheless applied, with the result that many human societies that did not fit the pattern were relegated to the category of hunter-gatherers or "savages," and denied the capacity to develop property rights, civil government, or commerce. The colonial history of Australia and New Zealand, however, parts company sharply at the point where Aboriginals are deemed hunter-gatherers, whose land is *terra nullius* and cannot be the source of right or law, whereas Maori are judged to have begun to appropriate land and develop civil government, and so to be capable of entering upon a treaty though not of claiming to enforce it.[15] The ambivalence of this judgement—the assertion of both Maori capacity and incapacity—lies at the base of all Treaty history. It provides the material for assertions of sovereignty by both sides in subsequent debate; and the continuing debate, partly because it cannot erase the fact of the original judgement, is in principle capable of no end.

A doctrine—in this case a grand narrative of history—that serves to dominate others is also an instrument that the dominators use to understand and debate with themselves; and it is vital to comprehend that they do not understand themselves solely in the role of dominators. This may entail denial of that role, but it does not follow that the denial invalidates their understanding of themselves in other roles; and they may have done and suffered many things in their history that they need to understand, and continue to debate, among themselves rather than in their encounters with others. It is futile to dismiss those debates as blinkered and ethnocentric; one cannot deny that human communities need to understand themselves without denying that they have selves to understand. The Enlightened stadial narrative was formulated by west Europeans (chiefly Frenchmen and Scots), who needed to understand how barbarian and nomad invasions had acted in the transformation of a classical slave economy into feudal and then into mercantile civil society; and they needed also to understand how civil society could be stabilized to the point where it overcame the danger of religious warfare fought over the role of churches and sects that might destabilize civil government. Then, even as a new understanding developed, between 1769 and 1840 Europe passed through the unexpected experience of wars of revolution that replaced the wars of religion.

To the Europeans who became the Pakeha, therefore, history—as understood by the unlearned when they thought about it, as well as by the learned whose business was to think—was not simply a reassuring narrative that enclosed itself, but a record of contestation, not only between seekers after power and survival, but between images, ideas, principles, and values. The most triumphalist whiggisms knew that they had had adversaries and might have others; Europe's was an adversarial and rhetorical culture in which every narrative could be told again and told differently. In some perceptions it was this deeply divided culture that Europeans were imposing upon others; why, Voltaire joined the K'ang-hsi emperor in wondering, did Christian missionaries expect the Chinese to attend to their theological disputes?[16] But Voltaire did not have much hope of reducing his own culture to one of philosophical indifference; and there was—perhaps there still is—the alternative of saying that precisely because European culture had been the victim of terrible and sometimes absurd internal divisions, of belief as well as interest, only Europeans understood or possessed the freedom that came of confronting these choices and overcoming them. Precisely at the points where their philosophers hated their own culture, Europeans acquired a capacity for living in a contested history, bringing them the power and perhaps the right to impose that history on the inert "oriental" or the innocent "savage;" self-criticism generated its own complacency and became an instrument of domination. The non-European might be faced with the alternatives of making choices imposed by others, or re-establishing a world in which they did not have to be made.

There was an alternative to this self-condemning yet self-exalting historicism; the whole enterprise of "history"—on which perhaps only Europeans had embarked—could be condemned as a departure from "nature," in which alone human beings had been happy, whereas in "history" they were condemned to pursue a happiness that they would never attain. Europeans had learned from Rousseau—as is evident in the journals of James Cook or the tragedy of Marion du Fresne[17]—to consider it the burden, and the duty, of the individual to be alienated from one's own society and to envy those who had not abandoned nature for the unhappiness of history. Here there arose the image of the "noble" or at least the happy "savage:" the noun denoting that he had never appropriated land or involved himself in the paradoxical divisiveness of society, the adjective that he had escaped alienation from his extra-historical essence. Maori laid little claim to this condition of unwarlike innocence, and it was a premise of the Treaty of Waitangi that they were "not savages living by the chase," but had embarked upon the appropriation of land, the erection of a civil government, and (though this was not stated) the enhancement of a considerable capacity for warfare (the state of war being the antithesis of a state of treaty).[18] Nevertheless, in making claims under the Treaty and explaining how an intimate relation with the land (*mana whenua*) arose and existed in pre-contact culture, Maori allege with justice the existence and survival of a view of the world that Pakeha thinking once ascribed to the "noble savage," and are still inclined to ascribe to "indigenous" peoples whom Pakeha view as their own antiselves. The concept of history now becomes problematic to both sets of participants in the debate, and the element of contestability takes on a new dimension.

V

Maori as participants in this debate need to articulate—to one another and to other participants—their understanding of sovereignty, or of whatever term in either language they wish to employ in its stead; and

Pakeha need to understand their employment of the term, or rather the limits within which Pakeha may expect to understand it. It is an essential feature of all communication that it takes place between actors who do not fully understand one another, and of all communication between communities that each is addressing its own members as much as members of the other. Each, that is to say, needs to speak its own language and discourse in order to assure its members that it continues to exist and make its own history; but it also wishes to convey messages to the other, which the latter must understand even if the understanding is imposed by the primary speaker. The other is entitled both to ask for means of understanding the messages conveyed, and to employ its own language and self-understanding in interpreting them. Translations must therefore be negotiated, and we have need of the concept of a treaty between languages, or more precisely between language groups. On the assumption being used here—that every autonomous or sovereign entity must both articulate and enact a history—there is need also of the concept of a treaty between histories, as they are used in speech and as they are enacted in decisions.

Translation is a mixed blessing, and also a necessity. A notoriously imperialist English poet once wrote:

> The men of my own stock,
> They may do ill or well,
> But they tell the lies I am used to hear,
> They are used to the lies I tell,
> And we do not need interpreters
> When we go to buy and sell.
> The men of my own stock,
> Bitter bad they may be,
> But they know what I think of them
> And I know what they think of me.[19]

It is an unfortunate truth that these verses, in which there is much wisdom, go on to incite English-speaking Canadians to exclude Chinese immigrants; a fact tending to reinforce the self-destructive liberalism that insists that one cannot affirm an identity without creating an Other, about whom one makes statements both unjust to the latter and distorting of one's own self. But the politics of multiculturalism entail knowing that there is risk of paranoia and avoiding it; we need only know that this will be difficult. The condition of not needing interpreters is a valuable human liberty—when it is appropriate and available, which may not be very often. Much of what is best in conservative political philosophy amounts to an assertion of the value, even the necessity, of codes of conduct shared so fully that they do not need, and may not be susceptible of, constant explication; but situations constantly arise in a morally ambivalent world that require that the implicit must be rendered explicit.[20] When two communities, and consequently two languages or discourses, are in contact, the complexity of the situation is multiplied; language that should remain implicit must be not merely explicated but translated, and the politics of translation are seen to entail acts of power, in circumstances where power may already be most inequitably distributed. Since, too, we live in a globalized world where language is instantly distributed among many actors, there is serious danger of the translators and interpreters becoming more powerful, though not more valuable, than they ought to be. We look for ways in which language users may negotiate the terms on which they speak to one another, and the negotiators may remain in charge of the negotiation.

In the Treaty negotiation here set out as a model, we suppose Maori articulating a perception of sovereignty, in some sense or other of that term, which they affirm they brought to the Treaty and may still use in assessing how far the Crown has fulfilled an understanding to respect it. That perception may be said to have existed in two "histories": one that of the peoples of Aotearoa before, and at the moment of, contact with Europeans; the other that of the Maori people of New Zealand, a history shared with Pakeha settlers, in which many things have occurred that the Treaty is now being used to evaluate. The history, or rather the existence in what is perceived as history, of the pre-contact *tangata whenua* is therefore important; not the least because it supplies a language that Maori speak among themselves, use in making claims against the Pakeha, and affirm that the Treaty guarantees (and has failed to guarantee) to them. The problem arises that this language, and the view of the world that it entails, differ so sharply from what is implicit in Pakeha discourse that it may be asked at some point whether they entail a concept of "history" in any sense intertranslatable with Pakeha use of that term.

We have seen that Europeans in 1769–1840 conceived of both sovereignty and history as grounded in the appropriation of land, by procedures agricultural, commercial and increasingly capitalist. They conceded to Maori some capacity for appropriation and government, but did not recognize their capacity for agriculture and commerce (though in fact Maori were in their own way acquiring both). In response, Maori have affirmed, and are still affirming, that they acquired a relationship with land through an imaginative self-shaping around the linked concepts of *mana* and *whenua,* constructing statements of the order "the land is ours; we are the land's" by means of tradition, *whakapapa,* and significant narrative and myth; so that *poiesis* becomes an effective form of appropriation. Pakeha do not find this hard to understand, but they find it hard to enter into its discourse, to relate it to discourse of their own—on those occasions when they have sincerely tried to do so—or to understand the view of the world that it entails. It has seemed to them the thinking of an animist culture—one should add high and sophisticated rather than "primitive" or "barbaric"—in which the spiritual substance of the individual is connected with that of the universe by way of one's ancestors and their *whenua,* so that there are rhythms and patterns within which conflicts and resolutions are contained. In this universe, they are tempted to say, there is rhythm but not history; pasts may be narrated, but do not rest on radical conflicts of value, and there can be no such thing as the radical alienation from accepted values that obliges the individual to construct new systems. Here the voice of Rousseau may be heard asking whether the life in nature is not to be preferred; but the basic myths of European civilization begin from the expulsion from Eden and the fall of Troy, after which moral catastrophes occur—Cain and Abel, Orestes and Clytemnestra—that no *utu* can resolve and that necessitate the construction of new moral systems, themselves far from unproblematic. At this point the Pakeha is tempted to say that he lives in history and that the noble shaman (who has replaced the noble savage) does not, thus lacking the capacity to criticize his own culture. The Pakeha has at times been guilty of the supreme complacency of claiming to possess the only critical culture, entitling him to rule those who do not criticize, and therefore cannot rule, themselves. But even when willing to abandon this claim, he needs to ask what is being said to, and of, his still-powerful culture and his claim to self-criticism, by those articulating ideologies of their own. It may be that the encounter between "history" and that which is not history in the Pakeha sense merely reduplicates the encounter between values that he recognizes as "history."

Maori today are ready and entitled to assert that an animist and holistic view of the universe, the land, and human existence prevailed among their ancestors in Aotearoa before contact and remains basic to their culture in Aotearoa New Zealand under the Treaty. They appear to make use of this world view in several ways. It is integral to the discourse by which they lay claim to occupancy of the land on the bases of *whakapapa* and *poiesis;* it is integral to the culture in which the Treaty is read as guaranteed to them; and in so far as they have lost it and been deprived of the means of maintaining it, they claim it as one of the losses for which compensation is due. We may think of it as a history that has been lost, but which they empower themselves to recover by reciting the history of its loss. But the question remains: is it a history as Pakeha use that term or may be induced to extend its meanings? Te Maire Tau has contended that *matauranga Maori*—the language in which this world view is articulated—is not a history but an *episteme:* a system of speech designed to organize knowledge in a certain way, of which a dimension of history, assuming it to possess one, is not more than part.[21] To reformulate it as a series of statements about Maori history, he says, would be destructive of it, both in the sense that to do so would relegate *matauranga Maori* to a pre-contact past, and in the sense that it would assimilate Maori thinking to categories of historicity that are of Pakeha formulation and have been imposed on Maori by Pakeha action. Tau is aware that this may be what is going to happen, but his position is not immeasurably remote from the more radical contentions of Linda Tuhiwai Smith and others, who have contended that history, anthropology, and all disciplines that offer to examine a culture from outside are or have been instruments of domination, employed by those for whom knowing (or claiming to know) a culture is a means of ruling it.[22]

There is a hard core of truth in this. To know, or rather to say, anything about me is an act of power on your part; minimally, it extends your consciousness to cover mine. My only recourse is to say, and seek to know, something about you, thus hoping to equalize an exchange of power between us; but if the power relations existing among us are otherwise radically unequal, one of us—in this case me—will be at a disadvantage. Placing the discipline of history at the center of the argument, we must add that the only remedy is the establishment of a Habermasian ideal open society in which I am as free to write your history as you are to write mine, and each of us enjoys equal freedom to respond to the writing of his history by the other.[23] This ideal, however, is hard to realize for many reasons, one of which is that the history of every community serves two purposes and is recounted in two ways. In the first instance, it is recounted to its own members and is best understood by them because they know what is implicit and presumed in it; they are the "men of my own stock" who "do not need interpreters." Only in the second instance is it recounted to others and about others, becoming the record of dealings with them and opening up the possibilities that they may have histories of their own to recount, in which the history of the primary community is recounted in the others' own way. Once this has happened—and it may have happened because the primary community has annexed the secondary community and its history—there might be limits to the extent to which any community can or may claim to recount its history only to itself or demand that "they" attend and respond to our self-understanding, while "we" must attend and respond to their understandings both of us and of themselves. In so far as a Pakeha writer may say so, this appears to be the case even if "we" have so far been the dominated and repressed party; there does not seem to be any other way out of the situation of dominance.

If the Habermasian ideal were realized—as can never be fully the case—Maori would write Pakeha history in terms informed by Maori thinking, just as the reverse would obtain. The Pakeha, however, might observe that this would entail only historical thinking about both cultures, and that this thinking is already a characteristic of their highly historicist culture; Maori perceptions of history might amount to radical criticisms of Pakeha ways of writing it, but would not amount to a criticism of the notion of history itself. They would be claiming—and indeed they already are—that they live in a historical universe, where communities are formed by conflicts and contestations of value both within themselves and among each other; and the question would recur whether *matauranga Maori* does not presuppose a universe of another character. There have been claims to local monopolies of knowledge, where Maori culture is to be expounded only to Maori and by *matauranga Maori*, and other *epistemes* excluded; as well as claims that historical information concerning *hapu* is the property of that *hapu*, not to be disclosed unless the *hapu* authorities see fit.[24] The reasons for such claims are not only tactical. Clearly it can be to "our" advantage to refuse information, which "we" understand without needing interpreters, to others who need the interpreters whom we deny them or insist upon choosing ourselves; there is a case for holding that this was being done to the Nga Puhi chiefs at Waitangi. The issue deepens, however, when one hears of Maori who feel that certain kinds of *whakapapa*-derived information are so much part of their ancestral substance that they surrender themselves to others if they disclose them. Tactically and semiologically, they are quite right in thinking so; but this is a matter of culture, of who they are and what they have not ceased being. In the open society, we give ourselves away to one another, expecting that the power we surrender will not be misused; and we accept the implication that the selves we see ourselves as having are contingent and conditional on the perceptions, the actions, and the power of others. That appears to be the precondition of the construction of histories in the open, or multicultural society; but in saying this we are approaching a point at which "open" and "historical" appear to be interchangeable terms.

IV

There is a sternly Pakeha view of these matters—in New Zealand much associated with the writings of Peter Munz—that holds that only a fully historicized relation between cultures, in which every history is exposed to interpretation, criticism, and verification by the histories of every culture, qualifies as an open society, and that every culture in such a society must be content with a history provisional in the sense that it is constantly subject to such scrutiny.[25] Exponents of this powerful and valid position have been known to assert that a history intended only to maintain a particular society and culture in being is not history at all, but myth; and further, that *matauranga Maori* is myth in the sense that it articulates a world view formed in ancient Aotearoa by a human society that knew of the existence of no other society than itself. Exploring, settling, and conquering Europeans, with all their crimes on their heads, knew that there were many societies in the world and that one history might be challenged by another. Their offense against other peoples, including Maori, was that they excluded them from the history in which histories challenged one another; Glenelg's memorandum is a step toward including Maori, which was in many ways subsequently retracted. Maori, it might now be said, aim at inclusion in the history of multihistoricity, and the Treaty offers a means of achieving this. But they recount not only the history of the Treaty and its non-fulfilments and fulfilments; they must also bring to the debate (or treaty between histories) their own history as a people or peoples, and this is necessarily rooted in the culture and *episteme* of Aotearoa before contact, which they claim has not disappeared as a ground for argument. It therefore matters whether we hold this culture to be capable only of a mythic self-assertion, and whether we hold that myth must be altogether deconstructed and reconstructed as history. (There are of course those who hold that history is itself a myth liable to deconstruction, but it is not immediately necessary to consider them.)

Maori as well as Pakeha—though for reasons intimately theirs—need to decide whether the world view inherited from their pre-contact culture is radically unlike history or not, and what is to be done in the light of the answer. This is a question they need to decide among themselves, partly because the practical needs for an answer arise from their dealings with each other as well as with the Pakeha. The latter need to hear and respond to what Maori are saying on this matter, and at the level where there is debate about the meaning and status of "history," they find themselves possessed of power that has grown precarious. If the term means contact and conflict between cultures and value systems, it is they who imposed it on the Maori and are still in a position, recalling Glenelg's, to impose value on Maori claims to take part in it. They may assert that they have always known what history is, since their myths begin after the disruption of a mythic cosmos and—being the record of contestation over values within particular societies as well as between them—are not mere self-sustaining myths closed against criticism. In their culture it was always known what it was to be radically alienated from that culture; Marion du Fresne knew what it was even as the knowledge tragically entangled him in the transgressions of *tapu* that forced Te Kauri to kill him, but it is far from clear whether Te Kauri knew it.[26] At the risk of repeating the primary arrogance of asserting theirs to be the only self-critical and historical culture, they are obliged to ask whether Maori propose to engage in the activity of historical self-criticism, whether they propose to modify it, or whether they intend to deny its value (as a blend of postmodernism with nostalgia for the Dreamtime tempts Pakeha to do themselves). They are not entitled—by the terms of the treaty between histories—to empower themselves to judge whether Maori have entered historical discourse or not; but they need to respond in their own terms to what Maori are understood to be saying, and to separate judgment from the authority to give judgment is not an easy matter. This is one reason why there is need of a treaty between histories.

It would seem (to a Pakeha observer) that Maori are saying, and are perhaps self-obliged to say, that *matauranga Maori* is a necessary part of both their collective consciousness and their political situations; they need to assert it as a way in which they think and as a ground for their claims against the Crown. They agree that it was not, but is now, a historical contingency; that is, we are no longer in ancient Aotearoa, where it was the only *episteme* that could or did exist. Maori consequently find themselves in a world of history, and must view *matauranga Maori* in that context; but to the extent to which history was formerly imposed upon them by the Pakeha, they must now renegotiate their entry into it, and are now entitled to advance the nonhistoricity of an animist cosmos as a negotiating gambit in a treaty with history itself. This negotiation can only be recounted as a history; it is predetermined that Maori have entered history, and that they will enter it; but the terms of that entry will be and are being negotiated in a treaty to which they are parties. This negotiation, however, is not only one between Maori and Pakeha; it is one among Maori themselves, as their consciousness of who they are moves from a debate between indigenous peoples and the modern state, to one taking shape as both enter upon the postmodern and possibly posthistorical world of global capitalism, in which the settlement of their claims under the Treaty involves them, and as the Pakeha endeavor to cope with the same world in their way.

Te Maire Tau's essays may be read as debates over this problem as it appears to Maori and among them, and there are evident limits to what a Pakeha commentator may usefully say about it.[27] One or two observations may be cautiously put forward. One is that *matauranga Maori* appears (to a Pakeha eye) the ideology of a relationship through ancestors with land, but that the ancient peoples of Aotearoa were *tangata waka* as well as *tangata whenua;* they came by sea, in the sailing galleys called *waka,* and had ten or twelve centuries—a long but not a very long time—to build up *whakapapa* and connect themselves with a cosmos viewed primarily as land. It might be worth asking whether the precontact consciousness contained—as the Pakeha very differently does—the image of a remembered voyage and a cosmology of the ocean, compelling the reconstruction of cosmos as history; a modern Maori poet has written "the *waka* is a knife through time."[28] Another and more far-ranging observation is that before and after 1840, the *hapu* and *rangatira* did not by any means respond to Pakeha intrusion by retreating into a Dreamtime where only *whakapapa* counted. Relationships of a kind in which the Treaty figured were very much of their own choosing; they embraced culture contact and were not naïve about it; and there is a highly Maori history of a modernity that they debated and contested, sometimes violently, among themselves.[29] Here they inhabit history in the sense of a contestation of values and identities; Pakeha, Christianity, Treaty, and *whakapapa* are points on a parallelogram of forces from which they seek voice in determining their exit. These observations are meant to encourage the Pakeha in believing that Maori will debate their own history in a discourse to which one may be admitted by the steps one takes in entering upon someone's *marae.*

VII

As resurrected in the last quarter of the twentieth century, the Treaty of Waitangi may be imagined as instituting an ongoing negotiation, not likely to be brought to a closure, between concepts of sovereignty descended from those presented in the document of 1840. A continuing debate over the meaning of sovereignty does not so much replace, as become, the exercise of sovereignty itself, since the formal sovereign—the Crown incorporated with the Parliament and people of New Zealand—is required to hear constant challenges, both to its exercise in past and present and to the historical process by which it came into being. This debate over the nature of a state's sovereignty is not a prelude to the dissolution of that sovereignty; Aotearoa New Zealand is not situated in narrow seas, a constellation of offshore islands offered absorption into a continental empire of the market. In debating its sovereignty and rendering it debatable, the exercise of sovereignty is intensified, a significant and imaginative move in a world where sovereignty is everywhere challenged and threatened with suppression. A binational polity may be said to have reinstituted itself as a *marae,* that very Maori institution where challenge is constantly being turned into greeting and strangers into guests and fellow counselors. The situation is not idyllic but precarious; past antagonisms do not disappear when recounted, and opposed conceptions of sovereignty and history do not disappear when required to engage in negotiation. But the peoples concerned—it is a simplification to say there are two of them—have known and shaped each other for two centuries, and the antagonisms and incomprehensions between them do not altogether preclude that situation in which "they know what I think of them and I know what they think of me" and the relations between them are implicit as well as explicit. They may be imagined pursuing the state of things by recounting histories in one another's hearing.

This encounter is a treaty between histories rather than a mere dialogue, because in recounting such a history one affirms one's sovereignty and vice versa. But the treaty between histories is not a conversation in which one does not need interpreters, for the reason that a community recounts its history primarily to itself—with good cause—and only subsequently in the hearing of others; history legitimates, even when the legitimacy (and the sovereignty) can be contested from both within and without. In the history already known to the members of the community there is much that is implicit—not necessarily incontestable—and needs to be interpreted and translated when communicated to others. These may be imagined as endeavoring to connect the history they hear with one they know already, which legitimates them and their sovereignty to themselves and others; once again, the encounter must be imagined as a treaty, the proper form of an encounter between sovereigns. Like history, sovereignty comes in diverse forms; these mitigate and modify one another, and the debate among them may become a sharing of sovereignty.

At Enniscorthy in the Republic of Ireland, the Aras 98 Museum is charged with the historical exhibition of the Rising of 1798. It does not do so in simply nationalist terms or images, but presents it first as a chess game in which each piece has a voice, and then in a circular chamber in which the vertical panels display the several interpretations—rebel, Orange, Catholic, Nationalist, revisionist—of the history of 1798, while the cupola displays the words of Louis Cullen, doyen of Irish historians (and himself no neutral), to the effect that the interpretation of any complex historical event is never concluded but remains a debate. The Republic of Ireland—this tells us—is securely legitimated, by means that imply the paramountcy of one of these histories over others, to the point where it can afford to admit that its legitimacy can be interpreted and its history recounted in more ways than one; Ireland being Ireland, it does not look for a final resolution in which one master narrative absorbs the others. It will be a long time before an equivalent of Aras 98 exists in Northern Ireland, since no legitimated sovereign yet exists there, and if established will be the product of a treaty between communities whose histories have still to emerge from direct and violent conflict. There will have to be revision of both, or all, these histories; and historians—who are revisionists by vocation—aim to uphold a sovereign capable of admitting that its sovereignty has more than one history. They are not badly placed in Aotearoa New Zealand.

Notes

1. For preliminary studies, see J. G. A. Pocock, "The historian as political actor in polity, society and academy," *Journal of Pacific Studies*, 20 (1997): 89–112, and "The politics of history: the subaltern and the subversive," *Journal of Political Philosophy*, 6:3 (1998): 219–34.

2. I use "Aotearoa" to denote both the ancient world of these islands and its survival in the present day. On the history of names for New Zealand, see Tony Deverson, "From Staten Landt to Aotearoa New Zealand: the naming of 'Pacific's Triple Star'," *NZWords* 4 (New Zealand Dictionary Centre, Wellington, August 2000).

3. For these and other Maori terms, see Glossary.

4. For earlier attempts to formulate this presentation, see J. G. A. Pocock, "Law, sovereignty and history in a divided culture: the case of New Zealand and the Treaty of Waitangi," the Iredell Memorial Lecture, University of Lancaster, 1992, reprinted in *McGill Law Journal*, 43:3 (1998): 481–506; and in Pocock, *The Discovery of Islands* (Cambridge: Cambridge University Press, 2005), pp. 226–55; "Waitangi as mystery of state: some consequences of the ascription of federative capacity to the Maori," in *Political theory and the rights of indigenous peoples*, ed. Duncan Ivison, Paul Patton and Will Sanders (Melbourne: Cambridge University Press, 2000), 25–35.

5. Glenelg (Colonial Secretary), Memorandum, December 15, 1837, Colonial Office 209/2:409, quoted in P. G. McHugh, "Constitutional theory and Maori claims," in *Waitangi: Mâori and Pâkehâ perspectives of the Treaty of Waitangi*, ed. I. H. Kawharu (Auckland: Oxford University Press, 1989), 25–63 at p. 31: "They are not Savages living by the Chase, but Tribes who have apportioned the country between them, having fixed Abodes, with an acknowledged Property in the Soil, and with some rude approaches to a regular System of Government . . . therefore . . . Great Britain has no legal or moral right to establish a Colony in New Zealand, without the free consent of the natives, deliberately given, without Compulsion, and without Fraud."

6. See W. H. Oliver, "The future behind us: the Waitangi Tribunal's retrospective utopia," in *Histories, Power and Loss: uses of the past—a New Zealand commentary*, ed. Andrew Sharp and Paul McHugh (Wellington: Bridget Williams Books, 2001), 9–30.

7. See Judith Binney, "Te Umutaoroa: the earth oven of long cooking," in Sharp and McHugh, *Histories, Power and Loss*, 147–64.

8. Waikato Raupatu Claims Settlement Act 1995, No. 58, Part I—Apology by the Crown to Waikato. The context of the Act is set in Andrew Sharp, "Civil rights, amelioration and reparation in New Zealand," in *Government policies and ethnic relations in Asia and the Pacific*, ed. Michael E. Brown and Sumit Ganguly (Cambridge: MIT Press, 1997), 420–56 esp. at pp. 450–51.

9. For a summary account of the genesis of this method, see J. G. A. Pocock, *Barbarism and religion: II: narratives of civil government* (Cambridge: Cambridge University Press, 1999), 14–17.

10. J. G. A. Pocock, *The ancient constitution and the feudal law* (Cambridge: Cambridge University Press, 1957, 1987). For critical comment, see Glenn Burgess, *The politics of the ancient constitution* (London: Macmillan, 1992) and J. W. Tubbs, "Custom, time and reason: early seventeenth-century conceptions of the common law," *History of Political Thought*, 19:3 (1998): 363–406.

11. See P. G. McHugh, "A history of Crown sovereignty in New Zealand," in Sharp and McHugh, *Histories, Power and Loss*, 188–211.

12. McHugh, "A history," n. 10.

13. I use the word *waka* to denote (a) the ships in which Polynesians reached Aotearoa, (b) the claim to descent from a particular vessel, (c) the narrative of self-formation thus constructed.

14. For this view of history as it entered the Pacific Ocean, see J. G. A. Pocock, "Tangata whenua and enlightenment anthropology," *New Zealand Journal of History*, 26:1 (1992): 28–53, reprinted in *The Shaping of History: essays from The New Zealand Journal of History*, ed. Judith Binney (Wellington: Bridget Williams Books, 2001), pp. 38–61; "Nature and history, self and other: European perceptions of world history in the age of the encounter," in *Voyages and beaches: Pacific encounters, 1769–1840*, ed. Alex Calder, Jonathan Lamb, and Bridget Orr (Honolulu: University of Hawaii Press, 1999), 25–44; Pocock, *Barbarism and religion II*, chaps. 21, 22. It has been significantly developed with relation to Waitangi by Mark Hickford, "Making territorial rights of the natives:

Britain and New Zealand, 1830–1847" (D. Phil. diss., University of Oxford, 1999), and Patrick Moloney, "Early Victorian notions of savagery and civilisation," *New Zealand Journal of History*, 35:2 (October 2001). The first modern account was that of R. L. Meek, *Social science and the ignoble savage* (Cambridge: Cambridge University Press, 1976).

15. The writings of Henry Reynolds study this point of divergence. See, for instance, his *Frontier: Aborigines, settlers and land* (Sydney: Allen and Unwin, 1987); *Aboriginal sovereignty: reflections on race, state and nation* (St. Leonards, NSW: Allen and Unwin, 1996); *Why weren't we told?: a personal search for the truth about our history* (Ringwood, Vic.: Viking, 1999).

16. Voltaire, *Siècle de Louis XIV* (1751), the concluding chapter; Pocock, *Barbarism and religion II*, 7–102.

17. See n. 26 below.

18. Lord Glenelg, Colonial Office Memorandum, December 15, 1837. See note 5 above.

19. Rudyard Kipling, "The Stranger" (1908) in *Rudyard Kipling: the complete verse*, ed. M. M. Kaye (London: Kyle Cathie, 1990), 441.

20. I think particularly here of the works of Michael Oakeshott, especially *Rationalism in politics and other essays* (first published London: Methuen, 1962; new and expanded edition, Indianapolis: Liberty Press, 1991), and *On history and other essays* (Oxford: Basil Blackwell, 1983).

21. Te Maire Tau, "Mâtauranga Mâori as an epistemology," *Te Pouhere Kôrero*, 1:1 (1999):10–23. See further, n. 27 below.

22. Linda Tuhiwai Smith, *Decolonizing methodologies: research and indigenous peoples* (London: Zed Books, and Dunedin: Otago University Press, 1999). Reviews by Peter Munz, *New Zealand Books*, 9:5 (December 1999): 6, and Anna Green, *New Zealand Journal of History*, 33:2 (1999): 251–53.

23. See e.g. Jurgen Habermas, *Moral consciousness and communicative action*, trans. C. Lenhardt and S. W. Nicholsen. (Cambridge: Polity Press, 1990), though the issue gets more complex in multicultural societies, where strategies need to be in place for cultural protection; "Struggles for recognition in the democratic constitutional state," in *Multiculturalism: examining the politics of recognition*, ed. Amy Gutmann, (Princeton: Princeton University Press, 1994).

24. A useful introduction to these claims is Angela Ballara, "Who owns Mâori tribal tradition?" *Journal of Pacific Studies*, 20 (1996): 123–37.

25. Peter Munz, *When the Golden Bough breaks: structuralism or typology?* (London: Routledge and Kegan Paul, 1973); *The shapes of time: a new look at the philosophy of history* (Middletown: Wesleyan University Press, 1977); *Our knowledge of the growth of knowledge: Popper or Wittgenstein?* (London: Routledge and Kegan Paul, 1985). More immediately, "The purity of historical method: some sceptical reflections on the current enthusiasm for the history of non-European societies," *New Zealand Journal of History*, 5:2 (1971): 1–17; "The two worlds of Anne Salmond in post-modern fancy dress," *New Zealand Journal of History*, 28:1 (1994): 60–75; and Salmond's response in the same issue; Alan Ward, "Historical Method and Waitangi Tribunal claims," in *The certainty of doubt: tributes to Peter Munz*, ed. Miles Fairburn and W. H. Oliver (Wellington: Victoria University Press, 1996): 140–56.

26. Anne Salmond, *Two Worlds: first meetings between Maori and Europeans* (Auckland: Viking, 1991), chap. 13.

27. Te Maire Tau, "Matauranga Maori as an epistemology," in Sharp and McHugh, *Histories, Power and Loss*, 61–74; "The death of knowledge; ghosts on the plains," *New Zealand Journal of History*, 35:2 (October 2001): 131–52.

28. Robert Sullivan, *Star Waka* (Auckland: Auckland University Press, 1999), 3. Cf. Michael Oakeshott, "Political education," in *Rationalism in Politics and Other Essays* (New York: Basic Books, 1962; reissued Indianapolis: Liberty Press, 1991), 60: "there is neither harbour for shelter nor floor for anchorage, neither starting-place nor appointed destination. The enterprise is to keep afloat on an even keel; the sea is both friend and enemy, and the seamanship consists in using the resources of a traditional manner of behaviour in order to make a friend of every hostile occasion."

29. See Lyndsay Head, "The pursuit of modernity in Maori society: the conceptual bases of citizenship in the early colonial period," in Sharp and McHugh, *Histories, Power and Loss*, 97–122.

Glossary of Terms

HAPU: a Maori community possessing a shared lineage.

IWI: an association of *hapu* and the lineages they may share, perhaps reaching back to a common ancestor.

KAWANATANGA: a word coined by missionaries and used in the Maori text of the Treaty. It is a phonetic equivalent of "government" and had that meaning in the minds of Crown signatories. What it meant to Maori in 1840 is much debated.

MANA: charisma, authority, power, identity.

MANA WHENUA: the authority by which land is claimed.

MARAE: the space before the meeting-house of a *hapu*, across which strangers advance, are challenged, recognized and admitted.

MATAURANGA, MATAURANGA MAORI: the body of discourse by which a people declares itself and its place in the universe.

RANGATIRA: a chief or noble person.

RANGATIRATANGA: chieftanship, the authority of chiefs. Used in the Treaty in ways held to guarantee the continued possession by Maori of their land and culture.

TANGATA WHENUA, TANGATA WAKA: *Tangata*=man, men, people. *Whenua*=placenta, birthplace, land. *Tangata whenua*=the people of the land, its first occupiers and primary sovereigns, i.e. Maori, *Waka*, see below. *Tangata waka*=peoples of the ship.

TAPU: a thing forbidden or sacred; the language or ceremony defining it.

TE IWI PAKEHA: the Pakeha people or nation. Cf. *te iwi Maori*.

TE IKA A MAUI: Maui's fish: a traditional term for the North Island of New Zealand.

TE WAI POUNAMU: The Greenstone Rivers: a traditional term for the South Island.

TE REO MAORI: the Maori language.

TIKANGA: custom and culture.

UTU: redress, justice, revenge.

WAIKATO: a river in the North Island; the district named for it; the *hapu* and *iwi* inhabiting it. Invaded by Crown and colonial forces in 1864, starting a series of wars.

WAKA: see note 13.

WHAKAPAPA: the genealogy or recital of ancestors, possibly reaching back to remote and mythic times, by which a Maori establishes his identity. Some, known as "urban Maori," have lost *whakapapa* and must establish identity by other means.

Introductory Bibliography

Binney, Judith ed. *The Shaping of History:* essays from *The New Zealand Journal of History.* Wellington: Bridget Williams Books, 2001.

Brown, Michael E., and Ganguly, Sumit eds. *Government policies and ethnic relations in Asia and the Pacific.* Cambridge, Mass.: MIT Press, 1997.

Calder, Alex, Jonathan lamb, and Bridget Orr eds. *Voyages and Beaches: Pacific encounters, 1769–1840.* Honolulu: University of Hawaii Press, 1999.

Coates, Ken, and Paul McHugh, eds. *Living Relationships: Kokiri Ngatahi: The Treaty of Waitangi in the New Millennium.* Wellington: Victoria University Press, 1998.

Durie, Mason. *Te Mana, Te Kawanatanga: The Politics of Maori Self-Determination.* Auckland: Oxford University Press, 1998.

Kawharu, I. H., ed. *Waitangi: Māori and Pākehā Perspectives on the Treaty of Waitangi.* Auckland: Oxford University Press, 1989.

McHugh, Paul. *The Maori Magna Carta: New Zealand Law and the Treaty of Waitangi.* Auckland: Oxford University Press, 1991.

Orange, Claudia. *The Treaty of Waitangi.* Wellington: Allen, and Unwin, 1988.

Pocock, J. G. A. *The Ancient Constitution and the Feudal Law: A Study of English Historical Thought in the Seventeenth Century.* Cambridge: Cambridge University Press, 1957; reissued with a retrospect, 1987.

———. *Barbarism and Religion,* volume II: *Narratives of Civil Government.* Cambridge: Cambridge University Press, 1999. (Forthcoming: volume IV: *Barbarians, Savages and Empires.*)

———. *The Discovery of Islands: essays in British History.* Cambridge: Cambridge University Press, 2005.

Sharp, Andrew. *Justice and the Maori.* 2nd ed. Auckland: Oxford University Press, 1997.

Sharp, Andrew, and Paul McHugh, eds. *Histories, Power and Loss: uses of the past: a New Zealand commentary.* Wellington: Bridget Williams Books, 2001.

Ward, Alan. *An Unsettled History: Treaty Claims in New Zealand Today.* Wellington: Bridget Williams Books, 1998.

Notes on Contributors

JORGE CAÑIZARES-ESGUERRA is Professor of History at the University of Texas at Austin. He is the author of the prize-winning *How to Write the History of the New World: Histories, Epistemologies and Identities in the Eighteenth-Century Atlantic World* (2001), and has two forthcoming books: *Puritan Conquistadors: Iberianizing the Atlantic 1550–1700*, and *Nature, Empire and Nation: Explorations of the History of Science in the Iberian World.*

DANIEL CAREY is Lecturer at the National University of Ireland, Galway. He is editor, with François Boulaire, of *Les voyages de Gulliver: Mondes lointains ou mondes proches* (2002), sole editor of *Asian Travel in the Renaissance* (2004), and author of *Locke, Shaftesbury, and Hutcheson: Contesting Diversity in the Enlightenment and Beyond*, forthcoming.

COLIN KIDD is Professor of Modern History at the University of Glasgow. Recent publications include *British Identities before Nationalism: Ethnicity and Nationhood in the Atlantic World, 1600–1800* (1999) and *Subverting Scotland's Past: Scottish Whig Historians and the Creation of an Anglo-British Identity, 1689–c. 1830* (1993), as well as numerous articles on ethnicity, historiography and theology, and Enlightenment and political culture.

ANN MOYER is Associate Professor of History at the University of Pennsylvania. She is the author of *Musica Scientia: Musical Scholarship in the Italian Renaissance* (1992), *Raffaele Brandolini On Music and Poetry* (2001), and *The Philosophers' Game: Rithmomachia in Medieval and Renaissance Europe* (2001). Her current work focuses on the study of culture and the formation of cultural identity in sixteenth-century Tuscany.

J. G. A. POCOCK is Professor Emeritus of History at Johns Hopkins University. His most recent project is *Barbarism and Religion*, a multi-volume study of Edward Gibbon and his *Decline and Fall of the Roman Empire*; volumes one and two have been awarded the Jacques Barzun Prize in Cultural History from the American Philosophical Association.

JULIA RUDOLPH is Assistant Professor of History at the University of Pennsylvania, and author of *Revolution by Degrees: James Tyrrell and Whig Political Thought in the Late Seventeenth Century* (2002). Her current work explores the intersections between common law, science, gender, and history during the early Enlightenment in England.

Index

All numbers in bold face refer to illustrations in the text.